CW01647908

AN ACCOUNT OF THE GENUS MECONOPSIS

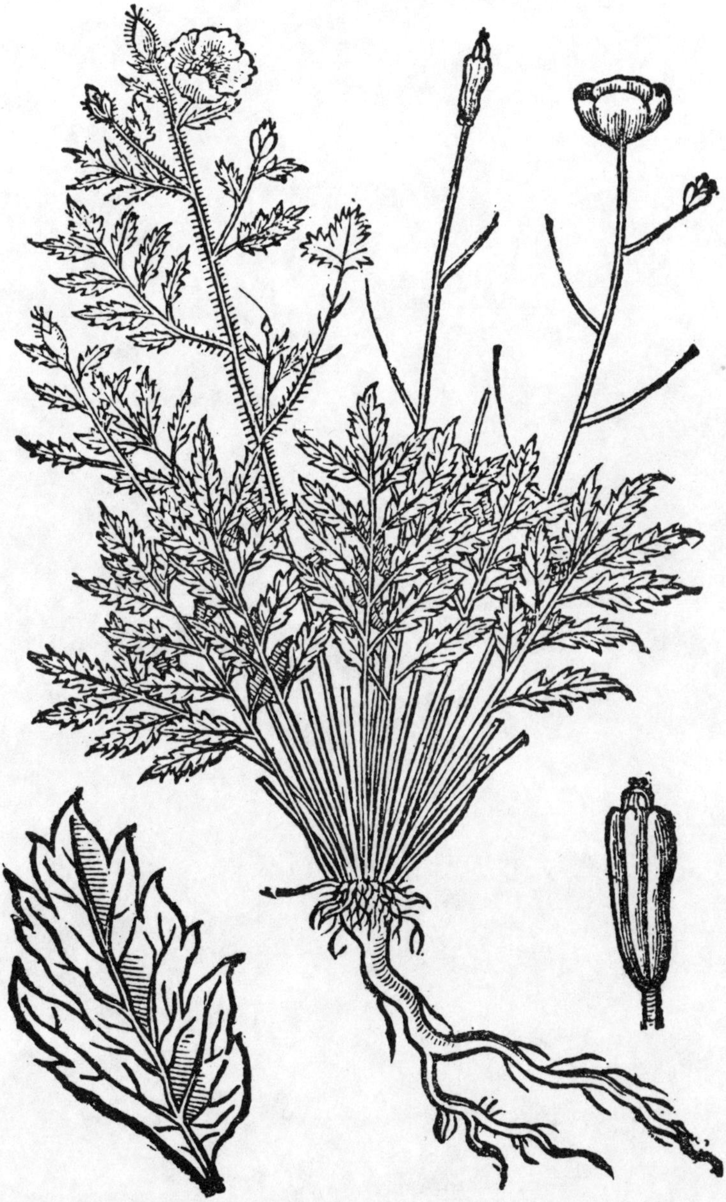

PARKINSON'S FIGURE OF *Meconopsis cambrica*, THE TYPE-SPECIES OF THE GENUS.
This figure, first published in 1640, is apparently the earliest known illustration of a *Meconopsis*.

AN ACCOUNT OF THE GENUS MECONOPSIS

BY

SIR GEORGE TAYLOR, K.B.E.

WITH NOTES ON THE CULTIVATION OF THE
INTRODUCED SPECIES BY

E. H. M. COX

WITH A FOREWORD BY

SIR WILLIAM WRIGHT SMITH

REGIUS KEEPER OF THE ROYAL BOTANIC GARDEN, EDINBURGH

WATERSTONE • LONDON

First published in 1934
This edition first published by Waterstone & Co. Limited 1985.
© Sir George Taylor.

All Rights Reserved.

The publishers are grateful to the Harry Smith
Horticultural Photographic Collection
for their kind permission to reproduce
colour plate numbers 1, 2, 4, 5, 7, 8, 9, 10, 11, 12, 13, 14, 16.

Cover Design by George Carter.

Printed and bound in Great Britain
by Richard Clay (The Chaucer Press) Ltd.,
Bungay, Suffolk.

Distributed (except in USA) by
Thames and Hudson Ltd.

ISBN 0 947752 31 5

FOREWORD

The genus *Meconopsis* has come very much to the forefront during the last thirty years of Horticulture, and deservedly so. A comprehensive statement of the present knowledge of the genus is consequently much to be desired and will be welcome to botanist and to gardener alike. The main authority in the past has been the admirable paper of Sir David Prain in the Kew Bulletin of 1915. Since that time keen explorers in western China, Tibet, and the Himalaya have added new members to the genus and to cultivation. It has also been possible in the intervening years through acquaintance with the plants in our gardens to come to some conclusions as to the validity of the various described species, to their interrelationships, to their tendency to variation, and to their possibilities in hybridisation. Needless to say, all the problems therewith connected cannot as yet be solved. But Mr. George Taylor of the British Museum has had the good fortune to deal with reasonably adequate material of the great majority of the species as represented in the chief herbaria, and has had, moreover, the benefit of a close acquaintance with the plants in cultivation throughout the British Isles. He is therefore in a position to marshal in a convenient volume what is at present known of this very beautiful genus. Further, it is a laborious task to assemble and arrange the numerous references to *Meconopsis* in botanical and in horticultural literature, and for its satisfactory completion a debt of thanks is due to Mr. Taylor and to those who have collaborated in the production of this volume.

WILLIAM WRIGHT SMITH.

Royal Botanic Garden,
Edinburgh.

TO

SIR DAVID PRAIN, C.M.G., C.I.E., LL.D., F.R.S.,

WHOSE NAME IS SO CLOSELY ASSOCIATED WITH THE STUDY OF THE GENUS *MECONOPSIS*.

PREFACE

The purpose of this volume is to summarise in convenient form our present knowledge of the genus *Meconopsis*. Since the publication of the last authoritative enumeration, that of Sir David Prain issued in 1915, the continued discovery of new species and the introduction of some of them to gardens, together with the accumulation of much additional information regarding those already known, have emphasised the need for a new critical review and the necessity for a revision of certain opinions currently held. At the same time there appears to be little doubt that considerable modification of the system now presented will be necessary when botanical exploration is carried into the many areas not yet investigated.

Fortunately it has been found unnecessary to alter the names of any species on purely nomenclatural grounds, but certain specific names, well known to horticulturists, have for taxonomic reasons been reduced to synonymy; *M. Wallichii*, for example, is placed under *M. napaulensis*, while *M. Prattii*, *M. racemosa*, *M. rigidiuscula*, and *M. rudis* are all referred to *M. horridula*.

It has been possible to complete this volume only with the unstinted co-operation of many willing helpers. The basis of my studies in the genus *Meconopsis* was laid at the Royal Botanic Garden, Edinburgh, where the unrivalled collections of herbarium specimens and cultivated plants were placed freely at my disposal. For this privilege I would particularly thank Professor Sir William Wright Smith, who has also given me continued encouragement during the course of my investigations and has supplied a Foreword to the present volume. Occasion may also be taken to express my indebtedness to the late Mr. George Forrest, who by his magnificent collections added so materially to our knowledge of the genus and with whom I had many opportunities of discussing the behaviour of certain species in the field. It is interesting to mention that the conclusions reached in this work regarding the aggregate species *M. integrifolia* and *M. horridula*, plants with which Forrest had a very intimate acquaintance, met with his entire approval. Latterly, the study of the genus has been continued at the British Museum (Natural History), and my sincere thanks are due to Mr. J. Ramsbottom, Keeper of Botany, for his unfailing interest in the progress of the work and for the many facilities he has afforded. Mr. Ramsbottom has also read the complete manuscript and made many valuable suggestions. To my colleague Mr. J. E. Dandy I am under a deep debt of gratitude for his stimulating criticism and invaluable advice and assistance during the preparation of the volume. Special acknowledgment must be made to Mr. T. Hay, whose zealous interest in the genus has led to fruitful co-operation with Sir Clive Wigram, by which our gardens have been enriched by several new species. To these gentlemen I am indebted for the acquisition of field specimens from areas difficult of access and for opportunities of examining cultivated plants.

For loan of specimens I wish to express my thanks to the Regius Keeper, Royal Botanic Garden, Edinburgh; to the Director of the Royal Botanic Gardens, Kew; to Professor T. H. Goodspeed of the University of California; and to the Directors of the Paris Herbarium and the University Herbarium, Breslau. I would also thank the staffs of the libraries of the Royal Horticultural Society and the Linnean Society for their unfailing courtesy on the occasions when I have consulted works under their charge. Finally, I must thank the many horticulturists, too numerous to mention individually, who have either allowed me to inspect their collections of plants or who have sent me cultivated specimens for examination.

GEORGE TAYLOR.

British Museum (Natural History),
London.

CONTENTS

LIST OF ILLUSTRATIONS

AN ACCOUNT OF THE GENUS MECONOPSIS

INTRODUCTION

HISTORY OF THE GENUS MECONOPSIS AND ITS SUBDIVISIONS

THE genus *Meconopsis*, which belongs to the tribe *Papavereae* of *Papaveraceae*, was founded by Viguier in 1814, and as the original publication is not readily accessible the diagnosis given there is reproduced below.* It was based on the single species *Papaver cambricum*, and differentiated from typical *Papaver* by the presence of a short style and the complete absence of a sessile stigmatic disc surmounting the ovary. On these criteria, principally, Viguier proposed his new genus, regarding it as intermediate between *Papaver* and *Argemone*. It was some time before his view found acceptance, and for a number of years botanists regarded the genus *Meconopsis* as unnecessary or, if admitting it, generally obscured its identity by the inclusion of species which really did not belong to it.

The first Asiatic representative to be added was *M. napaulensis*, described in 1824 by De Candolle from material sent by Wallich, and in the following year two further Indian species, originally described under *Papaver*, but now included in *Meconopsis*, were proposed by D. Don; these were also based on Wallich specimens. By the addition of two species from California, Bentham in 1835 greatly extended the geographical and taxonomic limits of the genus. Recently, however, the exclusively Old World distribution of *Meconopsis* has been restored by the transference of Bentham's plants, now considered to be forms of a single species, to a new genus, *Stylomecon*. Further species from India, and later from China and intervening regions, were added at intervals, so that in 1896 Prain recognised twenty-three species.

Prain's paper of 1896 embodied the first detailed study of the genus, and contained a preliminary classification of the species. He then regarded them as conveniently divided into seven groups, which, sometimes with considerable modification, he retained in his subsequent revisions. A more comprehensive

* Calyx diphyllus, caducus; corolla tetrapetala; stamina numerosissima; antherae lateraliter dehiscentes; *stylus brevis*; stigmata radiantia, *convexa, libera, et non sessilia super discum*, persistentia. Capsula unilocularis, valvulis dehiscens; dissepimenta parva.

survey was possible in 1906, when Prain published an enumeration of all the known species. He then considered the genus to be composed of two sections—*Eumeconopsis* and *Polychaetia*—and under these he arranged nine subordinate groups. This treatment was substantially accepted by Fedde in his account of the *Papaveraceae* in " Das Pflanzenreich," published in 1909, but in that work Prain's sections were treated as subgenera, and his minor groups raised to the rank of sections. In Prain's latest revision, published in 1915, the classification of the genus, then considered to embrace forty-three species, was essentially the same as that propounded in 1906, with the addition of two new series and considerable remodelling of the existing ones by the inclusion of further species. Kingdon-Ward in 1926 offered certain criticisms of Prain's classification, and, in addition to certain modifications of the existing series, suggested the establishment of two new ones.

The classification of *Meconopsis* proposed in the present work differs fundamentally from that hitherto accepted. The two major groups now defined do not correspond in any way to Prain's sections, and are differentiated on entirely different characters. While the subordinate groupings approximate closely in both systems, their status and arrangement are here altered very materially.

In the definition of his sections Prain relied on the character of the pubescence—whether the hairs were simple (sect. *Eumeconopsis*) or barbellate (sect. *Polychaetia*). By use of this character, however, species obviously very closely related were placed in separate sections, the series *Cambricae* and *Chelidonifoliae* being examples of this. Further, interpretation of the structure of the hairs often presents difficulty, all transitions being found from simple setae to conspicuously barbed hairs.

It seems desirable, if possible, to find other criteria to facilitate the primary classification of the genus. In two species, placed by Prain in his series *Torquatae*, the presence of a disc extending over the apex of the ovary appears to be of fundamental taxonomic importance, and not only assists the classification of the genus, but represents an interesting structural development.* The formation of this disc is so exceptional, combined as it is with the presence of at least a short style, that the question of separate generic status for the two species has been considered. They occur, however, within the geographical range of *Meconopsis*, and present such a striking habit resemblance to some more typical members of the genus that it has been decided to retain them in *Meconopsis* as representing a distinct subgenus.

Thus in the classification proposed here *Meconopsis* is regarded as falling into two subgenera: *Eumeconopsis*, in which the style, when present, is never

* See figures of *M. discigera* in Ann. of Bot. xx: tab. 24 fig. 12 (1906) and in Journ. of Bot. lxviii: fig. 4 (1930); of *M. torquata* in Ann. of Bot. xx: tab. 24 fig. 11 (1906).

expanded into a disc, and *Discogyne*, a very natural group of two species in which the style is expanded into a disc at the base. In the subgenus *Eumeconopsis* three sections are recognised, *Cambricae*, *Eucathcartia*, and *Polychaetia*, determined primarily by habit, flower-colour, and pubescence characters. The section *Cambricae* comprises the single species *M. cambrica*, but *Eucathcartia* can be arranged in two series, *Chelidonifoliae* and *Villosae*, on account of a difference in habit. By far the greatest number of species are included in the section *Polychaetia*, and are grouped in two subsections: *Eupolychaetia*, in which the species retain a dense winter-rosette of leaves, and *Cumminsia*, in which the plants have a geophytic habit during winter. In *M. grandis* and *M. bella* the leaves are stated to persist during the winter, but never in a dense rosette as in section *Eupolychaetia*. The first of these subsections is composed of two series, *Superbae* and *Robustae*, defined according to leaf and pubescence characters. Six series are recognised in the subsection *Cumminsia*, the initial differentiation depending on the nature of the pubescence, whether of barbellate or of simple hairs. Only two of its series, *Simplicifoliae* and *Grandes*, are characterised by conspicuously barbellate hairs, and the former is distinguished by having the leaves all basal, cauline leaves being present in the *Grandes*. Of the remaining four series, the *Bellae* are at once recognised by their pear-shaped capsules borne on curved stalks. The *Primulinae* are separated from the *Delavayanae* and *Aculeatae* by having the flowers borne in the axils of the upper stem-leaves, while the *Delavayanae* are at once differentiated from the *Aculeatae* by their branching caespitose rootstock. A conspectus of the classification adopted, showing the various groups and their constituent species, is set out on p. 13.

DELIMITATION OF THE SPECIES

The taxonomist's difficulty with *Meconopsis* lies less in the grouping of the species than in their individual delimitation. This observation does not apply with equal force to all the series, but in the two largest, *Robustae* and *Aculeatae*, it is often a matter of extreme difficulty to arrive at a convenient definition of certain species, and for some it cannot be claimed that the specific limits proposed here are entirely satisfactory. Many species are so highly polymorphic and unstable under cultivation that it may be permissible to treat the various forms merely as incipient taxonomic units which have not yet become sufficiently fixed to warrant nomenclatural recognition. The factors of time and geographical isolation may eventually bring such stability as will lead to an easier comprehension of their status. Alternatively, the flux of forms referred to certain species may be the result of continued interbreeding so that any specific differences which may formerly have existed have been obscured by repeated hybridisation.

Within what are here regarded as species an extraordinary range of variation is commonly found, a range which formerly would have been considered to transgress even the generic limits. Of all the species *M. paniculata*, *M. napaulensis*, *M. integrifolia*, *M. lancifolia*, and *M. horridula* exhibit the most striking degrees of variation. With the exception of *M. lancifolia* all these species are in cultivation. Usually the extreme forms are so distinct that, if dealing with these alone, one would scarcely hesitate to accord them separate specific rank. Between the limits of variation the forms pass so imperceptibly from one intermediate state to another that all must be embraced in a single species. In many instances it will be difficult to persuade horticulturists that certain forms which they may be growing are really not specifically distinct, but the interrelation of such forms often only becomes obvious on reference to a wide range of material, such as is furnished by herbarium specimens of wild plants. It appears that a proper conception of these variable species and their constituent forms will be possible only when sufficient cultural, genetical, and cytological data are available, supplemented by observation in the field.

RANGE OF HABIT IN MECONOPSIS

Within the genus a wide range of habit is displayed. The two sections *Cambricae* and *Eucathcartia* comprise polycarpic species bearing leafy flowering-stems. These in *M. cambrica* are freely produced from a branching base, but in the other species only a single flowering-stem is borne each year. In two species, *M. chelidonifolia* and *M. lyrata*, the production of vegetative buds in the axils of the stem-leaves represents an interesting development which appears to be quite exceptional in the *Papaveraceae*. This phenomenon is generally associated with alpine plants which must accomplish flowering, ensure fertilisation, and produce and disseminate their seeds in a very short season, and these may be the conditions in the species mentioned. The section *Polychaetia* contains a very polymorphic assemblage of plants. The majority are monocarpic, but a few are perennial. In the monocarpic members the tap-root may be short and napiform, or it may be stout, elongated, and succulent, attaining a foot or more in length. This latter condition, in which there is often a marked disproportion between root and shoot, is generally found in those species which inhabit screes at the highest altitudes. In the structure of the inflorescence a striking range may be observed, from plants bearing their flowers on basal scapes a few inches in height, such as *M. bella*, to those producing a copiously branched inflorescence often 6 feet in height, such as *M. napaulensis*.

It is a general feature of alpine plants that they produce comparatively large brilliantly coloured flowers, and the species of *Meconopsis* are no exception.

The more extensive exposure to light has been suggested as a reason, but it may also be partly accounted for as a device to increase the chances of insect visitation which must be at a premium under the extreme conditions existing at high altitudes.

AFFINITIES OF THE GENUS

The awkward problems attending a taxonomic study of the *Papaveraceae* are well known, and here and there in the family great difficulty is experienced in delimiting the genera. As some of these are interpreted at present, it is difficult to find satisfactory differences by which to separate them. Nevertheless, by the employment of an association of characters rather than any single one it is possible to arrive at a convenient, though admittedly arbitrary, classification. Of *Meconopsis* it can be said that its relationships with neighbouring genera are exceedingly close, but at the same time its limits are more or less clearly defined.

In the arrangement of the genera into tribes considerable diversity of opinion exists, and at present one cannot state that a really satisfactory grouping of the genera is available. One fundamental character in the interpretation of which there has been much confusion is that of the stigmatic structure. Thus *Meconopsis* was described by Bentham and Hooker* as having the stigmatic rays opposite the placentae, while Fedde,† although referring the genus to the tribe *Papavereae* (characterised by commisural stigmas), in his generic description clearly stated that the lobes alternate with the placentae. Further, while it is here proposed to unite the two genera *Cathcartia* and *Meconopsis*, in the most recent classification‡ these have been referred to distinct tribes partly on account of alleged differences in their stigmatic characters. Recent research on the carpel morphology of the *Papaveraceae*§ has led to the conclusion that, with the exception of the genera *Platystemon* and *Platystigma* and certain species of *Eschscholtzia*, the stigmas of the subfamily *Papaveroideae* are commisural. In any future classification of the family proper understanding of this character will lead to a better conception of the generic affinities.

It has been found necessary to absorb *Cathcartia* within *Meconopsis* as no real character can be found to separate them. Since Hooker described the former genus in 1851, basing it on the single species *C. villosa*, its limits have varied in a very elastic manner; several species have been described under *Cathcartia* which have since been referred to *Meconopsis*, and one has been described in *Meconopsis*, subsequently included in *Cathcartia*, and now replaced under *Meconopsis*. Prain in his 1915 revision of *Meconopsis* returned *Cathcartia* to its initial monotypic

* Bentham and Hooker, Gen. Pl. i: 52 (1862).
† Fedde in Engl., Pflanzenr. iv, 104: 247 (1909).
‡ Hutchinson in Bull. Misc. Inf. Kew 1925: 161 (1925).
§ Saunders in New Phytologist xxix: 51 (1930).

state, but the difficulty of its precise separation from *Meconopsis* still existed. He admitted that the original differentiating characters used by Hooker had broken down but, rather than regard the two genera as congeneric, he proposed further characters in support of their separation. The following statement may be quoted from his paper:* "There is no species of *Meconopsis* with a stigma like that of *Cathcartia villosa*, in which the valves of the capsule become separated from the placental ribs beyond the point at which these ribs begin to converge to the base of the style. It is therefore easy to keep up the genus *Cathcartia* for the type *C. villosa*." Examination of the entire range of fruiting material of *Meconopsis* and *Cathcartia* shows that this capsule character is not confined to *C. villosa*. In *M. integrifolia*, for example, some forms have capsule-valves extending beyond the base of the style. The capsule characters found in *Meconopsis* are notoriously variable, and conditions are found similar to those regarded by Prain as peculiar to *Cathcartia*. It is difficult to understand why such a species as *M. Oliverana* should be consistently referred to *Meconopsis* when in its capsule structure and habit it is essentially of the same type as *C. villosa*.

The removal of the several species displaying such characters from *Meconopsis* and their inclusion in *Cathcartia* has been suggested as a possible solution, but this is precluded by the obvious natural affinities of the species concerned. The adoption of such a course would necessitate the removal of *M. Oliverana* to *Cathcartia*, and thereby dissociate it from its closest ally, *M. chelidonifolia*, with which it is practically identical in all but fruiting characters. The degree of dehiscence has also been suggested as a differential character, *Cathcartia* generally being stated to have a capsule which dehisces from the apex to the base. This, however, occurs rarely, if ever, the splitting usually being arrested some distance from the bottom. Certainly in *Cathcartia* the valves split apart for a greater distance than in typical *Meconopsis*, but the degree of dehiscence depends on no structural character, and varies so considerably that this criterion cannot be used for differential purposes. In view of the extreme plasticity displayed by the capsules of *Meconopsis* there appears to be no valid reason why *Cathcartia* should not be included in that genus.

The genera which appear to be immediately related to *Meconopsis* are *Argemone*, *Papaver*, and *Stylomecon*. Comparison between species of *Argemone* and certain species of *Meconopsis* demonstrates at once the exceedingly close affinity between these genera; in fact, several authors, all with one exception pre-Linnean, have regarded *M. cambrica* as belonging to *Argemone*. The generic distinction generally considered as primary is a numerical one, the flowers of *Argemone* being trimerous, whereas those of *Meconopsis* are dimerous. This

* Prain in Bull. Misc. Inf. Kew 1915: 134 (1915).

distinction, however, is by no means absolute, and it seems better to rely on the structural character of the sepals. In *Argemone* the sepals appear to be constantly three, and are each surmounted by a horn-like appendage, while in *Meconopsis* the sepals are only exceptionally three, and never have the outgrowths characteristic of *Argemone*. It may also be mentioned that *Argemone* is exclusively a New World genus, although one of its members has become extensively naturalised in the Old World.

Since *Papaver* and *Meconopsis* (as represented by *M. cambrica*) were considered congeneric until 1814, it is only to be expected that the relationship between these genera is very close. Viguier, when he decided to base the genus *Meconopsis* on Linnaeus's *Papaver cambricum*, was most influenced by the presence of a distinct style in that species, in contrast to the condition found in *Papaver*, where the stigma is sessile with radiating lobes arranged on a disc surmounting the ovary. These distinctions served admirably to distinguish typical *Meconopsis* from typical *Papaver* until species of *Meconopsis* became known in which the stigma was sessile and in which the arrangement of the stigmatic rays approached very closely to the condition found in certain species of *Papaver*, particularly in the section *Miltantha* of that genus. This section is characterised to some extent by having stigmatic rays arranged on a pyramid or cone, but the condition may fairly be regarded as a modification of the more usual discoid type in which the disc is conical instead of being flat. In the astylar forms of *Meconopsis* the stigmatic rays are prominently decurrent over fluted stigmatic columns and there is no suggestion of a disc as in *Papaver*. The subgenus *Discogyne* of *Meconopsis*, distinguished by the presence of at least a short style and a well-developed (but not stigmatic) disc, may be regarded as a local derivative, and not directly related to *Papaver*.

The monotypic genus *Stylomecon* includes the Californian plants which have been referred to the series or section *Anomalae* in all previous revisions of *Meconopsis*. While the treatment accorded to these plants by American authors has varied considerably, it now seems to be generally accepted that they represent forms of a single species, and only the generic identity has latterly been disputed. Greene* referred the species to *Papaver*, a procedure which has been followed by later American authors with the notable exceptions of A. Gray† and Abrams.‡ The species, however, while closely resembling certain members of *Papaver*, cannot be satisfactorily included in that genus, on account of its definite style and mode of capsule-dehiscence. Further, this Californian species in its annual habit, bicoloured flowers, and general facies is easily distinguishable from the exclusively Old World genus *Meconopsis*, and these circumstances led the author§

* Greene, Pittonia i: 168 (1898).

† A. Gray, Synopt. Fl. N. Amer. i, 1: 89 (1898).

‡ Abrams, Fl. Los Ang.: 162 (1904).

§ G. Tayl. in Journ. of Bot. lxviii: 138 (1930).

to recognise it as representing a new genus. The relationship of *Stylomecon* with *Meconopsis* appears to be very close, but although there is really no obvious structural distinction between the two genera they can readily be separated by a very distinct habit difference. *Stylomecon*, on account of the flattening of the ovary at the apex, shows an approach to the condition found in the subgenus *Discogyne* of *Meconopsis*.

Some mention must be made of the affinity between *Meconopsis* and *Chelidonium*. Through the species with narrow capsules, and particularly *M. Oliverana*, the relationship appears to be intimate. Generally the almost constant presence of two capsular valves which split apart from the placental ribs along their entire length is sufficient to distinguish *Chelidonium*, for although in *Meconopsis* two-valved capsules are occasionally found, the valves rarely separate for more than one-third of the length of the capsules and never from apex to base.

GEOGRAPHICAL RANGE OF MECONOPSIS

In the last complete account of *Meconopsis*, as already mentioned, forty-three species were recognised. Of these, two have been removed to *Stylomecon*, ten are here reduced to synonymy, and one is regarded as a hybrid, while eleven further species are added. The genus is thus considered to embrace forty-one species which, with a single exception, are confined to south-central temperate Asia. From the southern boundary, extending from Chitral and Kashmir along the Himalayas and intervening ranges to northern Yunnan, the genus occurs through southern Tibet and the province of Szechuan to southern Kansu, central Shensi, and western Hupeh at altitudes above 6,000 feet. The extra-Asiatic representative, which is the type-species of the genus, forms a peculiar geographical outlier confined to western Europe.

The majority of the species of *Meconopsis* are extremely local in their geographical distribution, and only about nine can be regarded as widely dispersed. Of these *M. cambrica* extends from western England, Wales, and Ireland to northern Spain. *M. paniculata* is found along the Himalayas from eastern Nepal to north-western Assam. *M. napaulensis* occurs from central Nepal to western Szechuan; *M. punicea* and *M. quintuplinervia*, almost coinciding in their range, from north-eastern Tibet to central Shensi; *M. integrifolia* from eastern Tibet and western Kansu southwards to north-eastern Upper Burma; *M. lyrata* from north-western Yunnan to central Nepal. *M. lancifolia* is found from south-western Kansu to south-eastern Tibet, northern Upper Burma and north-western Yunnan; while *M. horridula*, the most widely dispersed of all, occurs from western Kansu to north-western Yunnan, through Upper Burma and along the Himalayas to central Nepal.

With the exception of *M. cambrica*, which inhabits damp, shady ravines at altitudes usually below 2,000 feet, the species of *Meconopsis* occur in the alpine woods and scrub, meadows, and scree-slopes above 6,000 feet. Several species attain to heights above 17,000 feet, and *M. horridula*, which has been recorded from 19,000 feet, in some areas reaches the highest limit of phanerogamic vegetation.

In the main enumeration the nature of the habitat, as far as it can be ascertained from field-notes, is given for each species. It appears that *M. Delavayi*, *M. venusta*, and perhaps *M. pseudovenusta* are entirely calcicolous, while *M. lancifolia*, *M. speciosa*, and *M. horridula* also may be found on limestone formations.

HISTORY OF THE GENUS IN CULTIVATION

Although particulars of the introduction of the cultivated species are given in the main enumeration, a brief historical summary may be given here.

The first exotic species to be introduced to our gardens were raised from seeds collected by J. D. Hooker during his botanical exploration of Sikkim, and the first definite record of flowering is that of *M. simplicifolia* in 1848. Hooker also sent seeds of *M. villosa*, which flowered in 1851; *M. napaulensis*, which flowered in 1852 and was figured under the name *M. Wallichii*; and *M. paniculata*, which, however, is not definitely known to have flowered until 1863, and was then generally called *M.* "*nipalensis.*" *M. napaulensis* is stated to have been cultivated in European gardens before 1831,* but the basis for this statement is obscure and it requires confirmation. The next Himalayan species to be introduced was *M. aculeata*, which flowered at Kew in 1864, the plants having been raised from seed sent by Cleghorn from north-western India. *M. grandis* appeared in this country about 1895 from seeds apparently sent by Prain, who described the species. As far as records are available, *M. quintuplinervia* was the first Chinese representative of the genus to be introduced to European gardens. This species flowered in St. Petersburg in 1876 and was actually described in that year from cultivated specimens raised from seed collected by Przewalski in Kansu. The species, however, did not become extensively established in this country until Farrer secured seeds during his 1914–1915 expedition in Kansu.

M. integrifolia flowered in Paris in 1896 from seeds sent by the Abbé Farges from north-eastern Szechuan. In this country, where its introduction created great interest, the species appeared in 1904, having been raised simultaneously from seed obtained by Koslov in south-eastern Tibet and by Wilson in Szechuan. Wilson was further responsible for the introduction of *M. punicea*, which flowered in 1904, but was subsequently lost to cultivation, and *M. Henrici*, which flowered

* Prain in Ann. of Bot. xx: 360 (1906).

in 1906, but since has disappeared from gardens although collected by Kingdon-Ward in 1921. Although precise details cannot be given, it appears that Wilson also introduced *M. chelidonifolia*, which he collected in Szechuan in 1904 and again in 1908. *M. punicea* was obtained also by Farrer in 1914, but did not become acclimatised and its present reintroduction is due to Rock. *M. horridula* in its various forms is now firmly established, and appears to be raised with ease from each fresh batch of seed from China, but it was not until 1904, despite repeated endeavours, that it was brought to maturity in this country.

Unfortunately no further success has attended efforts to acclimatise the charming species *M. bella* since it flowered in 1906. At present a few plants, raised from seed recently received from Nepal, lead a somewhat precarious existence, and it seems that this desirable species will become established only when its fastidious habits are more thoroughly understood. *M. latifolia*, by far the most attractive member of the series *Aculeatae*, reached this country through the good offices of Appleton in Kashmir and flowered in 1908. *M. Delavayi* is recorded as having flowered at Edinburgh in 1913, and it is most unfortunate that this very attractive perennial did not become established, although it is hoped that recent attempts may meet with more success.

No species has enjoyed more overwhelming popularity than *M. betonicifolia*, the credit for whose introduction belongs to Kingdon-Ward, who collected the species in 1924 in south-eastern Tibet in an area where it had been discovered by Bailey in 1913. *M. superba*, which was previously known only from a single collection made in the Chumbi district of Tibet, quite unexpectedly flowered in cultivation in 1927. The precise origin of the seeds and exactly how the plant was introduced are something of a mystery. Recent botanical exploration in Nepal, in addition to providing material of several previously imperfectly known species, has yielded four new ones, and of these *M. regia*, which flowered in 1931, and *M. Dhwojii*, which flowered in the following year, may be said to have become established. By the introduction of *M. violacea* Kingdon-Ward added another to the number of species under cultivation. This plant flowered in this country in 1929 from seeds obtained in Upper Burma and south-eastern Tibet in 1926. At present attempts are being made to establish several species which have not been seen, or only fleetingly, in our gardens, and these include *M. impedita*, *M. lancifolia*, *M. speciosa*, and the new species *M. Georgei*. It is hoped that records of the success or failure of these plants will be made available.

It is obvious that great tracts of country in which conditions are favourable for the occurrence of *Meconopsis* still await exploration, and it may be stated with some degree of confidence that the resources of the genus as a source of garden plants are not yet exhausted.

HYBRIDISATION WITHIN THE GENUS

Records exist of eleven hybrids within the genus, but our knowledge of many of these is very unsatisfactory and is based entirely on the original plants which have since passed out of cultivation. Only rarely have specimens been preserved, and thus no description, or only a very incomplete one, can be given of these in this work. With few exceptions the hydrids have arisen spontaneously and evidence of their parentage is therefore often hypothetical. No hybrid as yet has become generally established in gardens, apparently on account of the difficulty of propagation and limited capacity for producing seed.

With the steady increase in the number of species under cultivation it may be expected that attempts will be made to produce hybrids. To the hybridist the resources of the genus would appear to be definitely restricted, and, as the majority of the species are monocarpic, the most fruitful field for experiment is probably to be found in the production of polycarpic plants. No general conclusions can be drawn from the limited information available, but consideration of the known hybrids indicates that a species which is polycarpic impresses that character on any alliance it may enter with a monocarpic species. Further, it also appears that yellow-flowered parent in any combination determines the flower-colour of the hybrid.

The several known hybrids are enumerated under their respective parents.

PROPERTIES OF MECONOPSIS

Apart from its horticultural value the genus is of no economic importance. Narcotic properties are attributed to the roots of *M. aculeata*, while those of *M. napaulensis* and *M. paniculata* are stated to be poisonous.

MECONOPSIS

MECONOPSIS Vig., Hist. Pavot. et Argémon.: 48 (1814).

DESCRIPTION. *Sepals* normally 2 (but occasionally 3 or 4, particularly in terminal flowers), soon deciduous. *Petals* most commonly 4, but often more and varying up to 10. *Stamens* numerous, very rarely only about 12; filaments filiform, rarely linear in the lower half or throughout their length. *Ovary* subglobose or ovoid or obovoid to narrowly subcylindric; style usually distinct though often very short, occasionally obsolete, rarely expanded at the base to form a disc surmounting the ovary; stigmas free or confluent to form a capitate or subclavate structure, opposite the placental ridges, more or less decurrent at the base. *Capsule* subglobose or ovoid or obovoid to narrowly oblong or narrowly subcylindric, glabrous to densely tomentose, dehiscing by interplacental valves usually for a short distance from the apex or rarely almost to the base. *Seeds* ovoid or more or less reniform or falcate-oblong or ellipsoid-oblong, smooth or obscurely or prominently longitudinally pitted, sometimes densely papillose. *Monocarpic or polycarpic herbs*, usually bearing simple scapes or a single erect simple or branched flowering-stem but rarely caespitose and bearing several stems from a branching rootstock. *Leaves* sessile or petiolate, aggregated in a basal rosette or carried up the flowering-stem, sometimes persisting in a rosette stage throughout the winter; lamina entire or serrate at the margin or more or less deeply divided. *Flowers* borne on simple basal scapes or singly from a central flowering-stem or in axillary cymules in a branched inflorescence.

Species 41, one confined to western Europe, the others natives of south-central temperate Asia (see Fig. 1). Type-species: *Meconopsis cambrica* (L.) Vig.

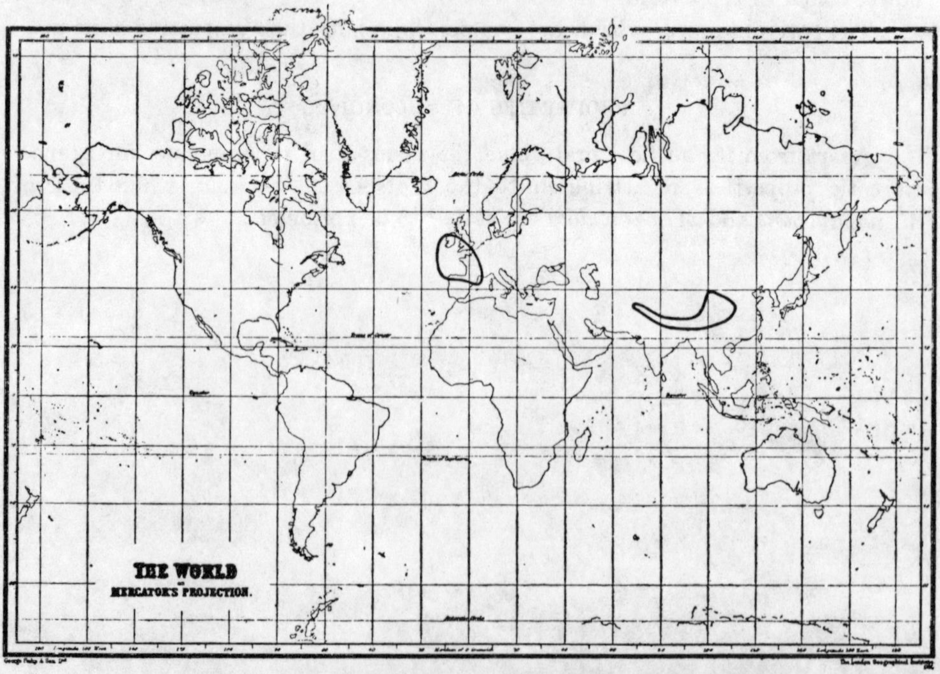

FIG. 1.—MAP SHOWING THE GEOGRAPHICAL RANGE OF *Meconopsis*.
The section *Cambricae*, comprising the type-species *M. cambrica*, is confined to western Europe, while the remaining forty species occur in south-central temperate Asia.

CONSPECTUS OF THE SPECIES AND THEIR GROUPS

Subgenus A. **EUMECONOPSIS**

Section I. **Cambricae**

1. *M. cambrica*

Section II. **Eucathcartia**

Series i. CHELIDONIFOLIAE

2. *M. chelidonifolia*, 3. *M. Oliverana*

Series ii. VILLOSAE

4. *M. villosa*, 5. *M. Smithiana*

Section III. **Polychaetia**

Subsection *a*. EUPOLYCHAETIA

Series i. SUPERBAE

6. *M. superba*, 7. *M. regia*

Series ii. ROBUSTAE

8. *M. robusta*, 9. *M. Dhwojii*, 10. *M. gracilipes*, 11. *M. paniculata*, 12. *M. longipetiolata*, 13. *M. violacea*, 14. *M. napaulensis*

Subsection *b*. CUMMINSIA

Series i. SIMPLICIFOLIAE

15. *M. simplicifolia*, 16. *M. quintuplinervia*, 17. *M. punicea*

Series ii. GRANDES

18. *M. integrifolia*, 19. *M. betonicifolia*, 20. *M. grandis*

Series iii. PRIMULINAE

21. *M. Florindae*, 22. *M. lyrata*, 23. *M. primulina*

Series iv. DELAVAYANAE

24. *M. Delavayi*

Series v. ACULEATAE

25. *M. Henrici*, 26. *M. Forrestii*, 27. *M. impedita*, 28. *M. venusta*, 29. *M. pseudovenusta*, 30. *M. Georgei*, 31. *M. lancifolia*, 32. *M. horridula*, 33. *M. latifolia*, 34. *M. speciosa*, 35. *M. aculeata*, 36. *M. neglecta*, 37. *M. sinuata*

Insufficiently known species of Series iii or v

38. *M. argemonantha*

Series vi. BELLAE

39. *M. bella*

Subgenus B. **DISCOGYNE**

40. *M. discigera*, 41. *M. torquata*

KEY TO THE SPECIES

A.

STYLE, when present, of uniform thickness throughout or swollen at the base but never expanded to form a disc surmounting the ovary. (Subgen. A. *Eumeconopsis.*)

Polycarpic; petals 4 (occasionally more in cultivated specimens), yellow.

Tufted base of plant glabrous or sparsely pubescent, the hairs simple or very minutely barbellate; species of western Europe. (Sect. I. *Cambricae.*) 1. *M. cambrica.*

Tufted base of plant beset with barbellate rufous hairs; species of the eastern Himalayas and western and central China. (Sect. II. *Eucathcartia.*)

Stem branched; branches leafy and usually bearing several flowers. (Ser. i. *Chelidonifoliae.*)

Ovary ellipsoid or ellipsoid-oblong, glabrous or very sparsely hairy . . 2. *M. chelidonifolia.*

Ovary narrowly oblong or subcylindric, glabrous . 3. *M. Oliverana*

Stem unbranched; flowers borne singly in the axils of the uppermost leaves. (Ser. ii. *Villosae.*)

Lamina ovate to suborbicular, deeply bipinnately lobed; ovary narrowly oblong or subcylindric, glabrous . . . . 4. M. *villosa.*

Lamina pinnately trifoliolate; ovary subglobose, densely hairy . . . 5. *M. Smithiana.*

Polycarpic (but then petals never yellow) or monocarpic; petals 4–10, yellow, blue, purple, red, or rarely white. (Sect. III. *Polychaetia.*)

a. Plants retaining a dense rosette of leaves during the winter. (Subsect. *a. Eupolychaetia.*)

Lamina of basal leaves not deeply lobed, oblanceolate, elliptic, or ovate-oblong, serrate at the margin and densely sericeous or appressed-tomentose. (Ser. i. *Superbae.*)

Flowers borne singly on axillary pedicels; petals white 6. *M. superba.*

Flowers, except the uppermost ones, borne on several-flowered axillary cymules; petals yellow . . . . 7. *M. regia.*

Lamina of basal leaves deeply lobed, generally bipinnatifid or bipinnatisect and more or less densely covered with spreading hairs. (Ser. ii. *Robustae.*)

Petals yellow or very rarely white.

Plants sparsely to densely bristly or occasionally glabrescent, the bristles of uniform length and often breaking off leaving subspinous bases.

Flowers borne singly on axillary pedicels . . 8. *M. robusta.*

Flowers borne on 1–3-flowered cymules.

Plants densely bristly, the bristles on the leaves commonly purple-black at the base . . . . 9. *M. Dhwojii.*

Plants sparsely bristly and ultimately glabrescent, the bristles light coloured throughout their length . 10. *M. gracilipes.*

Plants usually densely bristly and in addition very densely puberulous or with smaller barbellate hairs.

Bristles accompanied by a dense pubescence or tomentum of conspicuously branched hairs usually forming a substellate pubescence . . . . 11. *M. paniculata.*

Bristles accompanied by smaller minutely barbellate hairs . . . 12. *M. longipetiolata.*

Petals, red, purple, blue, or rarely white.

Flowers borne singly on axillary pedicels or rarely on 2–3-flowered cymules . . . . 13. *M. violacea.*

Flowers borne on copiously branched axillary cymules, the cymules (at least the lower ones) more than 3-flowered . . . . . 14. *M. napaulensis.*

b. Plants geophytic without a persistent dense rosette of leaves during the winter. (Subsect. *b. Cumminsia.*)

aa. Plants more or less densely bristly (the bristles barbellate), bearing a dense tuft of persistent leaf-bases interspersed with barbellate bristles, at the base contracted into a fibrous root-system or slender tap-root.

Leaves all basal; flowers borne on basal scapes. (Ser. i. *Simplicifoliae.*)

Petals blue; filaments filiform throughout their length.

Capsule sparsely covered with usually reflexed bristles . . . . 15. *M. simplicifolia.*

Capsule densely covered with appressed bristles . . . . . . 16. *M. quintuplinervia.*

Petals red; filaments expanded (linear) throughout their length . . 17. *M. punicea.*

Leaves basal and cauline, the uppermost aggregated in a false whorl at the level of which the upper flowers rise. (Ser. ii. *Grandes.*)

Petals yellow . . . . 18. *M. integrifolia.*

Petals blue, purple, or wine-purple.

Basal leaves truncate or cordate at the base 19. *M. betonicifolia.*

Basal leaves cuneate at the base . . . . . 20. *M. grandis.*

bb. Plants glabrous to densely bristly or spiny (the bristles or spines non-barbellate or rarely, in the series *Primulinae*, minutely barbellate but then the plants never densely bristly at the base), devoid of a dense tuft of persistent leaf-bases interspersed with bristles, at the base gradually tapering into a tap-root.

a. Capsule narrowly oblong, subglobose, or obovoid (in which case the leaves are entire or only slightly lobed), the stalk erect.

Flowers borne in the axils of the upper stem-leaves or when the flower is solitary, on a leafy peduncle; plants devoid of spines or subspiny bristles; tap-root napiform or narrowly elongated (not exceeding 3 in. in length). (Ser. iii. *Primulinae.*)

Petals yellow . . . . 21. *M. Florindae.*

Petals pale-blue (or very rarely pale-rose or white).

Tap-root swollen and usually napiform; ovary glabrous . . . 22. *M. lyrata.*

Tap-root slender and tapering; ovary usually sparsely pubescent 23. *M. primulina.*

Flowers borne on basal scapes or in ebracteate inflorescences, or in bracteate inflorescences and then the plants are usually beset with subspiny or spiny bristles and the tap-root usually stout and elongated (exceeding 3 ins. in length).

Polycarpic with the rootstock branched at the top, each branch bearing a rosette of entire leaves and terminating in a single 1-flowered scape. (Ser. iv. *Delavayanae.*) . . 24. *M. Delavayi.*

Monocarpic with the rootstock unbranched at the top (very rarely polycarpic in *M. venusta* with the rootstock branched); basal scapes, when present, usually several from each rosette; leaves entire to deeply divided. (Ser. v. *Aculeatae.*)

Filaments expanded (linear) below their middle . 25. *M. Henrici.*

Filaments filiform throughout their length.

I. Inflorescence ebracteate (but its stem occasionally leafy towards the base) or flowers borne on basal scapes.

* Flowers borne in ebracteate inflorescences.

Petals pale-blue; flowers borne on the upper part of the stem and without accompanying basal scapes; capsule narrowly subcylindric; style obsolete or nearly so . . 26. *M. Forrestii.*

Petals usually deep-purple (very rarely pale-blue); flowers usually borne throughout the length of the flowering-stem and almost always accompanied by basal scapes; capsule ellipsoid or ellipsoid-oblong to slightly obovoid; style distinct.

Leaves (at least some of them) pinnately or bipinnately lobed . . . . . . 29. *M. pseudovenusta* in part.

Leaves all entire or sinuate at the margin. . . . . 31. *M. lancifolia* (var. *solitariiflora*) in part.

** Flowers borne on basal scapes.

Capsule ellipsoid or ellipsoid-oblong; leaves sparsely to more or less densely covered with pungent spines.

Leaf-lamina entire or rarely slightly lobed at the margin 32. *M. horridula* in part.

Leaf-lamina deeply pinnatifid . . . 36. *M. neglecta.*

Capsule narrowly obovoid or subcylindric; leaves glabrous or sparsely bristly.

Tap-root napiform or shortly elongated and fusiform; number of basal scapes usually less than eight . . 33. *M. lancifolia* (var. *concinna*).

Tap-root stout and elongated; number of basal scapes (at maturity) usually more than 8.

Leaves at least sparsely bristly or spiny . . . . 27. *M. impedita.*

Leaves glabrous (very rarely sparsely bristly).

Capsule narrowly oblong or subcylindric, four to ten times as long as broad; petals 4 . 28. *M. venusta.*

Capsule narrowly obovoid to narrowly ellipsoid, scarcely attaining four times as long as broad; petals usually more than 4 . . . . 29. *M. pseudovenusta* in part.

II. Inflorescence bracteate at least at the base, the upper flowers usually without bracts; flowers never borne on basal scapes.

† Upper flowers ebracteate.

Petals yellow . . . . 30. *M. Georgei.*

Petals blue, purple, or wine-purple, rarely white.

Leaf-lamina entire or rarely pinnately lobed at the margin.

Lamina elliptic to oblanceolate or linear-oblong, rarely ovate or lanceolate, entire or lobed at the margin; petals blue to maroon.

Capsule narrowly oblong-ellipsoid to narrowly obovoid; bracts leafy . 31. *M. lancifolia* (var. *solitariiflora*) in part.

Capsule ellipsoid or ellipsoid-oblong to subglobose; lower bracts leafy, upper bracts reduced to scales 32. *M. horridula* in part.

Lamina more or less oblong to ovate, broadly crenate or more rarely pinnately or coarsely serrate at the margin; petals light-blue . . . 33. *M. latifolia.*

Leaf-lamina deeply pinnatifid or pinnatisect.

Style stout; spines on the ovary reddish-brown; species of western China . . . . . 34. *M. speciosa.*

Style slender; spines on the ovary golden-brown to straw-coloured; species of the western Himalayas 35. *M. aculeata.*

†† Upper flowers (like the lower ones) bracteate, but the bracts often displaced so that the flowers appear to be ebracteate 37. *M. sinuata.*

III. Character of inflorescence unknown; petals white; a species of doubtful affinity . . . . . 38. *M. argemonantha.*

β. Capsule pear-shaped or obovoid, often contracted at the base, the stalk curved; leaves finely divided. (Ser. vi. *Bellae.*) . . . . . 39. *M. bella.*

B.

Style abruptly expanded at the base into a broad glabrous disc surmounting the ovary and projecting beyond its edge. (Subgen. B. *Discogyne.*)

Style distinct, up to 0·25 in. in length; disc fringed at the margin; petals glabrous 40. *M. discigera.*

Style almost obsolete; disc sinuate and 8-angled at the margin; petals sparsely hairy on the outside . . . . 41. *M. torquata.*

ENUMERATION OF THE GROUPS, SPECIES AND HYBRIDS

SUBGEN. A. **EUMECONOPSIS**

MECONOPSIS subgen. EUMECONOPSIS (Prain) Fedde in Engl., Pflanzenr. iv, 104: 251 (1909) emend., excl. sect. 2.

Meconopsis sect. *Eumeconopsis* Prain in Ann. of Bot. xx: 343 (1906) pro parte, excl. ser. 2.

Species 39, arranged in 3 sections, one species native of western Europe, the others occurring in south-central temperate Asia. Type-species: *Meconopsis cambrica* (L.) Vig.

This subgenus is characterised by having the style, when present, of uniform thickness throughout its length or at least never expanded at the base into a disc surmounting the ovary and projecting beyond its margin. In those species in which the stigma is sessile the stigmatic lobes are usually radiating, but never over a flat or conical disc.

SECT. I. **CAMBRICAE**

MECONOPSIS sect. CAMBRICAE (Prain) Fedde in Engl., Pflanzenr. iv, 104: 251 (1909).

Papaver L., Sp. Pl. i: 506 (1753) et Gen. Pl., Ed. 5: 224 (1754) pro parte, quoad sp. 7.

Stylophorum Nutt., Gen. N. Amer. Pl. ii: 7 (1818) pro parte, quoad *Papaver cambricum*.

Cerastites Gray, Nat. Arrang. Brit. Pl. ii: 703 (1821) pro parte, quoad sp. 1.

[*Meconopsis* ser. *Chelidonifoliae* Prain in Journ. As. Soc. Bengal lxiv, 2: 311 et 313 in obs. (1896), *nomen nudum*, pro parte, quoad *M. cambrica*.]*

Meconopsis ser. *Cambricae* Prain in Ann. of Bot. xx: 343 (1906).

Species 1, *Meconopsis cambrica* (L.) Vig., confined to western Europe (see Fig. 1).

This section, which includes only the type-species of the genus, is characterised by its perennial habit, several leafy flowering-stems being produced from a tufted and usually glabrous base.

* Throughout this work square brackets are used in synonymy to indicate names which have no status under the International Rules of Botanical Nomenclature. These include *nomina nuda* (names published without a diagnosis or reference to diagnosis), *nomina synonyma* (names published as synonyms), and *nomina provisoria* (names published provisionally), together with misapplications and pre-Linnean names.

The extraordinary geographical segregation of the *Cambricae* from the area in south-central temperate Asia in which all the other species are found at once suggests separate taxonomic status for such widely separated groups. While, however, the majority of the Asiatic representatives are distinctive in their facies one series (*Chelidonifoliae*) agrees very closely with the European species. The possibility of combining this series with the section *Cambricae* as a separate genus has been entertained but no sufficiently important structural difference can be observed to warrant this. It is the close relationship between *M. cambrica* and the *Chelidonifoliae* which emphasises the desirability of accepting a wide definition for the genus *Meconopsis* and the inclusion of the Asiatic species within it.

1. MECONOPSIS CAMBRICA

Meconopsis cambrica (L.) Vig., Hist. Pavot. et Argémon.: 48, fig. 3 (1814). DC., Fl. Fr., Ed. 3, v: 586 (1815); Syst. Nat. ii: 87 (1821); Prodr. i: 120 (1824). Lindl., Syn. Brit. Bot. i: 17 (1829). Hook., Brit. Fl.: 256 (1830). Don, Gener. Syst. Gard. and Bot. i: 135 (1831). Baxt., Brit. Phanerogam. Bot. i: tab. 54 (1834). Mackay, Fl. Hibern.: 14 (1836). C. E. Sowerby, Illustr. Cat. Brit. Pl.: 17, tab. 49 (1841). Bab., Man. Brit. Bot.: 12 (1843). R. Hogg and G. W. Johnson, Wild Fl. Gr. Brit. i: tab. 21 (1863). Syme, Engl. Bot. Ed. 3: 94, tab. 63 (1863). D. Moore and A. G. More, Cybele Hibern.: 13 (1866). Hook. f., Stud. Fl.: 16 (1870). Robinson, Engl. Fl. Gard.: 183 (1883). Nicholson, Illustr. Dict. Gard. ii: 341 (1886). Rouy and Fouc., Fl. Fr. i: 163 (1893). Bois, Dict. Hort. ii: 821 (1893–99). L. H. Bailey, Cycloped. Amer. Hort. ii: 997 (1900); Man. Cult. Pl.: 299 (1924); Stand. Cycloped. Hort., New Ed. ii: 2017 (1927). Bulley in Fl. and Sylva iii: 82 (1905). Prain in Ann. of Bot. xx: 343 (1906); in Bull. Misc. Inf. Kew 1915: 142 (1915); in Countr. Life liv: 110 (1923). Fedde in Engl., Pflanzenr. iv, 104: 251, fig. 34 A–B (1909). Fitzherb. in Gard. Chron., Ser. 3, liv: 52, fig. 26 (1913). Farrer, Engl. Rock-Gard. i: 475 (1919). Moss, Cambr. Brit. Fl. iii: 161, tab. 171 (1920). G. Tayl. in Journ. of Bot. lxviii: fig. 5 (1930). L. H. and E. Z. Bailey, Hortus: 390 (1930). Wehrhahn, Gartenstaud. i: 467 (1930). Druce, Comit. Fl. Brit. Is.: 13 (1932).

[*Papaver erraticum Pyrenaicum luteo flore* C. Bauhin, Prodr. Theatr. Bot.: 92 (1620).]

[*Papaver errat. Pyrenaicum flore flavo* C. Bauhin, Pinax Theatr. Bot.: 171 (1623).]

[*Argemone lutea Cambro-Britanica* Parkinson, Theatr. Bot.: 369, fig. dextr. (1640). Morison, Pl. Hist. Univers. Oxon. ii: sect. 3, tab. 14 fig. 12 (1680).]

[*Argemone Cambro-Britanica lutea* Parkinson, *op. cit.*: 370 (1640). Ray, Hist. Pl. i: 856 (1686).]

[*Argemone Cambrobritannica lutea capite longiore glabro paucis spinulis ad loculamentorum juncturas ornato* Morison, *tom. cit.*: 279 (1680).]

[*Papaver luteum perenne, laciniato folio Cambro-britannicum* Ray, Syn. Meth. Stirp. Brit.: 122 (1690).]

[*Papaver cambricum perenne, flore sulphureo* Dill., Hort. Eltham. ii: 300, tab. 223 (1732).]

[*Papaver foliis pinnatis, fructu acuminato* L., Hort. Cliffort.: 201 (1737).]

Papaver cambricum L., Sp. Plant. i: 508 (1753). Sowerby, Engl. Bot.: tab. 66 (1790). Redouté, Choix Plus Bell. Fl.: tab. [92] (1827).

Papaver luteum Lam., Fl. Fr. iii: 173 (1778), *nomen illegitimum.*

Papaver flavum Moench., Meth. Pl.: 247 (1794), *nomen illegitimum.*

Papaver alpinum Salisb., Prodr. Stirp.: 377 (1796), *nomen illegitimum*—non *P. alpinum* L. (1753).

Argemone cambrica (L.) Desportes in Dict. Sci. Nat. ii: 481 (1804).

Cerastites cambrica (L.) Gray, Nat. Arrang. Brit. Pl. ii: 704 (1821).

Stylophorum cambricum (L.) Spreng. in L., Syst. Veg. Ed. 16, ii: 570 (1825).

Meconopsis cambrica formae *oxyphylla, oblita, hispanica, incisa, pyrenaica, borealis, tanacetoides, decipiens, inornata, gallica, nubilosa, arvernensis* Gandog., Fl. Europ. i: 330 (1883).

[*Meconopsis cambrica flore-pleno* Nicholson, Cent. Suppl. Dict. Gard.: 528 (1901).]

Meconopsis cambrica plena Hort. ex Stormonth in Garden lxvii: 157 (1905).

Meconopsis cambrica var. *aurantiaca* Hort. ex Wehrhahn, Gartenstaud. i: 467 (1930).

Description. *Polycarpic. Rootstock* branched, tufted, covered with persistent scaly leaf-bases. *Stems* erect, branched, leafy, glabrous or very sparsely hairy, attaining 2 ft. in height. *Basal leaves* (with long petioles) up to 8 in. in length; lamina pinnatisect towards the base and pinnatifid towards the apex, lower segments distant, segments pinnatifid or variously lobed, sparsely hairy or glabrous. *Upper cauline leaves* more shortly petiolate (uppermost occasionally subsessile), otherwise similar to the basal leaves. *Flowers* arising singly in the axils of the upper leaves, pedicels up to 10 in. in length, sparsely hairy or glabrous. *Petals* normally 4 (often multiplied in garden forms), obovate to suborbicular, up to 1·5 in. in length and 1·5 in. in breadth, yellow. *Stamens* numerous; filaments filiform, whitish; anthers yellow. *Ovary* ovoid to ellipsoid, glabrous; style short but distinct, up to 0·1 in. in length; stigma capitate, 4–6-lobed, green. *Capsule* ellipsoid-oblong, prominently 4–7-ribbed, splitting by 4–7 valves for about a quarter of its length. *Seeds* more or less reniform, testa with longitudinal rows of shallow pits. (Plate I.)

Geographical Range. Wales, western Ireland, south-western England and southwards through western France to northern Spain; in damp, shady, rocky places usually below 2,000 ft.; now extensively naturalised in many localities. Originally described from Wales.

The taxonomy and history of this species have been so fully discussed in the Introduction that only a few observations require to be made here. *M. cambrica* is the species on which Viguier founded the genus in 1814. Linnaeus had previously described the plant in 1753, referring it to *Papaver* although, in having a distinct style, it did not conform to his definition of that genus. The presence of a style led Viguier to remove the species from *Papaver* and regard it as typifying a separate genus. Thus *M. cambrica* is the type-species, although the significance of this has been overlooked by horticulturists in the stress which has been laid on the cultivated Asiatic species. Further, the introduction of these exotic plants has probably led to the indifference with which *M. cambrica* is now regarded.

In many gardens it is now considered an undesirable plant, but this reputation is scarcely merited and is probably to be accounted for by its tendency to increase so rapidly from self-sown seed, a property which is not shared to any great extent by its more desirable relatives. It is difficult to understand why *M. cambrica* sometimes fails to establish itself, for generally it is a most accommodating plant, adapting itself equally well to damp, shady woods or on dry walls and then providing with its attractive tufted habit and long-flowering season a desirable horticultural plant.

M. cambrica in its distribution forms an outlier remote from the circumscribed area in which the other members of the genus are found. Indeed, it has appeared possible that the genus *Meconopsis* might conceivably be restricted to the type-species, but the occurrence in Asia of species closely related to it has led to the conclusion that separate generic status is undesirable.

Parkinson, in 1640, recorded the plant, under the name *Argemone Cambro-Britanica lutea*, as occurring " in many places of Wales," precise localities being given. In this early publication there is also an excellent description of the species and a recognisable plate. (See Frontispiece.)

In addition to the typical form, *M. cambrica* is represented in cultivation by a double-flowered strain (" *M. cambrica flore-pleno* ") in which, as in the type, the flower-colour may be orange.

A hybrid has been recorded* between *M. cambrica* and *M. quintuplinervia*. It appeared spontaneously, where the two species had been growing in association, at Brockhurst, East Grinstead, Sussex, in 1919, but it died out and no specimens are available on which to base a proper description.

* *M. cambrica* × *M. quintuplinervia* Journ. Roy. Hort. Soc. xlv: cxiii (1920).

Sect. II. **EUCATHCARTIA**

Meconopsis sect. Eucathcartia (Prain) G. Tayl., comb. nov.

Cathcartia sect. *Eucathcartia* Prain in Ann. of Bot. xx: 368 (1906).

Species 4, each severally occurring in limited areas in western Hupeh and north-eastern Szechuan, western Szechuan, north-eastern Upper Burma and north-western Yunnan, and eastern Nepal to Bhutan. Type-species: *Meconopsis villosa* (Hook. f.) G. Tayl. (*Cathcartia villosa* Hook. f. ex Hook.).

Within the section *Eucathcartia* are included all the Asiatic species which combine the character of a polycarpic habit with 4-petalled yellow flowers. The four members are readily distinguished from the *Cambricae* by the usually dense pubescence of barbellate rufous hairs investing the tufted base of the plant and by the production of a single flowering-stem.

Ser. i. **CHELIDONIFOLIAE**

Meconopsis ser. Chelidonifoliae Prain in [Journ. As. Soc. Bengal lxiv, 2: 311 et 313 in obs. (1896), *nomen nudum*, pro parte, excl. *M. cambrica*] Ann. of Bot. xx: 364 (1906).

Meconopsis sect. *Polychaetia* Prain *tom. cit.*: 352 (1906) pro parte, quoad ser. 9.

Meconopsis subgen. *Polychaetia* (Prain) Fedde in Engl., Pflanzenr. iv, 104: 262 (1909) pro parte, quoad sect. 9.

Meconopsis sect. *Chelidonifoliae* (Prain) Fedde *tom. cit.*: 270 (1909).

Species 2, confined to central China (see Fig. 2). Type-species: *Meconopsis chelidonifolia* Bur. and Franch.

The two members of this series are characterised by their branching habit, the branches usually bearing several flowers. In their vegetative features the species are remarkably similar, but they can be readily separated by their very different fruits.

2. **MECONOPSIS CHELIDONIFOLIA**

Meconopsis chelidonifolia Bur. and Franch. in Journ. de Bot. v: 19 (1891); in Bonvalot, Tibet Inconnu: 467 (1892). Prain in Journ. As. Soc. Bengal lxiv, 2: 311 (1896); Novic. Ind.: 113 (1905); in Ann. of Bot. xx: 364 (1906); in Bull. Misc. Inf. Kew 1915: 177 (1915); in Countr. Life liv: 111 (1923). Bretschneider, Hist. Eur. Bot. Discov. China ii: 913 (1898). Bulley in Fl. and Sylva iii: 82 (1905). Fedde in Engl., Pflanzenr. iv, 104: 270, fig. 34C (1909). E. H. Wilson, West. China i: 127 (1913). Besant in Journ. Hortic. lxvi: 149 (1913). Ball in Gard.

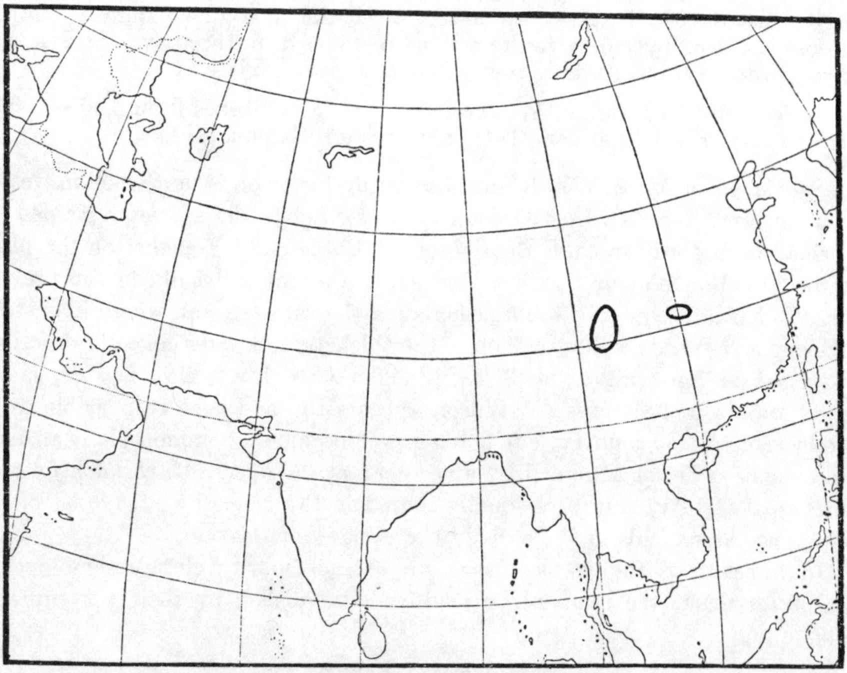

FIG. 2.—MAP SHOWING THE GEOGRAPHICAL RANGE OF THE SERIES *Chelidonifoliae*.
In their distribution the two species do not overlap; *M. chelidonifolia* is confined to western Szechuan while *M. Oliverana* occupies a more easterly area in eastern Szechuan and western Hupeh.

Chron., Ser. 3, lv: 248 (1914). Jenkins in Garden lxxviii: 240 (1914). Bull. Misc. Inf. Kew 1914, App.: 72 (1914). E. A. Bowles in Garden lxxx: 358, fig. (1916). Farrer, Engl. Rock-Gard. i: 475 (1919). Irving in Garden lxxxvii: 170, fig. (1923). Kingdon-Ward in Gard. Chron., Ser. 3, lxxix: 460 (1926). L. H. Bailey, Stand. Cycloped. Hort., New Ed. ii: 2017 (1927). Wehrhahn, Gartenstaud. i: 467 (1930). A. T. Johnson in Gard. Chron., Ser. 3, lxxxix: 126, 238 (1931); *op. cit.* xci: 423 (1932).

DESCRIPTION. *Polycarpic*. *Rootstock* covered with persistent leaf-bases interspersed with rufous bristles, passing below into a branched root-system. *Stem* erect, branched, up to 3 ft. in height, grooved, appressed rufous bristles present (at least towards the base). *Basal leaves* pinnatisect towards the base, pinnatifid towards the apex, the segments distant and pinnatifidly or pinnatisectly lobed, bristly on both surfaces and on the petiole, glaucous on the lower surface; not present at time of flowering. *Upper cauline leaves* sessile, tending to be trifoliolate or tripartite with the segments pinnately lobed, otherwise similar to the lower leaves. *Flowers* arising on slender pedicels borne singly in the axils of the upper cauline leaves. *Petals* 4, more or less obovate or suborbicular, up to 0·8 in. in length and 0·9 in. in breadth, yellow. *Stamens* numerous; filaments filiform; anthers narrowly oblong, yellow. *Ovary* ellipsoid, glabrous or sparsely bristly towards the base; style short but distinct; stigma capitate. *Capsule* ellipsoid, splitting by 5–6 valves for a short distance from the apex. *Seeds* falcate-oblong, testa with longitudinal rows of shallow pits. (Plate II.)

Geographical Range. Western Szechuan, at altitudes from 6,000–9,000 ft. Originally described from near Tatsienlu, western Szechuan.

Specimens of *M. chelidonifolia*, collected by Faber on Mount Omei in western Szechuan, were received in this country in 1887, but the species remained undescribed until 1891, and was then based by Bureau and Franchet on the plants obtained by Bonvalot and Prince Henri d'Orléans at Tatsienlu in the previous year. It has subsequently been gathered in the same region, where it is stated by Henry and Wilson to be common in the thickets, the latter collector describing the species as "growing about 3 ft. in height with clear yellow flowers, saucer-shaped and 2½ inches across." Wilson appears to have been responsible for its introduction to this country, but it has never become a common plant although its propagation is not attended by any apparent difficulty. *M. chelidonifolia* has the unusual faculty, only occasionally shared in the genus by *M. lyrata*, of producing vegetative buds in the axils of the upper stem-leaves.

In appearance the species bears an extraordinarily close resemblance to *M. Oliverana*, but the two can be readily distinguished by their very different fruits.

3. MECONOPSIS OLIVERANA

Meconopsis Oliverana Franch. and Prain ex Prain in Journ. As. Soc. Bengal lxiv, 2: 312 ("*Oliveriana*") (1896); Novic. Ind.: 114 (1905); in Ann. of Bot. xx: 365 (1906); in Bull. Misc. Inf. Kew 1915: 177 (1915); in Countr. Life liv: 111 (1923). Fedde in Engl., Pflanzenr. iv, 104: 270 (1909). Farrer, Engl. Rock-Gard. i: 478 ("*Olivieri*") (1919). L. H. Bailey, Stand. Cycloped. Hort., New Ed. ii: 2019 (1927).

Description. *Polycarpic. Rootstock* covered with persistent leaf-bases and rufous barbellate bristles. *Stem* erect, branched, leafy, glabrous or very sparsely bristly towards the base, conspicuously grooved, reaching 3 ft. in height. *Basal and lower cauline leaves* withered at time of flowering. *Upper cauline leaves* numerous, sessile or subsessile, somewhat stem-clasping; lamina pinnatisect towards the base, pinnatifid towards the apex (segments distant and pinnately lobed), up to 3·5 in. in length and 1·5 in. in breadth, more or less densely hairy and ultimately glabrescent on the upper surface, glaucous on the lower surface. *Flowers* arising singly on slender pedicels in the axils of the upper cauline leaves. *Petals* 4, suborbicular, about 0·75 in. in length and 0·75 in. in breadth, yellow. *Stamens* numerous; filaments filiform; anthers narrowly oblong, yellow. *Ovary* narrowly oblong or subcylindric, glabrous; style obsolete or very short; stigma 4–5-lobed, the lobes more or less decurrent. *Capsule* narrowly oblong or subcylindric, splitting for a short distance from the apex by 4–5 valves. *Seeds* falcate-oblong, testa with longitudinal rows of shallow pits.

GEOGRAPHICAL RANGE. Eastern Szechuan and western Hupeh. No altitudes are indicated by collectors. Originally described from Chengkow-ting, eastern Szechuan and Fang-hsien, western Hupeh.

This species has never been introduced into cultivation, but it resembles *M. chelidonifolia* so very closely that it would probably not make a very wide appeal to horticulturists. In its capsule-characters *M. Oliverana* closely approaches *M. villosa*, and it is remarkable that these species, until now, have been referred to different genera. When *M. Oliverana* was originally described the flower-colour was stated definitely not to be yellow, but Wilson in his field notes records the petals as being of that colour.

The species was based on specimens collected by the Abbé Farges in Szechuan and by Henry in Hupeh.

SER. ii. **VILLOSAE**

MECONOPSIS ser. VILLOSAE G. Tayl., ser. nov.

Cathcartia Hook. f. ex Hook. in Curt. Bot. Mag. lxxvii: sub tab. 4596 (1851).

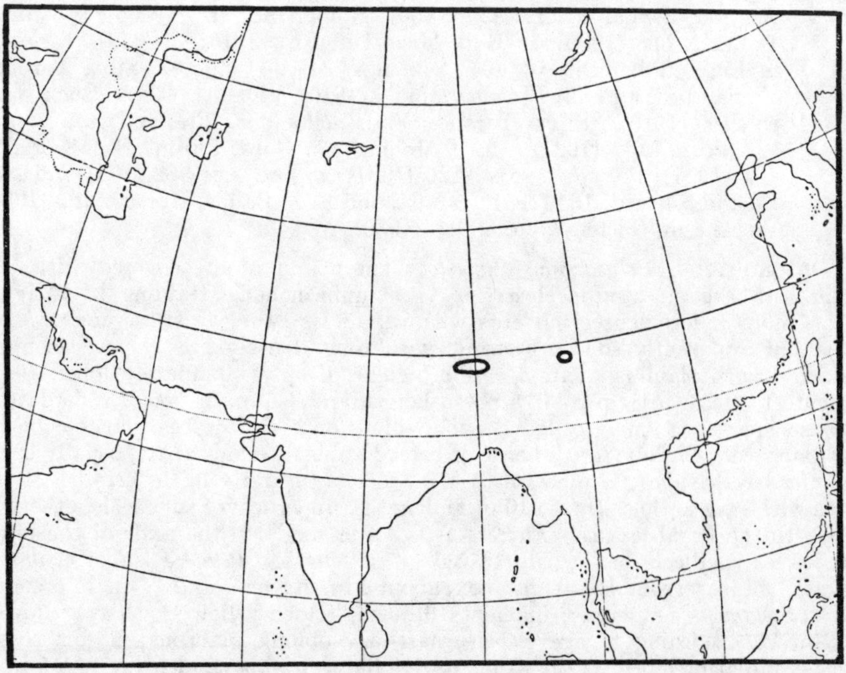

FIG. 3.—MAP SHOWING THE GEOGRAPHICAL RANGE OF THE SERIES *Villosae*.
M. villosa occurs from eastern Nepal to Bhutan, while M. *Smithiana* is found in a more limited westerly area in north-eastern Upper Burma and north-western Yunnan.

Species 2, one a native of the Indo-Himalaya from eastern Nepal to Bhutan, the other occurring in extreme north-eastern Upper Burma and north-western Yunnan (see Fig. 3). Type-species: *Meconopsis villosa* (Hook. f.) G. Tayl. (*Cathcartia villosa* Hook. f. ex Hook.).

In the series *Villosae* the stem is unbranched and the flowers are borne singly in the axils of the uppermost leaves. The association of these characters serves to separate this series from the preceding one, with which it is very closely related.

4. MECONOPSIS VILLOSA

Meconopsis villosa (Hook. f.) G. Tayl. comb. nov.

Cathcartia villosa Hook. f. ex Hook. in Curt. Bot. Mag. lxxvii: tab. 4596 (1851); Hook. f., Himal. Journ. ii: 198 (1854); Illustr. Himal. Pl.: frontisp. (1855). Lem., Jard. Fl. ii: 167 (1851). Planch. in Fl. Serr. vii: 115, tab. 686 (1851). B. J. in Cottage Gard. vii: 379, fig. (1852). Hook. f. and Thoms., Fl. Ind. i: 255 (1855); in Hook. f., Fl. Brit. Ind. i: 119 (1872). Walp., Ann. Bot. Syst. iv: 175 (1857). Nicholson, Illustr. Dict. Gard. i: 280 (1885). Garden xxxvi: 22 (1889). Prain in Journ. As. Soc. Bengal lxiv, 2: 325 (1896); Novic. Ind.: 127 (1905); in Ann. of Bot. xx: 368 (1906); in Bull. Misc. Inf. Kew 1915: 134 (1915). Fedde in Engl., Pflanzenr. iv, 104: 245, figs. 34 A–C (1909). Silva Tarouca, Freiland-Staud.: 59 ("*Catcarthia*") (1910). Farrer, Engl. Rock-Gard. i: 210 (1919). Silva Tarouca and Schneider, Freiland-Staud.: 145 ("*Catcarthia*") (1927). A. T. Johnson in Gard. Chron., Ser. 3, lxxxii: 484 (1927); *op. cit.* lxxxix: 126 (1931); *op. cit.* xc; 362 (1931); in New Fl. and Silva iii: 134 (1931). L. H. and E. Z. Bailey, Hortus: 128 (1930). Wehrhahn, Gartenstaud. i: 466 (1930).

Description. *Polycarpic*. *Rootstock* short and stout, covered with persistent leaf-bases and rufous bristles. *Stem* unbranched, attaining 15–24 in. in height, more or less densely covered with rufous spreading bristles. *Basal leaves* tufted but apparently soon withering, with long densely bristly petioles up to 8 in. in length; lamina ovate to suborbicular, deeply bipinnately lobed (lobes subacute to rounded), up to 4·75 in. in length and 4·5 in. in breadth, cordate at the base, sparsely to more or less densely villous on both surfaces, glaucous on the under surface. *Cauline leaves* borne at considerable intervals apart, usually larger than the basal leaves; lamina up to 4 in. in length and 4 in. in breadth; lower leaves with long petioles (up to 10 in. in length), upper leaves subsessile, otherwise similar to the basal leaves. *Flowers* 1–5, borne singly in the axils of the upper stem-leaves; pedicels bristly, up to 5·5 in. in length. *Petals* 4, suborbicular to obovate, obtuse to rounded at the apex, about 1 in. in length and 1·5 in. in breadth, yellow. *Stamens* numerous; filaments filiform, golden-yellow; anthers yellow to dark-brown according to age. *Ovary* narrowly oblong, glabrous; stigma sessile with 4–7 radiating lobes. *Capsule* narrowly oblong or subcylindric (up to 3·5 in. in length and 0·25 in. in breadth), splitting to more than half its length by 4–7 valves. *Seeds* falcate-oblong, testa with longitudinal rows of shallow pits. (Plate III.)

Geographical Range. Eastern Nepal to Bhutan, at altitudes from 9,000–14,000 ft. Originally described from Sikkim.

The remarks on p. 6 indicate the necessity for the transference of this species to *Meconopsis*. It is a plant of considerable horticultural merit. The perennial habit, rich yellow flowers and altogether attractive appearance are sufficient, one would have thought, to ensure for it a wider reputation than it enjoys at present. The species was discovered by J. D. Hooker in 1849 in eastern Sikkim, and flowered at Kew in 1851 from seeds sent home by him from that area. As *M. villosa* is most often treated as a woodland subject, it is interesting to note that Hooker found it growing in rock-clefts at an altitude of 10,000 ft. The species was collected by Cooper in Bhutan in 1913 and again in 1933 in the same country by Ludlow and Sherriff, who found it growing in open forest glades and also on shady banks in dense forest.

5. MECONOPSIS SMITHIANA

Meconopsis Smithiana (Hand.-Mazz.) G. Tayl. ex Hand.-Mazz. in Symb. Sin. vii: 337 (1931).

Cathcartia Smithiana Hand.-Mazz. in Anz. Akad. Wiss. Wien, Math.-naturv. Kl. lx: 182 (1923).

Description. *Polycarpic. Rootstock* short and stout, covered with persistent leaf-bases and rufous barbellate bristles, passing below into a fibrous root-system. *Stem* unbranched, attaining over 3 ft. in height, sparsely bristly (the bristles slightly reflexed) and ultimately more or less glabrescent, at the base invested with the remnants of persistent leaves. *Cauline leaves* borne at considerable distances from each other, lower leaves petiolate, upper leaves sessile or subsessile; lamina pinnately trifoliolate, up to 4·5 in. in length and 2·25 in. in breadth, covered with scattered appressed bristles on both surfaces; terminal leaflet more or less pinnately lobed, lobes rounded or subacute; basal leaflets about 1 in. distant from the terminal one, usually bipinnately lobed, lobes rounded or subacute; petiole about 4 in. in length, sparsely bristly. *Flowers* about 4, borne singly in the axils of the uppermost cauline leaves. *Petals* 4, broadly obovate and somewhat emarginate at the apex, about 0·75 in. in length and 0·75 in. in breadth, yellow. *Ovary* subglobose, densely covered with appressed rufous bristles; style obsolete or very short; stigma 5-lobed.

Geographical Range. Extreme north-eastern Upper Burma and north-western Yunnan, at altitudes from 10,000–12,000 ft. Originally described from Yunnan.

This species, an inhabitant of damp woods and alpine meadows, was discovered by Handel-Mazzetti in north-western Yunnan in 1916, and described by him some years later in the genus *Cathcartia*, the specific epithet honouring Sir

William Wright Smith, Regius Keeper, Royal Botanic Garden, Edinburgh. It has since been collected by Farrer in the same area, but on the Burmese side of the border, these being the only known records of the plant.

M. Smithiana is clearly allied to *M. villosa*, but is distinguished from that species by having trifoliolate leaves and a subglobose ovary. In the original description the species was stated to be monocarpic but the rootstocks show perennating buds, and these, together with the close affinity to *M. villosa*, suggest that it is polycarpic.

It is stated to be locally abundant on the stony alpine meadows, but as no ripe fruits and seeds have been collected its merit as a garden plant can be judged only from herbarium specimens. The resemblance to *M. villosa* suggests that *M. Smithiana* would be an equally desirable horticultural plant.

Sect. III. **POLYCHAETIA**

Meconopsis sect. Polychaetia Prain in Ann. of Bot. xx: 352 (1906) emend., excl. ser. 7 et 9.

[*Polychaetia* Wall., Numer. List: 277, sub n. 8125 (1832), *nomen synonymum*; ex Prain in Journ. As. Soc. Bengal lxiv, 2: 316 (1896), *nomen synonymum* —non *Polychaetia* Less. (1832).]

Meconopsis subgen. *Polychaetia* (Prain) Fedde in Engl., Pflanzenr. iv, 104: 262 (1909) pro parte, excl. sect. 7 et 9.

Meconopsis ser. *Decorae* Prain in Bull. Misc. Inf. Kew 1915: 143 (1915).

Species 3, arranged in two subsections, distributed from north-eastern Tibet, western Kansu and central Shensi to north-western Yunnan and northern Upper Burma, and westwards along the Himalayas and through southern Tibet to Kashmir and Chitral. Type-species: *Meconopsis paniculata* (D. Don) Prain (*Polychaetia paniculata* Wall. ex Prain).

The section *Polychaetia*, by far the largest in the genus, includes both polycarpic and monocarpic species, but when polycarpic, in contrast to the sections *Cambricae* and *Eucathcartia*, they never have yellow flowers.

Subsect. *a*. **EUPOLYCHAETIA**

Meconopsis subsect. Eupolychaetia G. Tayl., subsect. nov.*

Species 9, arranged in two series, occurring from Kumaun to western Szechuan and north-western Yunnan. Type-species: *Meconopsis paniculata* (D. Don) Prain.

All the species included in this subsection are monocarpic and, in retaining a dense rosette of leaves during the winter, form a very distinctive group of plants. They may take several years to reach maturity and the basal rosette of leaves persists throughout that period, ultimately producing a flowering shoot from the

* Species monocarpicae sect. *Polychaetiae*, foliis per hiemem persistentibus rosulatis.

centre and carrying up the inner leaves. The flowering-stem is most commonly tall and branched. In their winter state the cultivated species are extremely handsome and the appearance of the leaves is often enhanced by the presence of a dense pubescence. By using leaf and pubescence characters it is possible to recognise two series, *Superbae* and *Robustae*, within the subsection *Eupolychaetia*.

SER. i. SUPERBAE

MECONOPSIS ser. SUPERBAE Kingdon-Ward in Gard. Chron., Ser. 3, lxxix: [252 (err. "*Surperbae*") (Apr. 1926), *nomen nudum*] 460 in obs. (Jun. 1926) emend., quoad *M. superba*.

Meconopsis ser. *Robustae* Prain in Journ. As. Soc. Bengal lxiv, 2: 315 (1896) pro parte, quoad sp. 6.

Meconopsis sect. *Robustae* (Prain) Fedde in Engl., Pflanzenr. iv, 104: 267 (1909) pro parte, quoad sp. 22.

Species 2, occurring in central Nepal, the Chumbi region of Tibet and western Bhutan (see Fig. 4). Type-species: *Meconopsis superba* King ex Prain.

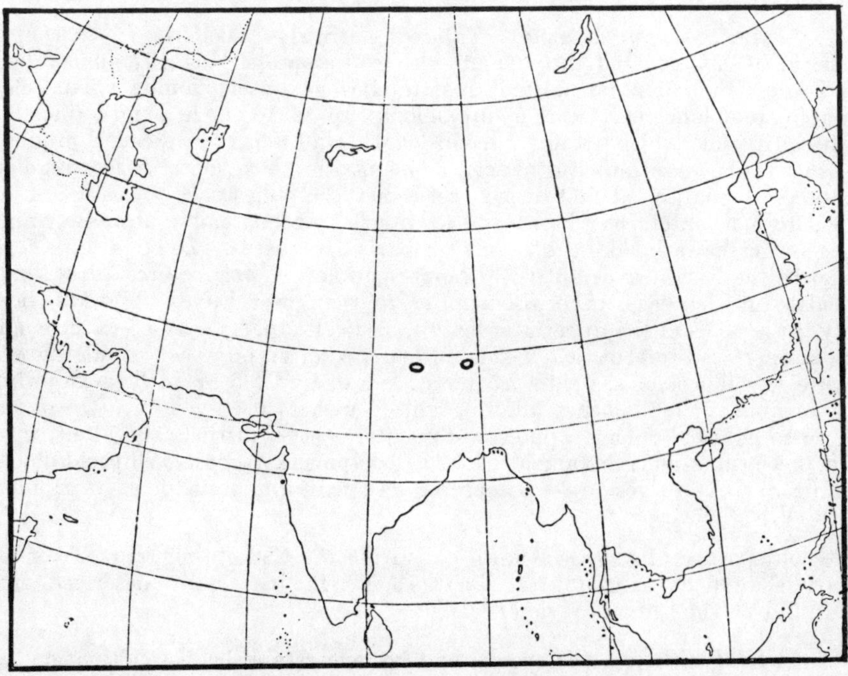

FIG. 4.—MAP SHOWING THE GEOGRAPHICAL RANGE OF THE SERIES *Superbae*.

The two species of this series inhabit distinct but apparently very limited areas. *M. regia* is known only from central Nepal and *M. superba* occurs to the east in the Chumbi region of Tibet and western Bhutan.

In this series the leaves are serrate at the margin and covered with a dense sericeous pubescence which gives to the plants, particularly in their winter conditions, a very characteristic appearance.

6. MECONOPSIS SUPERBA

MECONOPSIS SUPERBA King ex Prain in Journ. As. Soc. Bengal lxiv, 2: 317 (1896): Novic. Ind.: 119 (1905). King and Prain in Ann. Roy. Bot. Gard. Calcutta ix, 1: 4, tab. 2 (1901). Prain in Gard. Chron., ser. 3, xxxvii: 369 (1905); in Ann. of Bot. xx: 357 (1906); in Bull. Misc. Inf. Kew 1915: 170 (1915). Mottet in Jardin xx: 101 (1906). Fedde in Engl., Pflanzenr. iv, 104: 267 (1909). Farrer, Engl. Rock-Gard. i; 482 (1919). Kingdon-Ward in Gard. Chron., Ser. 3, lxxix: 460 (1926); in Ann. of Bot. xl: 545 (1926). L. H. Bailey, Stand. Cycloped. Hort., New Ed. ii: 2019 (1927). Lofthouse in Gard. Chron., Ser. 3, lxxxiii: 229, figs. 112–113 (1928); in New Fl. and Silva v: 203, fig. 71 (1933). Journ. Roy. Hort. Soc. liv: xxxii. figs. 96–97 (1929). J. T. Wall in Gard. Chron., Ser. 3, lxxxvii: 513, figs. 213–214 (1930). Harrow in New Fl. and Silva ii: 150 (1930). Hay in New Fl. and Silva ii: 169, fig. 63 (1930). Wehrhahn, Gartenstaud. i: 468 (1930).

DESCRIPTION. *Monocarpic. Tap-root* narrowly dauciform. *Plant* up to 3·5 ft. in height, covered throughout with soft appressed usually silvery hairs. *Basal leaves* in a dense persistent rosette during winter; lamina oblanceolate, oblanceolate-oblong, elliptic or ovate-oblong, up to 16 in. in length (including the broad petiole which attains 2 in. in length) and 3·5 in. in breadth, gradually tapering at the base into the petiole, acute at the apex, more or less regularly serrate at the margin, at first densely sericeous (the pubescence consisting of long barbellate hairs interspersed with shorter much-branched hairs), ultimately many of the longer hairs breaking off, leaving barbellate bases. *Lower cauline leaves* similar to the basal leaves but with shorter petioles. *Upper cauline leaves* sessile, auriculate at the base, otherwise similar to the lower leaves. *Flowers* borne singly in the axils of the uppermost leaves; pedicels stout, up to 4·5 in. in length, densely appressed-tomentose. *Petals* normally 4 (often 6 in the terminal flower), obovate to suborbicular, up to 2·5 in. in length and 2·5 in. in breadth, white. *Stamens* numerous; filaments filiform, white; anthers deep-yellow. *Ovary* subglobose to ellipsoid-oblong, appressed-tomentose; style distinct and stout, up to 0·4 in. in length; stigma prominently lobed, deep-purple. *Capsule* ellipsoid-oblong, splitting by 7–11 valves. *Seeds* more or less reniform, testa densely papillose. (Plate IV.)

GEOGRAPHICAL RANGE. Known only from the Chumbi region of Tibet and western Bhutan at altitudes of about 13,500 ft. Originally described from Ho-Ko-Chu in the Chumbi region of Tibet.

Until 1933, although the species had become established in cultivation, our knowledge of the plant in its natural state was derived solely from the original collections on which the species was based. These specimens were obtained by a native collector in 1884 at Ho-Ko-Chu in the Chumbi district of Tibet, portions of the type-collection being deposited in herbaria of this country. This remained the only known record of the natural occurrence of *M. superba* until it was discovered by Ludlow and Sherriff in June 1933 in western Bhutan, and an excellent series of specimens was obtained by these collectors. They noted that the species occurred above the snow line and were successful in securing an ample supply of seeds.

It is surprising that *M. superba* should unexpectedly appear in cultivation in this country and that the origin of the seeds should remain unknown. From the original plants, which flowered in 1927, seed was obtained, but the species is still rare in gardens, and does not appear to be so tolerant of cultural methods as its nearest relative *M. regia*. In the attractive winter rosette stage the two species are very similar and can be distinguished only by the more hoary appearance of *M. superba*, which has also more conspicuously barbellate hairs. In the flowering-stage, as indicated under *M. regia*, the two species are easily separable. Experience in cultivation has shown that *M. superba* is a less robust plant which fails to reach the size attained under natural conditions. In the original description it is stated to be "apparently 6 ft. high" with stem leaves "10–20 in. long."

M. SUPERBA × M. BETONICIFOLIA = 19C. × **M. Musgravei** G. Tayl. See p. 67.

7. MECONOPSIS REGIA

MECONOPSIS REGIA G. Tayl. in Journ. of Bot. lxvii: 259 (1929). Harrow in New Fl. and Silva ii: 150 (1930). Hay in New Fl. and Silva ii: 169, fig. 64 (1930); *op. cit.* iv: 44, tab. opp. 44 (1931); in Gard. Chron., Ser. 3, lxxxix: 354, figs. 178–179 (1931); *op. cit.* xcii: 392, fig. 196 (1932). Gard. Chron., Ser. 3, lxxxix: 343 (1931). G. C. Tayl. in Countr. Life lxix: liv, fig. (1931); *op. cit.* lxxiv: l, fig. (1933); *tom. cit.*: 310, fig. (1933). Journ. Roy. Hort. Soc. lvii: xxiii (1932). F. H. Fisher in Bull. Alp. Gard. Soc. i: 121, tab. 43 (1932).

DESCRIPTION. *Monocarpic*, covered throughout with soft hairs. *Tap-root* dauciform. *Basal leaves* persisting in a dense rosette throughout the winter, up to 16 in. in length (including the petiole) and about 3·5 in. in breadth; lamina narrowly elliptic, tapering equally towards the base and apex, more or less regularly and acutely serrate at the margin, decurrent into a broad short petiole at the base, densely covered on both surfaces with a silvery (or sometimes golden) felt of long appressed hairs. *Upper leaves* less densely hairy, sessile and more or less stem-clasping. *Flowering-stem* branched, attaining at least 2 ft. in height. *Flowers* numerous, borne on stout usually densely villous branches arising from the axils of the cauline leaves, the lower branches most often 4-flowered, the upper branches 1-flowered. *Petals* usually 4 (but terminal flower usually with 6 petals), suborbicular, up to 2·6 in. in length and 2 in. in breadth, yellow. *Stamens* numerous; filaments filiform, of the same colour as the petals; anthers deep-orange. *Ovary* globose or ovoid, densely covered with appressed bristles; style distinct, stout and thickened at the base, up to about 0·5 in. in length; stigma with 7–12 prominent lobes, reddish-purple. *Capsule* oblong-ellipsoid, densely covered with persistent appressed bristles, the persistent style prominently thickened towards the base, splitting by 7–12 valves. *Seeds* more or less reniform or ellipsoid-oblong, testa densely papillose. (Plate V.)

Geographical Range. Confined to central Nepal at altitudes from 12,000–15,000 ft. Originally described from Barpak and Michet, central Nepal.

The dimensions given above are taken from the available herbarium specimens and are usually much exceeded by cultivated plants. When well grown *M. regia* may attain a height of 5 ft., the leaves may be 28 in. in length while the flowers are occasionally 6 in. in diameter.

This very handsome species was first received in this country in 1928 from Barpak in central Nepal. It has since been sent from several Nepalese localities but has so far never been collected outside that kingdom. In appearance the species much resembles *M. superba,* the two being characterised by a dense covering of silky hairs on the serrate leaves. They are, however, easily distinguished as the flowers of *M. regia* are yellow and borne in an openly branched inflorescence, whereas those of *M. superba* are white and borne singly from the main axis.

The fruiting specimens show that in its natural state the hairs of *M. regia* turn to a rich golden-brown colour and this characteristic has been noted in cultivated plants, sometimes occurring in the juvenile state but usually only when the plants reach maturity. It appears that there are two strains in cultivation; one in which the golden hairs are present throughout the life of the plant, and the other more robust form in which the hairs are silvery at first but ultimately become golden-brown.

M. regia flowered for the first time in this country in 1931 and was then the object of wide admiration. Its merit as a garden plant is much enhanced by the beautiful dense rosette of persistent leaves produced during the winter months.

Ser. ii. **ROBUSTAE**

Meconopsis ser. Robustae Prain in Journ. As. Soc. Bengal lxiv, 2: 315 (1896) emend., excl. sp. 6.

Meconopsis sect. *Robustae* (Prain) Fedde in Engl., Pflanzenr. iv, 104; 267 (1909) pro parte, excl. sp. 22.

Species 7, distributed from Kumaun to western Szechuan and north-western Yunnan (see Fig. 5). Type-species: *Meconopsis robusta* Hook. f. and Thoms.

All the species included in this series have deeply lobed leaves and fall into two groups, one in which the flowers are yellow and the other in which the flowers

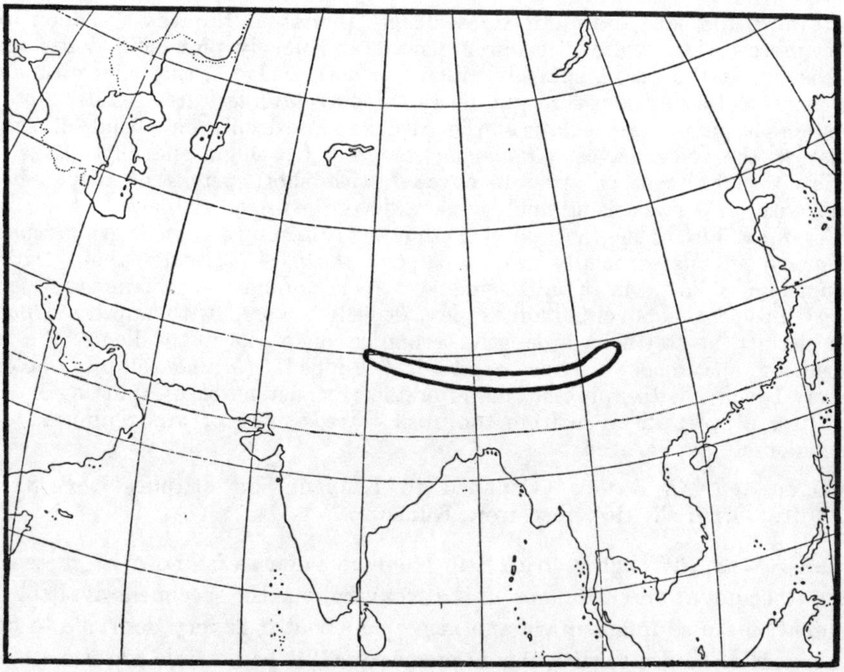

FIG. 5.—MAP SHOWING THE GEOGRAPHICAL RANGE OF THE SERIES *Robustae*.

are red, blue, purple, or rarely white. The five yellow-flowered species are very closely related, and when more fully known it is possible that some readjustment of the specific limits may be necessary.

8. MECONOPSIS ROBUSTA

MECONOPSIS ROBUSTA Hook. f. and Thoms., Fl. Ind. i: 253 (1855); in Hook. f., Fl. Brit. Ind. i: 118 (1872) pro parte. Walp., Ann. Bot. Syst. iv: 171 (1857). Prain in Journ. As. Soc. Bengal lxiv, 2: 315 (1896) pro parte; Novic. Ind.: 117 (1905) pro parte; in Gard. Chron., Ser. 3, xxxvii: 369 (1905); in Ann. of Bot. xx: 359 (1906) pro parte; in Bull. Misc. Inf. Kew 1915: 171, tab. opp. 176 fig. 2 (1915). Strachey, Cat. Pl. Kumaon: 10 (1906). Mottet in Jardin xx: 100 (1906); in Rev. Hort. xii: 204 (1912). Fedde in Engl., Pflanzenr. iv, 104: 268, fig. 34 D (1909) pro parte. Farrer, Engl. Rock-Gard. i.: 480 (1919) pro parte. Kingdon-Ward in Gard. Chron., Ser. 3, lxxix: 460 (1926) pro parte. Wehrhahn, Gartenstaud. i: 468 (1930). Hay in New Fl. and Silva iv: 225 (1932). G. Tayl. in Gard. Chron., Ser. 3, xcii: 41 (1932).

DESCRIPTION. *Monocarpic. Basal leaves* up to 13 in. in length (including the petiole, which may attain 5 in. in length) and 3 in. in breadth; lamina pinnatisect towards the base and more or less deeply pinnatifid towards the apex (segments more or less ovate, the lower distant and deeply pinnatifid, lobes acute to subacute at the apex), sparsely villous on both surfaces, the hairs ultimately breaking off, leaving short hispid bases. *Upper cauline leaves* sessile, more or less stem-clasping or auriculate at the base; lamina deeply pinnatifid, otherwise similar to the basal leaves. *Flowering-stem* 4–6 feet high, sparsely villous and ultimately glabrescent or sparsely covered with short persistent hispid bases of the hairs. *Flowers* arising singly in the axils of the upper cauline leaves; pedicels slender, up to 3 in. in length (becoming stout and attaining 8 in. in length in fruiting specimens), villous especially near the apex. *Petals* 4, obovate, about 1·25 in. in length and 0·75 in. in breadth, yellow. *Stamens* numerous; filaments filiform. *Ovary* ellipsoid to obovoid, more or less densely covered with appressed hairs; style distinct, up to 0·4 in. in length, becoming conspicuously swollen at the base in fruiting specimens; stigma capitate, 6–9-lobed. *Capsule* ellipsoid-oblong, sparsely covered with appressed hairs or their persistent bases, splitting by 6–9 valves for a short distance from the apex. *Seeds* more or less reniform, testa with a densely papillose coat.

Geographical Range. Confined to Kumaun, at altitudes from 8,000–10,300 ft. Originally described from Kumaun.

M. robusta, although restricted to Kumaun as far as is known at present, is stated to be not at all uncommon in that country, but the specimens available for examination are so fragmentary and incomplete that it is very desirable to have further material. Only when this is procured will it be possible to form an adequate conception of the species and ascertain its range of variation. Its salient characters are the single-flowered inflorescence branches and appressed hairs on the ovary and capsule. The species is easily separable from *M. paniculata*, of which at one time it was thought to be a geographical form, by the complete absence of a fine substellate pubescence.

Although all known specimens of *M. robusta* have one-flowered branches, they are from the upper part of the stem only, and it is possible that the lower branches may bear several flowers. Fruiting specimens, accompanied by an ample supply of seeds, were received in this country in the autumn of 1933 from near Pindari, Kumaun, and if plants can be successfully raised and brought to maturity, the uncertainty surrounding this species will be removed. The capsules of *M. robusta* are identical with those of *M. gracilipes* and, at present, the two species can be distinguished only by their inflorescence characters. When mature and complete specimens of *M. robusta* are available it may be necessary to merge the two species.

Several records exist of the occurrence of *M. robusta* in gardens, but it is doubtful if the species has ever been in cultivation and it is probable that some of the many forms of *M. paniculata* have been mistaken for it. The plant figured by J. D. Hooker as " *M. Nipalensis* " in " Curtis's Botanical Magazine " (tab.

5585) has been regarded as representing *M. robusta,* but the accompanying description clearly indicates that it is *M. paniculata* and the plate hardly differs from Hooker's illustration of that species (as "*M. nepalensis*") in his "Illustrations of Himalayan Plants."

9. MECONOPSIS DHWOJII

MECONOPSIS DHWOJII G. Tayl. ex Hay in New Fl. and Silva iv: 225, fig. 82 (July 8, 1932); in Gard. Chron., Ser. 3, xcii: 409, figs. 198–199 (1932). G. Tayl. in Gard. Chron., Ser. 3, xcii: 41 (July 16, 1932). F. H. Fisher in Bull. Alp. Gard. Soc. i: 163, tab. 66 (1932). Journ. Roy. Hort. Soc. lviii: xxxi (1933). G. C. Tayl. in Countr. Life lxxiii: xxvi, fig. (1933). Not. Roy. Bot. Gard. Edin. xviii: 64 (1933).

DESCRIPTION. *Monocarpic. Tap-root* dauciform. *Basal and lower cauline leaves* with long petioles, up to 13 in. in length (including the petiole); lamina pinnatisect towards the base and pinnatifid towards the apex (the segments roundly, obtusely, or subacutely lobed), sparsely bristly on both surfaces, the bases of the bristles usually purplish-black. *Upper cauline leaves* similar to the basal leaves but smaller. *Bracts* sessile, pinnatifidly lobed, more or less auriculate at the base. *Flowering-stem* branched, bristly with the bristles tufted immediately below the flowers, attaining 2 ft. in height. *Flowers* numerous, borne on axillary branches, the lower branches 3–5-flowered, the upper branches 1-flowered. *Petals* 4, obovate-orbicular, up to 1·5 in. in length and 1·5 in. in breadth, yellow. *Stamens* numerous; filaments filiform, whitish; anthers orange-yellow. *Ovary* globose or ellipsoid or ovoid, densely bristly, the bristles at first appressed but ultimately spreading; style slender or slightly thickened towards the base, about 0·25 in. in length; stigma capitate, green or yellowish-green. *Capsule* ellipsoid-oblong, splitting by 5–6 valves. *Seeds* ovoid or ellipsoid-oblong, testa densely papillose. (Plate VI.)

GEOGRAPHICAL RANGE. Restricted to eastern Nepal, at altitudes from 12,000–18,000 ft. Originally described from Sangmo, eastern Nepal.

This is one of the recent acquisitions from Nepal, and was described from a single gathering made at Sangmo by Lall Dhwoj, an officer in the Nepal Army, in whose honour the species was named.

M. Dhwojii is closely akin to *M. robusta,* a native of the neighbouring province of Kumaun, but unfortunately the material of that species available for comparison is very limited. From descriptions and the meagre material represented in herbaria, *M. robusta* appears to be a plant of considerable stature, and has flowers borne singly on axillary branches. The characters which serve to separate *M. Dhwojii* from *M. robusta* are the smaller stature, denser pubescence, more deeply divided leaves, the spreading hairs on the capsule and the unthickened style. Although the two species are widely separated geographically, it is possible that when fuller material of the Kumaun species becomes available a much closer taxonomic relationship will be recognised.

The seeds which accompanied the field specimens were successfully germinated, and the species flowered for the first time in this country in 1932. Particularly noteworthy features of *M. Dhwojii* are the finely cut leaves with dark-purple spots at the base of the bristles. The flowers are produced simultaneously from the axils of the basal and upper leaves.

10. MECONOPSIS GRACILIPES

Meconopsis gracilipes G. Tayl., sp. nov.*

Description. *Monocarpic. Basal leaves* unknown. *Upper cauline leaves* sessile; lamina auriculate at the base, obtuse to rounded at the apex, more or less deeply pinnately lobed at the margin (lobes acute to rounded at the apex), sparsely covered on both surfaces with barbellate hairs which break off, leaving persistent hispid bases, sometimes minutely puberulous. *Flowering-stem* branched, attaining at least 2 ft. in height, at first sparsely bristly but ultimately almost glabrescent. *Flowers* borne on slender axillary branches up to 15 in. in length, lower branches 3-flowered, upper branches 1-flowered. *Petals* 4, obovate or suborbicular, up to 1·25 in. in length and 1·0 in. in breadth, yellow. *Stamens* numerous; filaments filiform; anthers orange-yellow to dark-brown according to age. *Ovary* subglobose to ellipsoid, densely covered with appressed or obliquely spreading hairs; style distinct, up to 0·4 in. in length; stigma capitate. *Capsule* ellipsoid or oblong-ellipsoid, more or less densely covered with bristles or their persistent hispid bases, splitting by 4–7 valves for a short distance from the apex. *Seeds* more or less reniform, testa densely papillose.

Geographical Range. Central Nepal, at altitudes from 12,000–16,000 ft. Described from Khorlak, central Nepal.

The material on which this species is based consists of several portions of flowering-stems which cannot be satisfactorily identified as belonging to any described species in the series *Robustae*. It is possible that when fuller material of this new species and of *M. robusta* are available they will be found to merge but, at present, on account of their geographical segregation and certain morphological differences, it is more advisable to regard the two as distinct.

M. gracilipes is characteristic among the *Robustae* in having long slender branches and pedicels. In that group it is most closely related to *M. robusta* and *M. longipetiolata*, differing from the former in having the flowers borne on

* Inter species ser. *Robustarum* pedicellis gracillimis usque ad c. 37·5 cm. longis conspicua; *M. robustae* Wall. et *M. longipetiolatae* G. Tayl. peraffinis, sed a priori inflorescentia ramosa capsulaeque pubescentia magis densiore differt, et a *M. longipetiolata* habitu elatiore indumentoque sparsiore distinguitur. Typus in Herb. Mus. Brit., a Lall Dhwoj (n. 17) in Nepal anno 1928 lectus.

a branched inflorescence and in its capsule characters, while from the latter it is distinguished by its taller habit and sparse pubescence.

As seeds were sent from Nepal in 1928, the species has possibly been in cultivation.

11. MECONOPSIS PANICULATA

Meconopsis paniculata (D. Don) Prain in Journ. As. Soc. Bengal lxiv, 2: 316 (1896); Novic. Ind.: 118 (1905); in Gard. Chron., Ser. 3, xxxvii: 369 (1905); in Ann. of Bot. xx: 358 (1906); in Bull. Misc. Inf. Kew 1915: 170, tab. opp. 170 fig. 1 (1915); in Countr. Life liv: 110 (1923). Bulley in Fl. and Sylva iii: 84 (1905). T. Smith in Gard. Chron., Ser. 3, xlvi: 91 (1909). Fedde in Engl., Pflanzenr. iv, 104: 267, fig. 34 E (1909). Mottet in Jardin xx: 100 (1906); in Rev. Hort. xii: 204 (1912). Jenkins in Garden lxxviii: 240 (1914). Farrer, Engl. Rock-Gard. i: 478 (1919). Irving in Garden lxxxvii: 171 (1923). Harley in Garden lxxxix: 71, fig. (1925); in Journ. Roy. Hort. Soc. liii: 221, 226, fig. 29 (1928). Kingdon-Ward in Gard. Chron., Ser. 3, lxxix: 460 (1926); *op. cit.* lxxxii: 26 (1927); *op. cit.* lxxxvi: 111 (1929); in Garden xci: 340, fig. (1927); Plant Hunt. Edge World: 262 (1930). L. H. Bailey, Stand. Cycloped. Hort., New Ed. ii: 2019 (1927). Silva Tarouca and Schneider, Freiland-Staud.: 249 (1927). L. H. and E. Z. Bailey, Hortus: 390 (1930). Wehrhahn, Gartenstaud. i: 468 (1930). F. H. Fisher in Bull. Alp. Gard. Soc. i: 121, tab. 42 infr. (1932).

Papaver paniculatum D. Don, Prodr. Fl. Nepal.: 197 (1825), *nomen illegitimum*, pro parte.

Stylophorum nepalense (DC.) Spreng. in L., Syst. Veg., Ed. 16, iv, 2: 203 (1827) pro parte.

Stylophorum paniculatum (D. Don) Don, Gener. Syst. Gard. and Bot. i: 135 (1831), *nomen illegitimum*, pro parte.

[*Meconopsis napaulensis* (non DC.) Walp., Repert. Bot. Syst. i: 110 (1842) pro parte. Hook. f., Himal. Journ. ii: 53 ("*Nepalensis*") (1854); Illustr. Himal. Pl.: tab. 9 ("*nepalensis*") (1855); in Curt. Bot. Mag. xcii: tab. 5585 ("*Nipalensis*") (1866). Hook. f. and Thoms., Fl. Ind. i: 253 ("*Nipalensis*") (1855); in Hook. f., Fl. Brit. Ind. i: 118 ("*nipalensis*") (1872). Gard. Chron. 1855: 515 ("*Nipalensis*") (1855). Lem. in Illustr. Hort. iii: tab. 95 ("*nepalensis*") (1856). W. in Garden xiv: 280 ("*nepalensis*") (1878). Gard. Chron., New Ser., xi: 757 ("*nepalensis*") (1879). Towel in Gard. Chron., New Ser., xvii: 767 ("*nepalensis*") (1882). Robinson, Engl. Fl. Gard.: 183 ("*nepalensis*") (1883). Nicholson, Illustr. Dict. Gard. ii: 341 ("*nepalensis*") (1886). D. in Garden xliii: 81 ("*nepalensis*") (1893). Bois, Dict. Hort. ii: 821 ("*nepalensis*") (1893–99). Burbidge in Garden liii: 553 ("*nepalensis*") (1898). Bulley in Fl. and Sylva iii: 83 ("*nepalensis*") (1905). Kirtikar and Basu, Ind. Med. Pl. i: 83 ("*Nipalensis*"), tab. 56 (1918).]

Meconopsis Wallichii Hook. in Curt. Bot. Mag. lxxviii: tab. 4668 (1852) pro parte.

[*Meconopsis Wollastoni* Regel in Gartenflora xxv: 291 in obs. (1876), *nomen nudum.*]

[*Meconopsis robusta* (non Hook. f. and Thoms.) Prain in Journ. As. Soc. Bengal lxiv, 2: 315 (1896) pro parte. Fedde in Engl., Pflanzenr. iv, 104: 268 (1909) pro parte. Kingdon-Ward in Gard. Chron., Ser. 3, lxxix: 460 (1926) pro parte.]

Meconopsis paniculata var. *typica* Prain in Journ. As. Soc. Bengal lxiv, 2: 316 (1896).

[*Polychaetia paniculata* Wall. ex Prain *loc. cit.* (1896), *nomen synonymum.*]

Meconopsis paniculata var. *elata* Prain *loc. cit.* (1896). Fedde in Engl., Pflanzenr. iv, 104: 267, fig. 34 E (1909).

[*Meconopsis nepalensis* var. *elata* B. in Irish Gard. xiii: 103 (1918). Ellis in Journ. Roy. Hort. Soc. xliii: 563 (1919).]

Meconopsis himalayensis Hort. ex Hay in New Fl. and Silva ii: 170 in obs., fig. 67 ("*himalayense*") (1930).

Description. *Monocarpic. Tap-root* dauciform or narrowly elongated, up to 7 in. in length and 0·75 in. in thickness. *Basal leaves* in a dense rosette, up to 31 in. in length (including the petiole, which may attain 11 in. in length) and 8 in. in breadth; lamina very variable in shape, usually pinnatisect towards the base and more or less deeply pinnatifid towards the apex (segments lanceolate, oblong or deltoid, acute to rounded at the apex, entire or lobed at the margin, the lower segments distant), densely villous (at least when young) and usually densely covered with small much-branched hairs or substellately puberulous on both surfaces. *Lower cauline leaves* similar to the basal leaves but with shorter petioles. *Upper cauline leaves* sessile, more or less stem-clasping or auriculate at the base, otherwise similar to the lower leaves. *Flowering-stem* branched, attaining over 6 ft. in height, villous and densely puberulous. *Flowers* pendulous, arising singly in the axils of the uppermost leaves and in 2–6-flowered axillary cymules from the lower leaves; pedicels stout, up to 3·5 in. in length (attaining 8 in. in fruiting specimens), densely villous and puberulous. *Petals* 4 (rarely 5), obovate to suborbicular, up to 2 in. in length and 2 in. in breadth, yellow. *Stamens* numerous; filaments filiform, pale-yellow; anthers orange. *Ovary* globose or subglobose, densely covered with appressed golden-yellow hairs; style distinct, usually stout, up to 0·4 in. in length (attaining 0·6 in. and becoming conspicuously swollen towards the base in fruiting specimens); stigma with 6–12 prominent lobes, reddish-purple. *Capsule* ellipsoid-oblong, densely substellately puberulous and usually persistently villous, splitting by 6– (very rarely 4–) 12 valves for a short distance from the apex. *Seeds* reniform, testa densely papillose but commonly appearing to be pitted by the loss of the papillae. (Plate VII.)

Geographical Range. Eastern Nepal to north-eastern Assam, at altitudes from 10,000–14,500 ft. Originally described from Nepal.

This is one of the earliest species to be cultivated in this country, and it appears that its first introduction was due to J. D. Hooker, who collected and sent home seeds from Sikkim in 1849. It is known that plants were raised from these, but it is less certain whether they were ever brought to maturity, and the first record of the species flowering in this country seems to be that of 1863 mentioned under the figure of "*M. Nipalensis*" in "Curtis's Botanical Magazine" published in 1866.

Hooker believed that the plant which he had collected and figured so beautifully was *M. napaulensis* DC., and as such it was known both to botanists and horticulturists for many years. This confusion originated in the "Prodromus Florae Nepalensis," where, in describing the yellow-flowered *Papaver paniculatum*, D. Don included *M. napaulensis* as a synonym. Later authors, while accepting Don's opinion, adopted the earlier epithet of De Candolle for the species although, almost without exception, it was misspelt as "*nipalensis*" or "*nepalensis*." It was not until 1895, when Prain published his preliminary observations on the genus, that the proper identity of the species was clearly defined. Both *M. napaulensis* and *Papaver paniculatum* were based on Wallich specimens from Nepal, and examination of the types proved that they could be distinguished by their pubescence, capsule characters and flower-colour. Prain thus showed that Don was in error in considering the two plants to be conspecific, and he further pointed out that the plant generally known as *M. napaulensis* was really the original *P. paniculatum*, and this he transferred to *Meconopsis*.

Within recent years the known geographical range of the species has been very considerably extended. In herbaria it is adequately represented from Sikkim, and recent collections from Nepal have greatly augmented its representation from that country. The presence of *M. paniculata* in Bhutan has been established by Cooper, while Kingdon-Ward collected the species in the Delei Valley, north-eastern Assam, in 1928. This, at first sight, appears to be a surprising extension of its range. Although the species has not been recorded from the intervening areas, it may be expected to occur wherever ecological conditions are suitable.

In its leaf-characters *M. paniculata* displays considerable variation, and this most obviously in the attractive winter-rosette stage, but there is no other species in cultivation with which it may be confused. The yellow flowers borne on a copiously branched inflorescence and the presence of small much-branched hairs forming, usually, a more or less persistent substellate pubescence, are adequate characters by which to recognise the species. It should be noted that white forms occur in nature. The appearance of a white-flowered form in cultivation was recorded by Burbidge in 1898, and recently forms in which the flowers are spotted with bronze have been described. The leaves are provided with hairs of two kinds, long barbellate hairs and short much-branched hairs, which so clothe the surface of the leaves as to give the appearance of a fine substellate down.

In transferring *P. paniculatum* to *Meconopsis* Prain recognised two varieties whose separation depended on inflorescence characters. *M. paniculata* var. *typica* included forms in which the flowers were borne on paniculate cymes longer than the leaves and the sepals were sometimes puberulous only; while *M. paniculata* var. *elata* was distinguished by having flowers borne on simple cymes and these not or scarcely longer than the leaves. These two varieties, as Prain pointed out at the time of their definition, are completely connected by intermediate forms; the series is now so complete that no useful purpose is served by continuing to recognise them.

Collectors' notes indicate that in the lower altitudes *M. paniculata* is found in scrubby vegetation around pine forests, while at the higher levels it inhabits alpine meadows and peaty boulder slopes.

In 1883 a hybrid between *M. paniculata* (" *nepalensis* ") and *M. simplicifolia** was stated to be growing in the Royal Botanic Garden, Edinburgh, but I have been unable to confirm this record as no specimens of the plant were preserved.

? M. PANICULATA × M. BETONICIFOLIA = 19A. × **M. auriculata** Stapf. See p. 65.

12. MECONOPSIS LONGIPETIOLATA

MECONOPSIS LONGIPETIOLATA G. Tayl. ex Hay in New Fl. and Silva iv: 226, fig. 83 (July 8, 1932); in Gard. Chron., Ser. 3, xcii: 409, figs. 200–201 (1932). G. Tayl. in Gard. Chron., Ser. 3, xcii: 41 (July 16, 1932).

DESCRIPTION. *Monocarpic. Tap-root* dauciform. *Basal and lower cauline leaves* up to 13 in. in length (including the long bristly petioles); lamina pinnatisect towards the base and pinnatifid towards the apex (segments roundly, obtusely, or subacutely lobed), more or less densely covered on both surfaces with long bristles together with minute puberulous hairs. *Upper cauline leaves* similar to the basal leaves but smaller. *Bracts* sessile. *Flowering-stem* branched, bristly, attaining 18 in. in height. *Flowers* numerous, borne on axillary branches, the lower branches 3-flowered, the upper branches 1-flowered. *Petals* 4, obovate or suborbicular, about 1·5 in. in length and 1·5 in. in breadth, yellow. *Stamens* numerous; filaments filiform, whitish; anthers orange-yellow. *Ovary* ovoid, densely covered with appressed bristles; style slightly curved, up to about 0·25 in. in length; stigma capitate, 5-lobed, green.

GEOGRAPHICAL RANGE. Confined to Nepal. Originally described from a cultivated plant raised from seed received from Nepal.

This particularly graceful member of the genus originated from seed sent from Nepal and the original description was based on a plant which flowered in 1932. At that time the species could not be correlated with any field specimens, but more recent collections from Nepal include *M. longipetiolata*. In the original

* Owen in Gard. Chron., New Ser. xix: 799 (1883).

publication it was stated that the type-specimen was deposited in the British Museum (Natural History), but, by an unfortunate misunderstanding, the living plant on which the description was based was removed and has since been lost.

As the specific epithet implies, the species is distinguished by the unusually long petioles. It is probably most closely related to *M. paniculata*, and differs from that species in the incision of its leaves, its much longer petioles and absence of substellate pubescence on the leaves. *M. longipetiolata*, in its habit, is a much smaller and daintier plant than *M. paniculata*.

13. MECONOPSIS VIOLACEA

Meconopsis violacea Kingdon-Ward in Garden xci: 450 in obs., fig. (July 1927); in Gard. Chron., Ser. 3, lxxxii: 506 in obs. (Dec. 1927); in Ann. of Bot. xlii: 857, tab. 16 fig. 2 (1928); Pl. Hunt. Edge World: 262 (1930). T. W. Bolas in Gard. Chron., Ser. 3, lxxxvi: 343 (1929). Harrow in New Fl. and Silva ii: 150 (1930). Hay in New Fl. and Silva ii: 169, fig. 65 (1930); in Gard. Chron., Ser. 3, xciv.: 432, fig. 183 (1933). P. Moore in New Fl. and Silva ii: 232 (1930). F. H. Fisher in Bull. Alp. Gard. Soc. i: 121, tab. 42 supr. (1932). G. C. Tayl. in Countr. Life lxxiv: 1, fig. (1933).

[*Meconopsis* sp. Kingdon-Ward in Gard. Chron., Ser. 3, lxxxi: 433, fig. (1927).]

Description. *Monocarpic*. *Tap-root* dauciform, up to 6 in. in length and 0·5 in. in thickness. *Basal leaves* in a dense basal rosette, up to 9·5 in. in length (including the petiole, which may be 3 in. in length) and about 1·5 in. in breadth; lamina pinnatisect or deeply pinnatifid (segments oblong or lanceolate-oblong, acute at the apex, entire or irregularly lobed at the margin), covered on both surfaces (but especially on the midrib and on the margin) with long weak hairs intermingled with shorter and very short hairs. *Lower cauline leaves* similar to the basal leaves but with shorter petioles. *Upper leaves* sessile and more or less stem-clasping and auriculate at the base. *Uppermost leaves* pinnately lobed, otherwise similar to the lower leaves. *Flowering-stem* attaining 6 ft. in height, villous and puberulous. *Flowers* pendulous, borne singly in the axils of the upper leaves; pedicels slender, up to 2·5 in. in length (attaining 5 in. in fruiting specimens), densely hairy immediately below the flowers. *Petals* 4 (occasionally 5 or 6), obovate to suborbicular, about 1·5 in. in length and 1 in. in breadth, " bluish violet with a silky sheen, sometimes inclining to purple." *Stamens* numerous; filaments filiform, of the same colour as the petals except at the extreme base where they are white; anthers bright orange. *Ovary* ellipsoid to ellipsoid-oblong, densely covered with appressed or obliquely spreading pale-golden hairs; style distinct and usually slender, twisted, up to 0·3 in. in length; stigma subclavate or with the lobes more or less free, pale-green. *Capsule* ellipsoid-oblong, densely covered with persistent appressed hairs or their hispid bases, splitting by 7–9 valves for a short distance from the apex. *Seeds* ellipsoid-oblong to reniform, testa densely papillose. (Plate VIII.)

Geographical Range. Northern Upper Burma and south-eastern Tibet, at altitudes from 10,000–13,000 ft. Originally described from the Seinghku Valley and Diphukha La pass, Upper Burma and south-eastern Tibet.

This species was discovered by Kingdon-Ward in Upper Burma and more sparingly over the border in south-eastern Tibet in 1926. It is now well established in gardens in this country and the first record of flowering appears to be 1929.

In describing the plant the collector states that " in its first year it produces an enormous crown of pale sea-green leaves encased in golden hairs of silken texture " and the " leafy crown survives the winter under the snow." *M. violacea* inhabits steep alpine meadows and gravel slopes.

The most distinctive features of the species are the display of the flowers on simple axillary pedicels (rarely in cultivated specimens 3-flowered cymules are produced in the axils of the lower leaves), and the finely cut foliage, both characters serving to distinguish *M. violacea* from its nearest relative *M. napaulensis.*

M. violacea × M. betonicifolia = 19b. × **M. Coxiana** G. Tayl. See p. 66.

14. MECONOPSIS NAPAULENSIS

Meconopsis napaulensis DC., Prodr. i: 121 (1824). Walp., Repert. Bot. Syst. i: 110 (1842) pro parte. Prain in Journ. As. Soc. Bengal lxiv, 2: 317 (1896); Novic. Ind.: 119 (1905); in Gard. Chron., Ser. 3, xxxvii: 369 (" *nepalensis* ") (1905); in Ann. of Bot. xx: 359 (1906); in Bull. Misc. Inf. Kew 1915: 174, tab. opp. 176 fig. 1, tab. opp. 177 fig. 2 (1915); in Countr. Life liv: 110 (1923). Bulley in Gard. Chron., Ser. 3, xxvii: 388 (" *nepalensis* ") (1900). Mottet in Jardin xx: 100 (" *nepalensis* ") (1906); in Rev. Hort. xii: 204 (" *nepalensis* ") (1912). Fedde in Engl., Pflanzenr. iv, 104: 269, fig. 35 A (1909). W. W. Smith in Rec. Bot. Surv. Ind. iv: 348 (1913). Farrer, Engl. Rock-Gard. i: 478 (1919). Harley in Garden lxxxix: 643, fig. (" *nepalensis* ") (1925); in Journ. Roy. Hort. Soc. liii: 226 (" *nepalensis* ") (1928). Kingdon-Ward in Gard. Chron., Ser. 3, lxxix: 460 (1926); *op. cit.* lxxxii: 26 (1927); in Ann. of Bot. xl: 545 (1926). Hay in New Fl. and Silva ii: 170, fig. 66 (" *nepalensis* ") (1930).

Papaver paniculatum D. Don, Prodr. Fl. Nepal.: 197 (1825) pro parte.

Stylophorum nepalense (DC.) Spreng. in L., Syst. Veg., Ed. 16, iv, 2: 203 (1827) pro parte.

Stylophorum paniculatum (D. Don) Don, Gener. Syst. Gard. and Bot. i: 135 (1831) pro parte.

Meconopsis Wallichii Hook. in Curt. Bot. Mag. lxxviii: tab. 4668 (1852) pro parte. Floricult. Cab. xx: 265, tab. opp. 265 fig. 1 (1852). Planch. in Fl. Serr. viii: 5, tab. 753 (1852-53) pro parte. Lem. in Jard. Fl. iii:

tab. 315 (1853) pro parte. Thomps. Engl. Fl. Gard. ii: 23, tab. opp. 17 (1853). Morren in Belg. Hort. iv: 294, tab. 47 (1854). Hook. f. and Thoms., Fl. Ind. i: 254 (1855) pro parte; in Hook. f., Fl. Brit. Ind. i: 119 (1872) pro parte. Gouas in Rev. Hort. viii: 270, fig. 82 (1858). Garden xii: 105, fig. (1877). W. in Garden xiv: 280 (1878). Sadler in Garden xix: 308, tab. opp. 276 ("*Wallichiana*") (1881). Robinson, Engl. Fl. Gard.: 183, tab. 165 (1883). Journ. Hort., Ser. 3, vii: 144, fig. 27 (1883). Dod in Gard. Chron., New Ser., xxiv: 106 (1885). Nicholson, Illustr. Dict. Gard. ii. 341 (1886). Garden xlii: 42 ("*Wallichiana*") (1892). D. in Garden xliii: 81, fig. (1893). Bois, Dict. Hort. ii: 822, fig. 573 (1893–99). Prain in Journ. As. Soc. Bengal lxiv, 2: 318 (1896); Novic. Ind.: 120 (1905); in Gard. Chron., Ser. 3, xxxvii: 369 (1905); in Ann. of Bot. xx: 360, tab. 24 fig. 6 ("*Wallichiana*") (1906); in Bull. Misc. Inf. Kew 1915: 175 (1915): in Countr. Life liv: 110 (1923). Journ. Hort., Ser. 3, xxxvii: 72, fig. 11 (1898). Bulley in Fl. and Sylva iii: 84, fig. on 83 (1905). Mottet in Jardin xx: 100, fig. 57 (1906); in Rev. Hort. xii: 203, figs. 63–64 and tab. opp. 204 (1912). Page-Roberts in Garden lxxi: 626, fig. (1907). T. Smith in Gard. Chron., Ser. 3, xlvi: 91 (1909). Fedde in Engl., Pflanzenr. iv, 104: 369, fig. 35 B (1909). Silva Tarouca, Freiland-Staud.: 150 (1910). T. Young in Gard. Chron., Ser. 3, lii: 138 (1912). W. V. in Gard. Chron., Ser. 3, liii: 147, fig. 66 (1913). Fitzherbert in Garden lxxvii: 348, fig. (1913). Jenkins in Garden lxxviii: 240 (1914). Gard. Chron., Ser. 3, lviii: 329 (1915). Garden lxxix: 175, fig. (1915). Kirtikar and Basu, Ind. Med. Pl. i: 84, tab. 57 (1918). Farrer, Engl. Rock-Gard. i: 482 (1919). Garden lxxxiv: 384, 439 (1920). Kingdon-Ward, Farth. Burma: 130 (1921); in Gard. Chron., Ser. 3, lxxix: 460 (1926); in Garden xci: 340 (1927). Canning-Wright in Garden lxxxvi: 177, fig. (1922). Irving in Garden lxxxvii: 171 (1923). Sarsons in Garden lxxxviii: 736, fig. (1924). Harley in Garden lxxxix: 71 (1925); *op. cit.* xc: 474 (1926); in Journ. Roy. Hort. Soc. liii: 227, fig. 30 (1928). L. H. Bailey, Stand. Cycloped. Hort., New Ed. ii: 2017 (1927). Silva Tarouca and Schneider, Freiland-Staud.: 249 (1927). New Fl. and Silva i: 95, fig. 27 (1929). L. H. and E. Z. Bailey, Hortus: 390 (1930). Wehrhahn, Gartenstaud. i: 468 (1930). F. H. Fisher in Bull. Alp. Gard. Soc. i: 121, tab. 43 (1932).

[*Meconopsis robusta* (non Hook. f. and Thoms. 1855) Hook f. and Thoms in Hook. f., Fl. Brit. Ind. i: 118 (1872) pro parte.]

Meconopsis Wallichii var. *fuso-purpurea* Hook. f. in Curt. Bot Mag. cx: tab. 6760 (1884). Nicholson, Illustr. Dict. Gard. ii: 341 (1886). Prain in Bull. Misc. Inf. Kew 1915: 176 (1915). Forrest in Countr. Life liv: 614 (1923). Kingdon-Ward in Gard. Chron., Ser. 3, lxxix: 460 (1926); in Ann. of Bot. xl: 545 (1926); *op. cit.* xlii: 855 (1928).

[*Meconopsis Wallichii* var. *rubrofusca* Prain in Journ. As. Soc. Bengal lxiv, 2: 315 (1896), *laps. pro fusco-purpurea*; in Ann. of Bot. xx: 360 (1906).]

Meconopsis Wallichii forma *purpurea* Bulley in Fl. and Sylva iii: 84 in obs. (1905).

Meconopsis Wallichii forma *fusco-purpurea* Bulley, *loc. cit.* (1905).

Meconopsis Wallichii var. *typica* Prain in Bull. Misc. Inf. Kew 1915: 176 (1915).

Description. *Monocarpic. Tap-root* usually dauciform, up to 6 in. in length and 1 in. in thickness. *Basal leaves* in a dense rosette, up to 21 in. in length (including the petiole, which may attain 9 in. in length) and 7 in. in breadth; lamina very variable in shape, usually pinnatisect towards the base and pinnatifid towards the apex, the segments usually pinnately lobed (lobes acute to rounded at the apex), sparsely to more or less densely setose-villous (at least when young) and very sparsely to densely (rarely substellately) puberulous on both surfaces. *Lower cauline leaves* similar to the basal leaves but with shorter petioles. *Upper cauline leaves* sessile; lamina lanceolate, entire or pinnately lobed at the margin or deeply pinnatifid, cuneate to auriculate at the base, otherwise similar to the lower leaves. *Flowering-stem* branched, attaining 8 ft. in height, more or less densely setose-villous and puberulous. *Flowers* pendulous, arising singly in the axils of the uppermost leaves and in branched cymes bearing up to 17 flowers arising in the axils of the lower leaves; pedicels slender or stout, up to 3 in. in length (attaining 8 in. in fruiting specimens), sparsely to densely setose-villous and puberulous, becoming more or less hispid on account of the persistent hair bases. *Petals* 4, more or less obovate to suborbicular, up to 1·75 in. in length and 1·5 in. in breadth, red to purple or blue, occasionally white. *Stamens* numerous; filaments filiform, of the same colour as or darker than the petals; anthers orange-yellow. *Ovary* subglobose or ovoid to ellipsoid, densely covered with bristles (usually appressed but often spreading); style distinct, slender, up to 0·5 in. in length, remaining slender or becoming slightly swollen at the base in fruiting specimens; stigma capitate or subclavate, more or less prominently 5–8-lobed, dark-green. *Capsule* oblong to ellipsoid-oblong, densely covered with appressed or more or less spreading bristles or their persistent hispid bases, splitting by 5–8 (rarely 4–10) valves for a short distance from the apex. *Seeds* ovoid to broadly ellipsoid-oblong, testa densely papillose. (Plate IX.)

Geographical Range. Central Nepal to western Szechuan, at altitudes from 9,000–17,000 ft. Originally described from Nepal.

It appears that the confusion surrounding the proper identification of this species is again referable to the original error made by D. Don in considering *M. napaulensis* DC. as synonymous with his *Papaver paniculatum.* Before this tangle was satisfactorily unravelled by Prain, *M. Wallichii* and its variety *fusco-purpurea* had been described by the Hookers, who had accepted Don's opinion, and thus the affinity of their plants with the true *M. napaulensis* remained unrecognised. The closest relation was considered to be with *M. paniculata,* which was then masquerading under the name " *M. nepalensis.*"

J. D. Hooker, in describing *M. Wallichii* var. *fusco-purpurea,* emphatically stated that there was no structural difference between the variety and the type of the species, the only distinction residing in the colour of the flowers. Later Prain accepted this view but pointed out that the variety *fusco-purpurea* was indistinguishable from *M. napaulensis*, and, although he suggested that it might be taxonomically correct to include *M. Wallichii* also in that species, he hesitated to do so on account of the apparent difference in flower-colour and supposed geographical isolation. In a later publication he greatly modified this opinion. Two varieties were recognised in *M. Wallichii*: var. *typica* with sky-blue flowers and var. *fusco-purpurea* with dark-red or purple flowers. *M. napaulensis* was no longer considered identical with the latter variety and a definite opinion on that species was deferred " until direct testimony as to the colour of the petals becomes available."

Recent collections from Nepal have filled the gaps in our knowledge of the species. Specimens have been sent from that country which are identical with the type-collection of *M. napaulensis*, and the flower-colour is now definitely known to be red, purple, blue, or occasionally white. Further, *M. Wallichii* in all its forms shows no character sufficient to merit taxonomic separation. It is necessary, therefore, as has been foreshadowed by previous writers, to accept the older name *M. napaulensis* for the species and the one in current usage, *M. Wallichii*, must be relegated to synonymy.

In this widespread and variable species I have been unable to find any satisfactory characters by which to differentiate the several strains. Here, as in other members of the genus, there is a flux of forms which so intergrade as to make precise definition impossible. It appeared that there might be some correlation between the geographical distribution and the form assumed, but investigation did not substantiate this. For instance, the majority of the plants collected by Forrest in Yunnan are characterised by pinnatifid upper leaves with broad and usually rounded lobes, by cymes which are short and not conspicuously spreading, and pedicels which are very densely covered with appressed hairs. This combination of characters gives to Forrest's plants a distinctive facies, but examination of the entire range of material shows that similar forms occur in Sikkim and the intervening areas. This form of Forrest's has been introduced into cultivation and growers of it will no doubt be puzzled that it should be referred to *M. napaulensis*, but no other course is open when the wide range of variation is realised. Similarly the forms collected by Wilson in Szechuan seemed to be easily separable from the other gatherings of the species on account of their deeply divided leaves and bracts. It was found, however, that similar plants had been collected in Sikkim, and these were so interrelated with other forms as to show a complete transition to the typical plant.

The flower-colour has played such an important part in the recognition of varieties that some observations on this subject appear to be desirable. When *M. napaulensis* was first described from Wallich's specimens its flower-colour was unknown, but recently it has been conclusively shown that in Nepal the species may have red, purple, or occasionally white flowers. No record of blue flowers from that area is as yet known, and indeed the familiar blue-flowered form appears to be confined to certain areas in Sikkim and again in western Szechuan. Hooker noted that the plants which he collected in Sikkim had flowers of a dull purple, whereas the plants raised from seed sent home by him had very pale-blue flowers. This variability in colour has been commonly experienced in gardens in this country, and it appears that no reliance can be placed on flower-colour as a differential character.

It has been stated that *M. napaulensis* was known in cultivation before 1831, but the evidence for this is unconvincing, and it appears that the first record of the species flowering in this country is in 1852. One of the plants raised then was described and figured by W. J. Hooker in "Curtis's Botanical Magazine" under the name *M. Wallichii*.

M. napaulensis, in spite of its tendency to vary and give flowers of a disappointing colour, has established itself as a species of high merit. The more attractive features of the plant are the beautiful leaf-rosette which persists during the winter and the numerous flowers which are produced over a comparatively long period. Under favourable conditions the species may attain a height of eight feet and bear as many as three hundred flowers each three inches across.

In the rosette stage it is difficult, without careful examination, to distinguish *M. napaulensis* from *M. paniculata*. In the latter species the hairs usually give the plants a hoary appearance in contrast to the red-brown pubescence of *M. napaulensis*. This is by no means a constant distinction, and a more reliable character is to be found in the shorter puberulous pubescence which in *M. paniculata* is almost always substellate but is never so obviously so in *M. napaulensis*.

In its natural habit *M. napaulensis* is found on open stony slopes on the margins of scrub or pine forests, by the banks of mountain streams, and in rocky situations in shady gullies.

M. NAPAULENSIS × M. LATIFOLIA = 33A. × **M. decora** Prain. See p. 97.

SUBSECT. *b*. CUMMINSIA

MECONOPSIS subsect. CUMMINSIA (Prain) G. Tayl., subsect. nov.

Cathcartia sect. *Cumminsia* Prain in Ann. of Bot. xx: 368 (1906).

[*Cumminsia* King ex. Prain *tom. cit.*: 369 (1906), *nomen synonymum*.]

Meconopsis ser. *Cumminsia* (Prain) Prain in Bull. Misc. Inf. Kew 1915: 142 (1915).

Species 25, arranged in 6 series, occurring from north-eastern Tibet, western Kansu and central Shensi to north-western Yunnan and Upper Burma and westwards along the Himalayas and through southern Tibet to Kashmir and Chitral. Type-species: *Meconopsis lyrata* (Cummins and Prain) Fedde ex Prain (*Cathcartia lyrata* Cummins and Prain=*Cumminsia* King ex Prain).

This is much the larger subsection of sect. *Polychaetia*, and the 25 species which form it exhibit a very wide range of form. Both monocarpic and polycarpic plants are represented, but the common character distinguishing the subsection is the absence of a conspicuous basal rosette of leaves during the winter months.

SER. i. **SIMPLICIFOLIAE**

MECONOPSIS ser. SIMPLICIFOLIAE G. Tayl. ser. nov.*

Meconopsis ser. *Grandes* Prain in Journ. As. Soc. Bengal lxiv, 2: 320 (1896) pro parte, excl. sp. 10.

Meconopsis sect. *Grandes* (Prain) Fedde in Engl., Pflanzenr. iv, 104: 262 (1909) pro parte, quoad spp. 17–19.

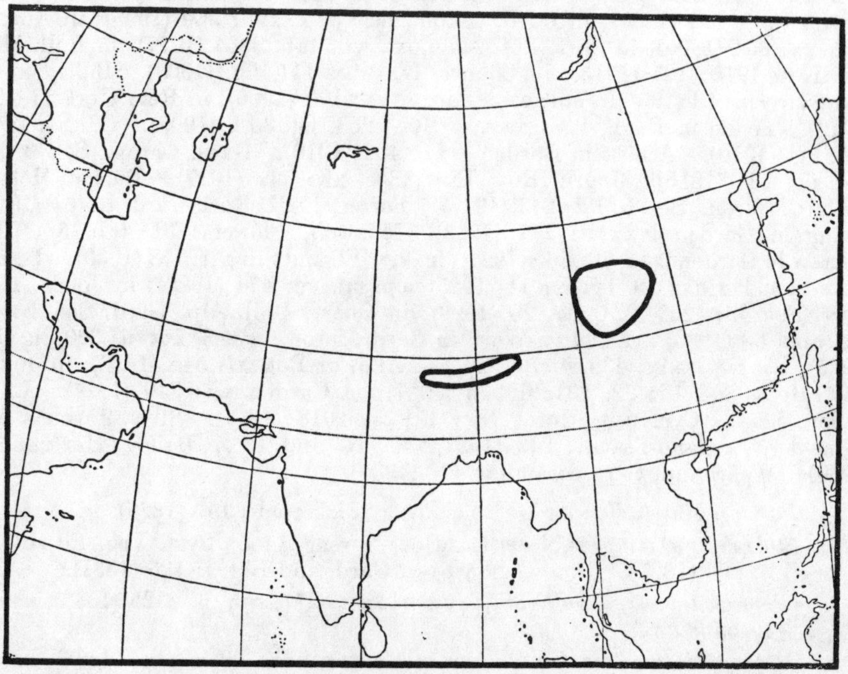

FIG. 6.—MAP SHOWING THE GEOGRAPHICAL RANGE OF THE SERIES *Simplicifoliae*. *M. simplicifolia* occupies the more south-westerly area, from central Nepal to south-eastern Tibet.

* Series subsect. *Eupolychaetiae*, foliis rosulatis et scapis basalibus longis l-floris distinguitur.

Species 3, two occurring in north-eastern Tibet, southern Kansu, central Shensi and north-western Szechuan, the other distributed from central Nepal to south-eastern Tibet (see Fig. 6). Type-species: *Meconopsis simplicifolia* (D. Don) Walp.

The species comprising this series are all at least potentially polycarpic and recognised by having a dense rosette of persistent leaf-bases interspersed with barbellate bristles. The entire or slightly lobed leaves are aggregated in a basal rosette, and the flowers are borne singly on long, slender basal scapes.

15. MECONOPSIS SIMPLICIFOLIA

Meconopsis simplicifolia (D. Don) Walp., Repert. Bot. Syst. i: 110 (1842). Hook. f. and Thoms., Fl. Ind. i: 252 (1855); in Hook. f., Fl. Brit. Ind. i: 118 (1872). Hook. f., Illustr. Himal. Pl.: tab. 8 (1855). Gard. Chron. 1855: 515 (1855). Lem. in Illustr. Hort. iii: tab. 114 (1856). Van Houtte in Fl. Serr. xiii: 61, tab. 1324 (1860). Journ. Hort. Prat. Belg., New Ser., iv: tab. 3 (1860). W. in Garden xiv: 280 (1878). Robinson, Engl. Fl. Gard.: 183 (1883). Nicholson, Illustr. Dict. Gard. ii: 341 (1886). Prain in Journ. As. Soc. Bengal lxiv, 2: 321 (1896); Novic. Ind.: 123 (1905); in Gard. Chron., Ser. 3, xxxvii: 369 (1905); in Ann. of Bot. xx: 354 (1906); in Curt. Bot. Mag. cxxxvii: tab. 8364 (1911); in Bull. Misc. Inf. Kew 1915: 167 (1915); in Countr. Life liv: 111, fig. (1923). Bulley in Fl. and Sylva iii: 84 (1905). Mottet in Jardin xx: 100 (1906); in Rev. Hort. xii: 203 (1912). Fedde in Engl., Pflanzenr. iv, 104: 263, fig. 35 F (1909). Garden lxxx: 295, fig. (1916). Arnott in Garden lxxx: 402 (1916). Gard. Chron., Ser. 3, lix: 314, fig. 137 (1916). Journ. Roy. Hort. Soc. xlii: clx (1917). Buchan-Heburn in Gard. Chron., Ser. 3, lxi: 245 (1917). Farrer, Engl. Rock-Gard. i: 481 (1919). Irving in Garden lxxxvii: 171 (1923). Maxwell, Flowers: 51, tab. 5 (1923). Harrow in Garden lxxxviii: 360 (1924); in New Fl. and Silva ii: 153 (1930). Harley in Garden lxxxix: 70, fig. on 71 (1925); *op. cit.* xc: 474 (1926); in Journ. Roy. Hort. Soc. liii: 223, 224, fig. 28 (1928); in Quart. Bull. Alp. Gard. Soc. ii: 54, tab. opp. 58 (1933). Kingdon-Ward in Gard. Chron., Ser. 3, lxxvii: 320, fig. 178 (1925); *op. cit.* lxxix: 439, 459 (1926); in Ann. of Bot. xl: 545 (1926); in Journ. Roy. Hort. Soc. lii: 23, 231, fig. 73 (1927); in Garden xci: 340 (1927). L. H. Bailey, Stand. Cycloped. Hort., New Ed. ii: 2018 (1927). Silva Tarouca and Schneider, Freiland-Staud.: 249 (1927). L. H. and E. Z. Bailey, Hortus: 390 (1930). Wehrhahn, Gartenstaud. i: 470 (1930).

Papaver simplicifolium D. Don, Prodr. Fl. Nepal.: 197 (1825).

Stylophorum simplicifolium (D. Don) Spreng. in L., Syst. Veg. Ed. 16, iv, 2: 203 (1827). Don, Gener. Syst. Gard. and Bot. i: 135 (1831).

[*Polychaetia scapigera* Wall., Numer. List: 277, sub. n. 8125 (1832), *nomen synonymum.*]

Meconopsis uniflora Gumbleton in Garden xxii: 90 in obs. (1882), *nomen illegitimum.*

[*Meconopsis simplicicaulis* Wood in Garden xxiv: 115 (1883), *laps. pro simplicifolia.*]

1 MECONOPSIS CAMBRICA

'A most accommodating plant, adapting equally well to damp, shady woods or on dry walls and then providing with its attractive tufted habit and long flowering season a desirable horticultural plant.'

2 MECONOPSIS REGIA
'Flowered for the first time in this country in 1931 and was then the object of wide admiration. Its merit as a garden plant is much enhanced by the beautiful dense rosette of leaves persisting during the winter months.'

3 MECONOPSIS PANICULATA
In its natural habitat, photographed by the author.
'This is one of the earliest species to be cultivated in this country, and it appears that its first introduction was due to J.D. Hooker, who collected and sent home seeds from Sikkim in 1849.'

4 MECONOPSIS NEPAULENSIS

'When Meconopsis nepaulensis was first described from Wallio's specimens its flower colour was unknown, but it had been conclusively shown that in Nepal the species may have red purple or occasionally white flowers.'

5 MECONOPSIS NEPAULENSIS
'In the rosette stage.'

6 MECONOPSIS SIMPLICIFOLIA
In its natural habitat, photographed by the author.
'Cooper collected it in Sikkim and Bhutan during 1913 and 1914 and many of the plants in gardens have been raised from his seeds'.

7 MECONOPSIS QUINTUPLINERVIA

'Predominantly a plant of alpine meadows, often among Rhododendron scrub, and it is so abundant in some localities as to form a "shimmering turf".'

8 MECONOPSIS INTEGRIFOLIA
'It appears that the first introduction of Meconopsis integrifolia to European gardens was due to Abbé Farges, who sent seed from Szechwuan from which plants were raised in Paris and flowered for the first time in 1896.'

9 MECONOPSIS BETONICIFOLIA

'It is given to few plants to attain such popularity so rapidly and to establish itself so firmly in the estimation of horticulturalists as Meconopsis betonicifolia.'

10 MECONOPSIS BETONICIFOLIA

Lilac form

'It is certainly a species of extreme merit, the usually perennial habit and ease of cultivation being factors which have no doubt contributed to its reputation.'

11 MECONOPSIS GRANDIS

'Found in (Sikkim) only as a cultivated plant about the dwellings used in summer by shepherds. They are not primarily concerned with the aesthetic qualities of the plant but grow it rather for the extraction of oil from the seeds . . .'

12 MECONOPSIS GRANDIS

'In Nepal the plant does not appear to be so robust as in Sikkim, and the colour of the flowers is given as purple, in contrast to the blue colour usually attributed to the Sikkim species.'

13 MECONOPSIS HORRIDULA

'This species in addition to being the most widely distributed member of the genus occurs throughout the greatest altitudinal range and indeed reaches the upper limits of flowering plant vegetation.'

14 MECONOPSIS HORRIDULA
'The species was described in 1855 from specimens collected in Sikkim.'

15 MECONOPSIS HORRIDULA

In its natural habitat, photographed by the author.

'Even if seed is carefully saved from good forms it is rarely possible to raise a uniform batch of plants.'

16 MECONOPSIS LATIFOLIA

'. . . always found growing in the crevices of rocks or among loose piles of stone débris . . . It likes the full sun and springs to full growth after the snow melts off, while the ground is still damp.'

17 MECONOPSIS CAMBRICA

18 MECONOPSIS CHELIDONIFOLIA

19 MECONOPSIS VILLOSA
In natural habitat

20 MECONOPSIS SUPERBA

21 MECONOPSIS REGIA

23 MECONOPSIS VIOLACEA

24 MECONOPSIS NAPAULENSIS

25 MECONOPSIS BELLA
In natural habitat

26 MECONOPSIS QUINTUPLINERVIA

27 MECONOPSIS PUNICEA

28 MECONOPSIS INTEGRIFOLIA
In natural habitat

29 MECONOPSIS GRANDIS

30 MECONOPSIS DELAVAYI
In natural habitat

31 MECONOPSIS HORRIDULA
The form which was described as Meconopsis rudis Prain
growing in its natural habitat.

32 MECONOPSIS LATIFOLIA

Meconopsis simplicifolia Baileyi Farrer, Engl. Rock-Gard. i: 481 in obs. (1919).

Meconopsis simplicifolia var. *Baileyi* Kingdon-Ward in Gard. Chron., Ser. 3, lxxix: 340 in obs., 459 in obs. (1926); in Garden xc: 115 in obs. (1926).

DESCRIPTION. *Monocarpic or polycarpic. Tap-root* slender, up to 6 in. in length and 0·2 in. in thickness, sometimes absent, and the root-system is then fibrously branched. *Stem* short and thick, concealed by the dense rosette of basal leaves and in the lower part densely covered by rufous or golden-brown bristles and membranous, usually densely hairy, persistent leaf-bases. *Leaves* all basal, subsessile or petiolate, with linear petioles up to about 8 in. in length and widened at the base; lamina usually more or less oblanceolate, but varying to lanceolate and ovate-lanceolate, up to 6·5 in. in length and 2 in. in breadth, gradually tapering at the base into the petiole, acute to rounded at the apex, entire or irregularly serrate or lobed at the margin, sparsely to densely covered on both surfaces with long weak bristles. *Flowers* semipendulous, borne singly on basal pedicels; pedicels 1–5 produced from each rosette (according to Ward up to 8), up to 25·5 in. in length (in fruit attaining 34·5 in.), more or less densely bristly, the bristles at first appressed or more or less spreading, ultimately reflexed. *Petals* 5–8, up to 2 in. in length and 1·5 in. in breadth, more or less obovate, purple to sky-blue. *Stamens* numerous; filaments narrowly linear, of the same colour as the petals (very rarely colourless); anthers orange. *Ovary* narrowly ellipsoid to oblong-ellipsoid, glabrous to densely bristly; style occasionally almost obsolete, usually distinct, slender to very stout, up to 0·3 in. in length (in fruiting specimens attaining 0·6 in.); stigma capitate or subclavate, 4–9-lobed, lobes more or less decurrent, green. *Capsule* erect, narrowly oblong to oblong-ellipsoid, glabrous to more or less densely covered with reflexed bristles, splitting by 4– (rarely 3–) 9 valves to about one-third of its length. *Seeds* irregular in shape but generally somewhat ellipsoid-oblong to reniform, testa densely papillose. (Plate X.)

GEOGRAPHICAL RANGE. Central Nepal to south-eastern Tibet, at altitudes from 11,000–17,500 ft. Originally described from Nepal.

M. simplicifolia is very closely related to *M. grandis* and, although it is always possible to distinguish the species in gardens, it is sometimes difficult to differentiate them from herbarium specimens. Their separation depends more on a combination of characters than on any single diagnostic mark. In *M. simplicifolia* the flowers are constantly borne on simple basal pedicels and the flowers have five or more petals. Further, the filaments of the stamens are, almost without exception, of the same blue colour as the petals, and these characters in association are sufficient to diagnose *M. simplicifolia.* The short stem in *M. simplicifolia* is usually more densely hairy and the leaves more densely tufted than in *M. grandis.*

In cultivation *M. simplicifolia* exists in two more or less well defined strains: one in which the flowers are deep-blue or purple and which is usually polycarpic, the other, with sky-blue flowers, which is usually monocarpic, although not invariably so. The introduction of the latter form is usually attributed to Bailey, who sent seeds to this country from south-eastern Tibet in 1913. It appears, however, that the plate given by Prain in "Curtis's Botanical Magazine" in 1911 represents this form, the seeds from which the "strictly monocarpic" plants were raised having been obtained from the Royal Botanic Gardens, Calcutta. In its typical form the species has been known in cultivation since J. D. Hooker introduced it from Sikkim in 1848, but it has been reintroduced several times since then. Cooper collected it in Sikkim and Bhutan during 1913 and 1914, and many of the plants at present in gardens have been raised from his seeds. Within the last few years the species has been extensively collected in Nepal and seeds have accompanied the specimens sent to this country.

Herbarium specimens show that *M. simplicifolia* in its natural state is generally polycarpic. In addition to the pedicels of the present year's flowers, those of the past year are often present and many specimens show the formation of offsets for the following year.

The species was originally described under *Papaver* from Wallich specimens collected on Gossain Than in Nepal. It is stated to inhabit alpine slopes and to grow in *Rhododendron* scrub, among boulders, and in the shelter of rocks.

M. SIMPLICIFOLIA × M. GRANDIS = 20B. × **M. hybrida** Puddle. See p. 71.

M. SIMPLICIFOLIA × M. INTEGRIFOLIA = 18A. × **M. Harleyana** G. Tayl. See p. 62.

M. SIMPLICIFOLIA × M. PANICULATA. See under *M. paniculata* (p. 42).

16. MECONOPSIS QUINTUPLINERVIA

MECONOPSIS QUINTUPLINERVIA Regel in Gartenflora xxv: 291, tab. 880 figs. b.c.d. (1876). Maxim., Fl. Tangut. i: 34, tab. 23 fig. 27 (1889). Prain in Journ. As. Soc. Bengal lxiv, 2: 321 (1896); Novic. Ind.: 123 (1905); in Ann. of Bot. xx: 354 (1906); in Bull. Misc. Inf. Kew 1915: 168 (1915); in Countr. Life liv: 111 (1923). Nicholson, Cent. Suppl. Dict. Gard.: 528 (1901). Diels in Engl., Bot. Jahrb. xxix: 354 ("*quintuplinervis*") (1901); *op. cit.* xxxvi, Beibl. 82: 46 ("*quintuplinervis*") (1905). Bulley in Fl. and Sylva iii: 84 (1905). Mottet in Jardin xx: 100 (1906); in Rev. Hort. xii: 203 (1912). Fedde in Engl., Pflanzenr. iv, 104: 264, fig. 35 G ("*quintuplinervis*") (1909). Farrer in Gard. Chron., Ser. 3, lvi: 318, fig. 126 ("*quintuplinervis*") (1914); *op. cit.* lvii: 1 ("*quintuplinervis*") (1915); *op. cit.* lix: 86 ("*quintuplinervis*") (1916); in Journ. Roy. Hort. Soc. xlii: 84 (1916); *tom. cit.*: 339 (1917); Eav. World ii: 9, tab. opp. 10 (1917); Engl. Rock-Gard. i: 479, tab. 48 dextr. (1919); *op. cit.*: 479, 506 (1919); Rainbow Br.: 223 (1921); apud Irving in Bull. Alp. Gard. Soc. i: 194, tab. 94 (1932). Limpr. f. in Fedde, Repert. Sp. Nov., Beih. xii: 383 (1922). Irving in Garden lxxxvii: 171 (1923). Harley in Garden lxxxix: 72, fig. on 71 (1925); in Journ. Roy. Hort. Soc. liii: 225, fig. 32 (1928). Kingdon-Ward in Gard. Chron., Ser. 3, lxxix: 439 (1926); in Garden xci: 340, fig. (1927). Brooker in Gard. Chron., Ser. 3, lxxx: 11, fig. 7 (1926).

Silva Tarouca and Schneider, Freiland-Staud.: 249 (1927). Johnson in Gard. Chron., Ser. 3, lxxxvii: 304 (1930); *op. cit.* lxxxix: 276 (1931). Harrow in New Fl. and Silva ii: 149 (1930). Wehrhahn, Gartenstaud. i: 469 ("*quintuplinervis*") (1930). Cox, Pl. Introd. Farrer: 42 (1930). Rehder and Kobuski in Journ. Arn. Arboret. xiv: 15 (1933).

Meconopsis punicea var. *Limprichtii* Fedde, Repert. Sp. Nov. xvii: 197 (1921). Limpr. f. in Fedde, Repert. Sp. Nov., Beih. xii: 383 (1922).

Description. *Polycarpic. Root-system* fibrous. *Stem* densely covered at the base with persistent leaf-bases and bristles. *Leaves* aggregated in basal rosettes, up to almost 10 in. in length (including the petiole) and 1·5 in. in breadth; lamina obovate to narrowly oblanceolate elliptic or lanceolate, longitudinally (commonly 3–5-) nerved, gradually tapering at the base into a long petiole which is membranous and flattened at the base, acute to obtuse at the apex, entire at the margin, more or less densely covered with straw-coloured bristles on both surfaces. *Flowers* pendulous, borne on basal scapes; scapes usually arising singly from each rosette of leaves but sometimes up to 3, attaining over 1 ft. in height, usually ribbed and more or less densely covered with slightly reflexed bristles. *Petals* 4, but occasionally 6, more or less obovate or suborbicular and rounded at the apex, up to about 1·5 in. in length and 1·5 in. in breadth, pale lavender-blue or purplish. *Stamens* numerous; filaments filiform throughout their length, of the same colour as the petals or whitish; anthers pale-yellow or buff-coloured. *Ovary* subglobose, ovoid, oblong or turbinate, densely bristly, the bristles appressed; style short and up to 0·25 in. in length or obsolete; stigma capitate and 3–6-lobed, when sessile, the lobes radiating. *Capsule* erect, ellipsoid or oblong-ellipsoid, splitting by 3–6 valves. *Seeds* falcate-oblong, testa reticulated or corrugated. (Plate XII.)

Geographical Range. North-eastern Tibet, through southern Kansu and north-western Szechuan to central Shensi, at altitudes from 7,500–14,000 ft. Originally described from cultivated specimens raised from seed collected in Kansu.

M. quintuplinervia was discovered by Przewalski in Kansu in 1880, and described from cultivated specimens raised from seed which he had sent to St. Petersburg. The species has proved very amenable to cultivation in this country, and its extensive introduction was due to Farrer, who sent home seeds from Kansu in 1914 and 1915. It is interesting to note that he observed albino forms in the field, but so far as I am aware, no record exists of these in cultivation. The chief merits of the species are the perennial habit and dainty carriage of the flowers.

Ample descriptions of the species, as it is found in its natural habitat, are given by Farrer in various publications. It is predominantly a plant of alpine meadows, often among *Rhododendron* scrub, and it is so abundant in some localities as to form a "shimmering surf." Occasionally it may encroach upon cultivated land and under these conditions it forms clumps a foot across, bearing forty to fifty blooms on scapes two to three feet in height.

There has been some misunderstanding regarding the stylar character of

M. quintuplinervia. The accuracy of the figure in "Gartenflora" has been questioned, but there is no doubt, as field specimens clearly show, that there may be a distinct style or a style may be absent and the stigmatic rays radiate on the top of the ovary. This condition is precisely similar to that found in *M. integrifolia*, where the variation from a sessile stigma to one borne on a long style is more marked.

The obvious affinity of the species is with *M. punicea*, a plant inhabiting the same area, but it can be distinguished from the latter by the smaller size, shape and colour of the petals, and, whereas in *M. punicea* several scapes are produced commonly from each basal rosette, in *M. quintuplinervia* there is usually only one. The difference in the staminal filaments is also diagnostic. In cultivated specimens the number of petals is very often multiplied and phyllody of the stamens frequently occurs.

The type-specimen of *M. punicea* var. *Limprichtii* which I have had the opportunity of examining is a luxurious plant of *M. quintuplinervia*.

M. QUINTUPLINERVIA × M. CAMBRICA. See under *M. cambrica* (p. 23).

17. MECONOPSIS PUNICEA

MECONOPSIS PUNICEA Maxim., Fl. Tangut. i: 34 (1889). Prain in Journ. As. Soc. Bengal lxiv, 2: 321 (1896); Novic. Ind.: 123 (1905); in Gard. Chron., Ser. 3, xxxvii: 369 (1905); in Ann. of Bot. xx: 355 (1906); in Curt. Bot. Mag. cxxxiii: tab. 8119 (1907); in Bull. Misc. Inf. Kew 1915: 169 (1915); in Countr. Life liv: 111 (1923). Bretschneider, Hist. Eur. Bot. Discov. China ii: 971 (1898). Masters in Gard. Chron., Ser. 3, xxxvi: 282, fig. 130 (1904). Bulley in Fl. and Sylva iii: 84 (1905). Bull. Misc. Inf. Kew 1905, App: 82 (1905). E. H. Wilson in Journ. Roy. Hort. Soc. xxix: 660 (1905); West. China i: 138 (1913); *op. cit.* ii: 9 (1913); Pl. Hunt. ii: 168 (1927). Garden xlvii: 318, tab. (1905). J. H. Veitch, Hort. Veitch.: 424 (1906). Mottet in Jardin xx: 101 (1906); in Rev. Hort. xii: 205 (1912). Riebe in Gartenw. x: 273 (1906). Journ. Roy. Hort. Soc. xxxi: cxxvii (1906). Fedde in Engl., Pflanzenr. iv, 104: 265, fig. 35 H (1909). Silva Tarouca, Freiland-Staud.: 150, fig. 200 (1910). Farrer in Journ. Roy. Hort. Soc. xlii: 86 (1916); in Gard. Chron., Ser. 3, lvii: 1 (1915); Eav. World ii: 129 (1917); Engl. Rock-Gard. i: 479 (1919); *op. çit.* 507 (1919); apud Irving in Bull. Alp. Gard. Soc. i: 193 (1932). Irving in Garden lxxxvii: 171 (1923). Kingdon-Ward in Gard. Chron., Ser. 3, lxxix: 439 (1926). L. H. Bailey, Stand. Cycloped. Hort., New Ed. ii: 2018 (1927). Silva Tarouca and Schneider, Freiland-Staud.: 249, fig. 271 (1927). Harrow in New Fl. and Silva ii: 149, fig. 57 (1930). Wehrhahn, Gartenstaud. i: 469 (1930). Cox, Pl. Introd. Farrer: 41 (1930). McDouall in Gard. Chron., Ser. 3, xcii: 336, fig. 162 (1932). Rehder and Kobuski in Journ. Arn. Arboret. xiv: 14 (1933).

[*Cathcartia punicea* Maxim., Fl. Tangut. i: 35, 111, tab. 23 figs. 12–21 (1889), *nomen synonymum.*]

DESCRIPTION. *Monocarpic or polycarpic. Tap-root* very slender, up to 2 in. in length and 0·25 in. in thickness. *Leaves* aggregated in a basal rosette, up to

15 in. in length (including the petiole) and 1·25 in. in breadth; lamina more or less oblanceolate, with several more or less prominent longitudinal nerves, gradually tapering at the base into the petiole, which is expanded and somewhat sheathing at the base, entire at the margin, more or less densely hairy on both surfaces. *Flowers* pendant, borne on simple basal scapes; scapes up to 6 from each rosette and attaining 2·5 ft. in height, usually ribbed and densely covered with slightly reflexed bristles. *Petals* normally 4, but occasionally 6, apparently rhombic-elliptic, acute at the apex or rarely suborbicular and rounded at the apex, up to 4 in. in length and 2 in. in breadth, intense red. *Stamens* numerous; filaments flattened and linear throughout their length, reddish; anthers yellow. *Ovary* broadly oblong, densely bristly, the bristles appressed; style very short or obsolete; stigma with 3–5 radiating lobes. *Capsule* ellipsoid-oblong, glabrous to densely bristly, splitting for a short distance from the apex by 3–5 valves. *Seeds* densely papillose but commonly appearing as pitted owing to loss of the papillae. (Plate XIII.)

Geographical Range. North-eastern Tibet, southern Kansu and north-western Szechuan, at altitudes from 9,500–14,500 ft. Originally described from north-eastern Tibet and northern Szechuan.

No species has drawn such superlative and almost extravagant epithets as *M. punicea.* Those who have had the privilege of seeing the species in its natural habitat, where it brightens the copses and meadows with splashes of the most vivid colour, are unanimous in their eulogies, and one feels from the descriptions that the ecstatic joy of a first acquaintance with the plant is warranted. Unfortunately, in this country, we must be content at present to nurse a few isolated specimens which lead a precarious existence in one or two of the more favoured gardens. The species appeared in cultivation as the result of Wilson's efforts in north-western Szechuan in 1903. He made a journey of about six weeks' duration for the specific purpose of obtaining seed of this poppy, and in this he was successful. It flowered in a private garden in 1904, but it appears to have died out shortly after that date. The species has been reintroduced within the last few years, the seeds having been obtained by the American collector Rock in south-western Kansu.

The dimensions given in the specific description are taken from herbarium specimens in conjunction with field notes. In cultivation the species is commonly more floriferous, bearing up to thirty blooms on each plant, and these sometimes show multiplication in the number of the petals. Farrer has stated that *M. punicea* is monocarpic, but it is recorded that plants have flowered in two successive years in a Scottish garden and have all the appearance of continuing to do so.

The species was discovered by Przewalski in north-eastern Tibet in 1884 and by Potanin in northern Szechuan a year later. These collections formed the basis for Maximowicz's description, and apparently the author was uncertain whether the species should be referred to *Meconopsis* or *Cathcartia*, as he actually described it under the former genus, while the accompanying plate bears the title *C. punicea.*

M. punicea is unique in the genus in having brilliant red flowers which are borne in a pendulous manner from basal scapes. In fruit the capsule assumes an erect position, and it should be noted that Farrer has mentioned plants in which the capsules are devoid of hairs.

The species is most closely related to *M. quintuplinervia*, with which it agrees in habit, but in addition to differences in the shape and colour of the petals *M. punicea* is distinguished by having the staminal filaments flattened and linear.

Field notes indicate that the species grows in association with *Rhododendron* and *Salix* in damp meadows and grassy slopes, shaded from the direct rays of the sun.

SER. ii. GRANDES

MECONOPSIS ser. GRANDES Prain in Journ. As. Soc. Bengal lxiv, 2: 320 (1896) emend., quoad sp. 10.

Meconopsis sect. *Grandes* (Prain) Fedde in Engl., Pflanzenr. iv, 104: 262 (1909) pro parte, excl. spp. 17–19.

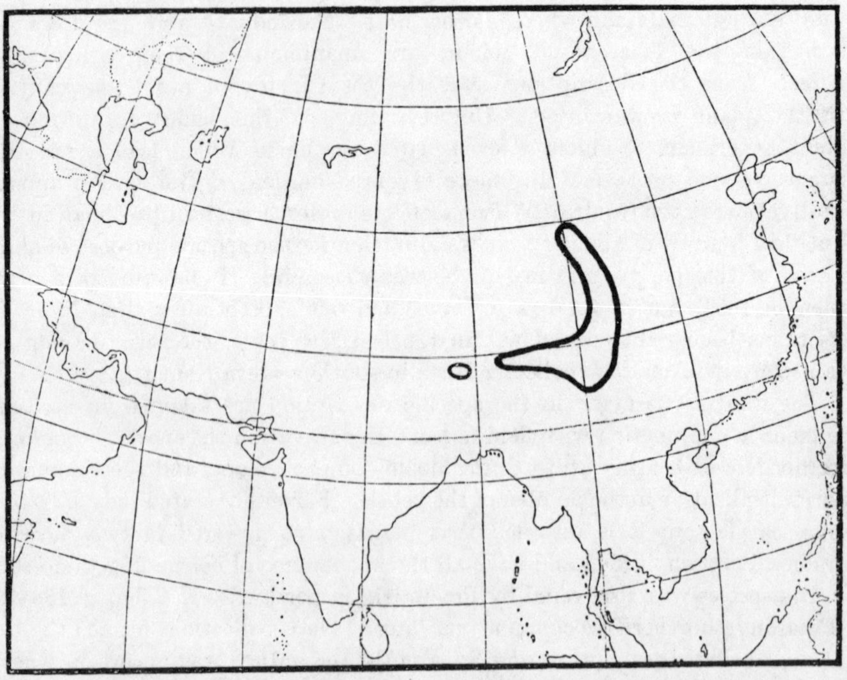

FIG. 7.—MAP SHOWING THE GEOGRAPHICAL RANGE OF THE SERIES *Grandes*. The smaller area represents the distribution of *M. grandis*.

Meconopsis ser. *Integrifoliae* Kingdon-Ward in Gard. Chron., Ser. 3, lxxix: 252, 253 in obs. (1926).

Meconopsis ser. *Superbae* Kingdon-Ward *tom. cit.*: [252 (err. " *Surperbae* ") (Apr. 1926), *nomen nudum*] 460 in obs. (Jun. 1926) pro parte, excl. *M. superba*.

Species 3, occurring from north-eastern Tibet and western Kansu to north-eastern Upper Burma and in central Nepal, western Sikkim and south-central Tibet (see Fig. 7). Type-species: *Meconopsis grandis* Prain.

The series is very closely related to the preceding one, differing from it principally in having cauline leaves of which the uppermost are aggregated in a false whorl and bear flowers in their axils. Of the three species, *M. integrifolia* is the only truly monocarpic member of the series.

18. MECONOPSIS INTEGRIFOLIA

Meconopsis integrifolia (Maxim.) Franch. in Bull. Soc. Bot. Fr. xxxiii: 389 (1886); Pl. Delav. i: 41 (1889). Maxim., Fl. Tangut. i: 35 (1889). Prain in Journ. As. Soc. Bengal lxiv, 2: 311 (1896); Novic. Ind.: 113 (1905); in Gard. Chron., Ser. 3, xxxvii: 369 (1905); in Ann. of Bot. xx: 352, tab. 24 figs. 7–8 (1906); in Bull. Misc. Inf. Kew 1915: 165 (1915); in Countr. Life liv: 110, fig. (1923). Coutts in Gard. Chron., Ser. 3, xxxvi: 198 (1904). Gard. Chron., Ser. 3, xxxvi: 240, fig. 97, tab. opp. 240 (1904). Mottet in Jardin xviii: 328 (1904); *op. cit.* xx: 100, 101, fig. 58 (1906); in Rev. Hort. xii: 204 (1912). Bull. Misc. Inf. Kew 1905, App: 82 (1905). Hemsley in Curt. Bot. Mag. cxxxi: tab. 8027 (1905). Bulley in Fl. and Sylva iii: 80, tab. opp. 80 (1905); *tom. cit.*: 191, fig. (1905). E. H. Wilson in Gard. Chron., Ser. 3, xxxvii: 291, fig. 121 (1905); in Journ. Roy. Hort. Soc. xxix: 660 (1905); West. China i: 138 (1913); *op. cit.* ii: 9 (1913); Pl. Hunt. ii: 163, tab. 105 (1927). Tallack in Gard. Chron., Ser. 3, xxxvii: 317 (1905). Garden xlvii: 286, fig. (1905). Meyer in Gartenw. ix: 534, tab. opp. 534 (1905). Weathers in Gard. Alb. i: 20, tab. 5 (1906). J. H. Veitch, Hort. Veitch: 95, 424, tab. opp. 424 (1906). Journ. Roy. Hort. Soc. xxxi: cxxv (1906). Pynaert in Rev. Hort. Belg. xxxiii: 189, fig. 43 (1907). Trib. Hort. iii: 169, tabs. 90–91 (1908). Fedde in Engl., Pflanzenr. iv, 104: 262, fig. 35 E (1909). Silva Tarouca, Freiland-Staud.: 150, tab. iv. sinistr. (1910). Gard. Chron., Ser. 3, l: 339, tab. opp. 339 (1911). Kingdon-Ward, Land Blue Poppy: 271 (1913); Myst. Riv. Tibet: 126, tab. opp. 176 (1923); Rom. Pl. Hunt.: 200 (1924); in Gard. Chron., Ser. 3, lxxix: 340 (1926); *tom. cit.*: 438, fig. 222 sinistr. (1926); in Ann. of Bot. xl: 543 (1926); in Garden xci: 340, fig. on 323 (1927). Jenkins in Gard. Chron., Ser. 3, xlvi: 146, fig. 60 (1909); in Garden lxxviii: 216, fig. on 217 (1914); *tom. cit.* 240 (1914). Hadden in Garden lxxx: 322, fig. (1916). Farrer in Journ. Roy. Hort. Soc. xlii: 84 (1916); *tom. cit.*: 338 (1917); Eav. World i: 270 (1917); Engl. Rock-Gard. i: 476 (1919). Forrest apud Prain in Bull. Misc. Inf. Kew 1918: 211 (1918); in Countr. Life liv: 614, figs. 1–2 (1923). Limpr. f. in Fedde, Repert. Sp. Nov., Beih. xii: 383 (1922). Irving in Garden lxxxvii: 170 (1923). Harley in Garden lxxxix: 70, fig. on 71 (1925); *op. cit.*: 541, fig. (1925); *op. cit.* xc: 135, fig. (1926); in Gard. Chron., Ser. 3, lxxxii: 109, fig. 46 (1927); in Journ. Roy. Hort. Soc. liii:

220, 223, fig. 27 (1928); in Quart. Bull. Alp. Gard. Soc. ii: 54, tab. opp. 55 supr. (1933). L. H. Bailey, Stand. Cycloped. Hort., New Ed. ii: 2018 (1927). Silva Tarouca and Schneider, Freiland-Staud.: 249 (1927). L. H. and E. Z. Bailey, Hortus: 390 (1930). Wehrhahn, Gartenstaud. i: 468 (1930). Hand.-Mazz., Symb. Sin. vii: 337 (1931). New Fl. and Silva iv: fig. 70 (1932). Rehder and Kobuski in Journ. Arn. Arboret. xiv: 14 (1933).

Cathcartia integrifolia Maxim. in Bull. Acad. Imp. Sc. St. Pétersb. xxiii: 310 (1877); Fl. Tangut. i: 36, tab. 9 figs. 7–12, tab. 23 figs. 22–25 (1889). Bretschneider, Hist. Eur. Bot. Discov. China ii: 971 (1898).

Meconopsis pseudointegrifolia Prain in Ann. of Bot. xx: 353, tab. 25 (1906); in Bull. Misc. Inf. Kew 1915: 167 (1915); in Countr. Life liv: 111 (1923). Bull. Misc. Inf. Kew 1907, App.: 72 (1907). Fedde in Engl., Pflanzenr. iv, 104: 263 (1909). Farrer in Engl. Rock-Gard. i: 479 (1919). Forrest in Countr. Life liv: 614 (1923). Kingdon-Ward in Gard. Chron., Ser. 3, lxxix: 438, fig. 222 med. (1926); *op. cit.* lxxxii: 506 (1927); in Garden xc: 96, fig., fig. on 97 (1926); *op. cit.* xci: 340 (1927); in Ann. of Bot. xl: 543, tab. 16 fig. 4 (1926). Besant in Gard. Chron., Ser. 3, lxxxi: 371, fig. 175 (1927). L. H. Bailey, Stand. Cycloped. Hort., New Ed. ii: 2018 (1927). Wehrhahn, Gartenstaud. i: 468 (1930). Hand.-Mazz., Symb. Sin. vii: 337 (1931). Gard. Chron., Ser. 3, xci: 428, fig. 200 (1932).

Meconopsis integrifolia var. *Souliei* Fedde in Engl., Pflanzenr. iv, 104: 262 (1909). Prain in Bull. Misc. Inf. Kew 1915: 166 (1915). Kingdon-Ward in Gard. Chron., Ser. 3, lxxix: 438, fig. 222 med. (1926); in Ann. of Bot. xl: 543 (1926).

Meconopsis Souliei (Fedde) [Farrer, Engl. Rock-Gard. i: 482 (1919), *nomen provisorium*] Kingdon-Ward, Rom. Pl. Hunt.: 205 in obs. (1924); in Gard. Chron., Ser. 3, lxxvii: 394 in obs. (1925).

[*Meconopsis integrifolia* var. *microstigma* Prain ex Kingdon-Ward in Gard. Chron., Ser. 3, lxxix: 438 in obs. (1926), *nomen synonymum*; in Ann. of Bot. xl: 543 in obs. (1926), *nomen synonymum*.]

[*Meconopsis pseudointegrifolia* var. *brevistyla* Prain ex Kingdon-Ward *locis cit.* (1926), *nomen synonymum*.]

[*Meconopsis integrifolia* var. *brevistyla* Balf. f. ex Kingdon-Ward *locis cit.* (1926), *nomen synonymum*.]

Meconopsis brevistyla [Hort. ex Prain in Countr. Life liv: 112 in obs. (1923), *nomen provisorium*] Kingdon-Ward in Gard. Chron., Ser. 3, lxxviii: 191 in obs. (1925); *op. cit.* lxxix: 438, fig. 222 dext. (1926); *op. cit.* lxxxii: 26 (1927); in Ann. of Bot. xl: 544 (1926). Harley in Garden lxxxix: 541, fig. (1925).

Meconopsis pseudointegrifolia var. *gracilis* Kingdon-Ward in Gard. Chron., Ser. 3, lxxxii: 506 in obs. (1927); in Ann. of Bot. xlii: 861 (1928).

[*Meconopsis integrifolia* var. "*Aberuchill*" Jameson in New Fl. and Silva iv: 38, fig. 16 (1931).]

Description. *Monocarpic*, more or less densely covered throughout with soft spreading rufous or golden-yellow hairs. *Tap-root* narrowly dauciform, up to 4 in. in length, or root system fibrous. *Stem* stout, more or less densely hairy, (the hairs spreading or slightly reflexed), striate, from 5 in. to 3 ft. in height. *Basal leaves* aggregated in a dense rosette (often intermixed with small densely sericeous scale leaves), up to 15 in. in length (including the petiole) and 2 in. in breadth; lamina oblanceolate or obovate to almost linear, gradually tapering at the base into a broad linear petiole which is conspicuously veined and expanded at the base, acute to rounded at the apex, entire at the margin, at first densely hairy on both surfaces but ultimately more or less glabrescent, usually with 3 or more prominent longitudinal nerves and with the midrib slightly keeled on the under surface. *Lower cauline leaves* similar to the basal leaves but with shorter and less expanded petioles. *Upper cauline leaves* subsessile, narrowly elliptic or lanceolate or oblanceolate or linear. *Uppermost leaves* usually aggregated in a false whorl at the level of which the flower-stalks arise. *Flowers* up to 6 in. in diameter, most commonly numbering 4 or 5, produced in succession from the axils of the uppermost stem leaves and occasionally of the lower stem leaves, rarely borne on simple basal scapes; pedicels attaining 21 in. in length (at least in fruiting specimens). *Petals* normally 6–8, suborbicular to obovate, up to 2·5 in. in length and 2·5 in. in breadth, yellow or rarely white.* *Stamens* numerous; filaments linear or filiform, of the same colour as the petals; anthers orange, yellow, or black according to age. *Ovary* broadly ellipsoid-oblong, ovoid or ellipsoid, usually densely hairy (with the golden-yellow hairs appressed) but varying through all degrees of pubescence to glabrous; style obsolete or when present up to 0·5 in. in length; stigma capitate with the 4–9 stigmatic rays variously decurrent on the style and passing through intermediate stages to a depressed sessile condition in which the rays are radiating and more or less decurrent on the ovary. *Capsule* broadly ellipsoid-oblong to ellipsoid, splitting by 4–9 valves to about one-third of its length. *Seeds* more or less reniform, testa prominently longitudinally pitted. (Plate XIV.)

Geographical Range. North-eastern Tibet and western Kansu, through Szechuan to north-western Yunnan and north-eastern Upper Burma, at altitudes from 9,000–17,000 ft. Originally described from Kansu.

It is unfortunate that this well-known plant should have been the source of so much misunderstanding and, as a consequence, should be burdened with such a cumbrous synonymy. In dealing with this species most authors have apparently concentrated on finding differences between the various forms, neglecting the intermediate conditions and thus failing to recognise the very close resemblances which they show. As it is proposed that these should be included in one species, in contrast to the opinions currently held, it is desirable to recapitulate the history of *M. integrifolia* and examine the facts which have led to the conclusion that this flux of forms is really one species subject to extreme variation. It is possible to recognise certain foci around which the specimens examined tend, more or less, to become aggregated, but there is so much intergrading that it is impossible to segregate any stable units by means of constant structural characters.

* In a specimen collected by Rock in 1932 the colour of the petals is given as pink.

M. integrifolia was first collected by Przewalski in Kansu in 1872 and again in 1873. The species was briefly described by Maximowicz in 1877 and he included it in *Cathcartia*, although he subsequently accepted Franchet's opinion that it was more properly referable to *Meconopsis*.

In its distribution the species is one of the most widespread of the genus, extending from Kansu in the north to south-eastern Tibet. It appears to be most abundant in north-western Yunnan, where it was discovered by Delavay on the Likiang Range in 1899 and has subsequently been copiously collected there by Forrest and others. At first sight it seemed that there was a significant correlation between the stylar character and the geographical distribution. It was observed that in the specimens from Kansu and northern Szechuan the stigma almost without exception was of the depressed sessile type, while in the south-western area of its range there was a higher proportion of stylar forms. The bulk of the material examined is from the intermediate province of Yunnan, and here it is found that the entire range of forms is found growing in association.

As originally figured, *M. integrifolia* was shown as having no style, but Franchet in identifying Delavay's plant with this species noted the presence of a distinct though short style, and as he had the type-collection for comparison he evidently regarded the stylar character as of no taxonomic importance.

In 1904 plants which were at first referred to *M. integrifolia* and figured under that name flowered simultaneously in two gardens in this country. The seed from which these had been raised was derived from independent sources; the one set of seeds was from the Koslov expedition to south-eastern Tibet and the other from Wilson collected at Tatsienlu in western Szechuan. Both plants were figured in "Flora and Sylva" and comparison suggested that they belonged to different species. The Koslov plant as grown had the flowers borne singly on basal scapes and characterised by the presence of a prominent style; that of Wilson had the flowers raised on a stem and had sessile stigmas with conspicuous radiating lobes. The question of the identity of these plants was referred to Prain who decided that the latter was typical *M. integrifolia* while the former, in virtue of its habit and conspicuous style, he described as a new species under the name *M. pseudointegrifolia.* Forrest and Monbeig subsequently collected forms in Yunnan in which the flowers in addition to having conspicuous styles were borne in a cluster on the stem. It was then realised that the separate identity of *M. pseudointegrifolia* depended only on the presence of a long style. Among Forrest's specimens were others corresponding to the original Delavay gathering in which the style was very short or almost obsolete. Prain suggested that these forms might equally well be regarded as varieties either of *M. integrifolia* or of *M. pseudointegrifolia.* Actually the plants were distributed under the name *M. integrifolia* var. *brevistyla*, although no description of that variety can be traced.

Thus at this stage three plants were recognised differing only in their stylar characters. This position has recently been accepted by Kingdon-Ward, who has suggested that the intermediate variety should be given specific rank. Further, he advances differences in habit, degree of pubescence, shape of the flowers and number of capsular valves, to support his opinion. Careful examination of the copious field material and observation of cultivated specimens has shown that there is no justification for retaining specific or varietal status for these forms. It is true that the extremes of variation afford a very striking contrast, but they are so closely intergraded by intermediate types that it is impossible to recognise any clearly defined units within the aggregate. Indeed, it can be demonstrated that flowers which have a conspicuous style are present on the same plant with flowers in which the stigma is almost sessile. Further evidence of the unreliability of the stylar character as a criterion for separation is afforded by the species *M. quintuplinervia*, in which there is found the same range from a capitate stigma on a well-defined style to a condition in which the stigma is of the depressed sessile radiating type.

As might be expected, certain of the forms, if more or less isolated in gardens, come true from seed, and the belief that these represent distinct species is understandable until they are compared with the entire range. It is then seen that there are no concrete characters by which to separate them. The separate existence of these forms depends on cultural methods, and if it is desired to designate them by names then the procedure adopted in a recent number of "The New Flora and Silva," where a form is named after the garden in which it was raised, is to be recommended. Latin epithets should be avoided unless the plant is sufficiently distinct to be typified and given a proper diagnosis.

It appears that the first introduction of *M. integrifolia* to European gardens was due to Abbé Farges, who sent seed from Szechuan from which plants were raised in Paris and flowered for the first time in 1896. Wilson was responsible for the successful introduction of the species into this country in 1904. An isolated plant flowered in 1903 from the Koslov seed mentioned above, but the credit of its extensive and permanent introduction belongs to Wilson. In its wild state *M. integrifolia* is found abundantly in alpine meadows, rocky slopes and boulder screes. It is recorded that the species may attain a height of three feet, may produce as many as eighteen flowers and these may be from eight to ten inches in diameter.

M. INTEGRIFOLIA × M. BETONICIFOLIA = 19D. × **M. Sarsonsii** Sarsons. See p. 68.

M. INTEGRIFOLIA × M. GRANDIS = 20A. × **M. Beamishii** Prain. See p. 70.

18A. ×**MECONOPSIS HARLEYANA**

(*M. integrifolia* (Maxim.) Franch. ♂ × *M. simplicifolia* (D. Don) Walp. ♀)

×MECONOPSIS HARLEYANA G. Tayl. in New Fl. and Silva vi.: 48 (1933).

Meconopsis simplicifolia Bailey's var. × *Meconopsis integrifolia* Brooker in Gard. Chron., Ser. 3, lxxxiii: 353, fig. 167 (1928).

Meconopsis simplicifolia var. *eburnea* Hort. ex Harley in New Fl. and Silva iv: 199, fig. 74 (1932); in Quart. Bull. Alp. Gard. Soc. ii: 54, tab. opp. 59 (1933).

DESCRIPTION. *Polycarpic*. *Leaves* all basal; lamina lanceolate to oblanceolate, up to 6 in. in length (including the linear petiole which may attain 2·5 in. in length and 0·3 in. in breadth) and 1 in. in breadth, gradually tapering at the base into the petiole, acute to rounded at the apex, entire at the margin, more or less densely covered on both surfaces with soft hairs. *Flowers* borne singly on basal scapes; scapes 1–4 from each rosette, up to 18 in. in length, more or less densely covered, especially towards the apex, with soft reflexed hairs. *Petals* 6–9, ovate to obovate or suborbicular, up to about 2·5 in. in length and 1·8 in. in breadth, pale-yellow. *Stamens* numerous; filaments narrowly linear, of the same colour as the petals; anthers orange. *Ovary* ovoid, densely covered with golden-brown appressed hairs; style up to 0·25 in. in length; stigma capitate with 3–4 more or less decurrent lobes. *Capsule* ellipsoid-oblong, densely covered with spreading hairs, splitting by 3–4 valves.

GEOGRAPHICAL RANGE. A garden hybrid of spontaneous origin but possibly occurring naturally in south-eastern Tibet.

The occurrence of this plant in cultivation was first recorded by R. L. Harley* in 1926, and he then regarded it as a yellow-flowered variety of *M. simplicifolia*, although suggesting that it might possibly be a hybrid between that species and *M. integrifolia*, as both were growing in close proximity in his garden. It was raised from seed saved from Bailey's form of *M. simplicifolia* and flowered for the first time in 1925.

The plant appeared spontaneously, and there appears to be no doubt that it is a hybrid between the parents suggested. The yellow flower-colour and dense covering of hairs on the ovary are derived from *M. integrifolia*, while *M. simplicifolia* is probably responsible for the perennial habit. Seeds have been produced, though sparingly, and the hybrid appears to be so fixed as to breed true.

It is possible that the plant collected by Kingdon-Ward† at Temo La in Tibet in 1924 and designated the "Ivory Poppy" is *M. Harleyana*. This plant was growing in company with the sky-blue-flowered form of *M. simplicifolia*, although Kingdon-Ward records that *M. integrifolia* was found in close proximity.

* Harley in Garden xc: 474, fig. (1926); in Gard. Chron., Ser. 3, lxxxi: 71, fig. 28 (1927); in Journ. Roy. Hort. Soc. liii: 224 (1928).

† Kingdon-Ward in Garden xc: 115, fig. (1926); in Ann. of Bot. xl: 536, tab. 16 fig. 2 (1926); in Gard. Chron., Ser. 3, lxxxi: 72, fig. 30 (1927).

19. MECONOPSIS BETONICIFOLIA

Meconopsis betonicifolia Franch., Plant. Delav. i: 42, tab. 12 (1889). Bretschneider, Hist. Eur. Bot. Discov. China ii: 886 (1898). Prain in Bull. Misc. Inf. Kew 1915: 143 (1915). Forrest in Countr. Life liv: 614 (" *betonicifolius* ") (1923). Harrow in New Fl. and Silva ii: 151 (1930). L. H. and E. Z. Bailey, Hortus: 390 (1930). Chittenden in Journ. Roy. Hort. Soc. lvi: 80 (1931).

Cathcartia betonicifolia (Franch.) Prain in Ann. of Bot. xx: 369 (1906). Fedde in Engl., Pflanzenr. iv, 104: 245, fig. 33 D (1909). Farrer, Engl. Rock-Gard. i: 210 (" *betonicaefolia* ") (1919).

Meconopsis Baileyi Prain in Bull. Misc. Inf. Kew 1915: 161 (1915). Farrer, Engl. Rock-Gard. ii: 477 (1919). Kingdon-Ward in Garden xc: 96, fig. (1926); *op. cit.* xci: 340, 450, fig. (1927); in Gard. Chron., Ser. 3, lxxix: 340, fig. 171 (1926); *op. cit.* lxxxii: 26 (1927); in Ann. of Bot. xl: 541, tab. 16 fig. 3 (1926); in Journ. Roy. Hort. Soc. lii: 23, 233, fig. 72 (1927). J. E. G. White in Gard. Chron., Ser. 3, lxxxi: 449, fig. 217 (1927). Harley in Journ. Roy. Hort. Soc. liii: 226, fig. 33 (1928). G. Tayl. in Gard. Chron., Ser. 3, lxxxv: 66 (1929).

Meconopsis Baileyi var. *pratensis* Kingdon-Ward in Gard. Chron., Ser. 3, lxxxii: 506 in obs. (1927); *op. cit.* xciii: 367 (1933); in Ann. of Bot. xlii: 856, tab. 16 fig. 1 (1928). Pl. Hunt. Edge World: tab. opp. 96 (1930).

Meconopsis betonicifolia var. *Baileyi* (Prain) [Edwards in Gard. Chron., Ser. 3, lxxxv: 473 in obs. (1929), *nomen nudum*] L. H. and E. Z. Bailey, Hortus: 390 (1930).

Meconopsis betonicifolia forma *Baileyi* (Prain) Cotton in Gard. Chron., Ser. 3, lxxxv: 143 in obs. (1929). Stapf in Curt. Bot. Mag. cliii: tab. 9185 (1930). Kingdon-Ward, Pl. Hunt Edge World: 301 (1930).

Meconopsis betonicifolia forma *Franchetii* Stapf in Curt. Bot. Mag. cliii: sub tab. 9185 in obs. (1930).

[*Meconopsis betonicifolia* var. *Franchetii* (Stapf) L. H. and E. Z. Bailey, Hortus: 390 (1930), *nomen synonymum.*]

Description. *Monocarpic or polycarpic. Rootstock* short and stout, densely covered with dark-brown bristles and invested with the remnants of persistent petioles interspersed with barbellate rufous bristles. *Stem* rigidly erect, glabrous or with scattered, spreading rufous hairs, attaining up to 5 ft. in height. *Basal and lower cauline leaves* petiolate (petiole up to 8 in. in length and widened at the base into a sheath); lamina oblong to elongate-oblong, up to 6 in. in length and 3 in. in breadth, truncate or slightly cordate at the base and more or less decurrent on the petiole, subacute or obtuse or rounded at the apex, usually with broad obtuse serrations at the margin but sometimes coarsely and irregularly serrate and even lobed; rufous bristles scattered on both surfaces and particularly obvious on the margin. *Upper cauline leaves* sessile, more or less auriculate at the base and stem-clasping, otherwise similar to the lower leaves. *Uppermost leaves* aggregated in a false whorl, at the level of which the flower-stalks arise. *Flowers* usually few (commonly not more than 6), semi-pendulous, produced in succession from the axils of the uppermost leaves and occasionally from the axils of lower cauline leaves; pedicels (at least in fruiting specimens) up to 11 in. in length. *Petals* typically 4 (commonly 5–6 in the terminal flower), broadly obovate or suborbicular or ovate, up to 2 in. in length and 2 in. in breadth, rounded (rarely acute) at the apex, ranging in colour from rose-lavender to satiny-sky-blue. *Stamens* numerous; filaments filiform or very rarely narrowly linear, white; anthers orange or golden-yellow. *Ovary* ellipsoid-oblong, glabrous to densely covered with rufous bristles; style not exceeding 0·25 in. in length; stigma 4–7-lobed, pale-green. *Capsule* oblong to oblong-ellipsoid, splitting by 4–7 valves for about one-third of its length. *Seeds* more or less reniform, testa with longitudinal rows of shallow pits. (Plate XV.)

Geographical Range. South-eastern Tibet, north-western Yunnan and northern Upper Burma at altitudes from 10,000–13,000 ft. Originally described from north-western Yunnan.

It is given to few plants to attain such popularity so rapidly and to establish themselves so firmly in the estimation of horticulturists as *M. betonicifolia*. It is certainly a species of supreme merit, the usually perennial habit and ease of cultivation being factors which have no doubt contributed to its reputation. Unfortunately there has been considerable controversy regarding the identity of the plant in cultivation and it seems desirable to offer some comments on this subject, after making careful examination of the field specimens and cultivated plants.

Credit for the discovery of this species belongs to Père Delavay, who collected it in woods near Hokin and at San-tcha-ho in north-western Yunnan in 1886. His specimens were described and figured by Franchet three years later. Forrest and Rock have since collected the species in the same area.

The specimens on which Prain based *M. Baileyi* were sent by Bailey from Lunang, Kongbo, in south-eastern Tibet, but the material was so incomplete and fragmentary that the author did not recognise the proper affinity of his species. Only one or two flowers were collected, and thus a proper conception of the vegetative parts was possible only when Kingdon-Ward, in June 1924, returned to the same locality and obtained ample material. He subsequently identified his specimens with *M. Baileyi* and the extensive introduction of the plant under that name was due to him. Further, Kingdon-Ward supplied an amplified description of the species but at that time drew no comparisons with *M. betonicifolia*.

Separation of the two species has been suggested on account of habit differences and relative lengths of the style and degree of hairiness of the ovary. The first two characters at once proved untrustworthy, but the pubescence character of the ovary appeared more significant, and it is on this alleged distinction that the specific status of *M. Baileyi* depends. While it is to be admitted that the pubescence on the ovary in Kingdon-Ward's specimens is generally much more dense than in the Yunnan forms, and that this character is retained in cultivated plants, it is possible to obtain a range from a glabrous or sparsely hairy condition to the densely hairy state ascribed to *M. Baileyi*. That the two plants are conspecific seems evident, and I have expressed the opinion* that they may be regarded as geographical forms of the same species. Stapf has since accepted this view by identifying the cultivated plant as *M. betonicifolia* forma *Baileyi*, and for the other form, on which the species was founded, he has proposed the name *M. betonicifolia* forma *Franchetii*.

The behaviour of the species in cultivation appears to differ somewhat from that in the natural state. Herbarium specimens and field photographs of *M. betonicifolia* show that the flowers are produced only from the uppermost leaves and, almost without exception, have only four petals. As cultivated, flowers normally arise also in the axils of the lower stem leaves and not infrequently the number of petals is multiplied. The form in cultivation is that which was described as *M. Baileyi* with a densely hairy ovary and generally short style. If plants are allowed to flower during the second year from seed they are very generally monocarpic, but if flowering is inhibited they usually form offsets and become polycarpic.

Collectors' notes indicate that *M. betonicifolia* is a plant of shady woods and thickets, or of lush alpine meadows along the watercourses, usually in sandy soils.

19A. ×**MECONOPSIS AURICULATA**

(? *M. betonicifolia* Franch. × *M. paniculata* (D. Don) Prain)

Meconopsis auriculata Stapf in New Fl. and Silva ii: 272 (1930). Hay in New Fl. and Silva ii: 273, fig. 103 (1930); in Gard. Chron., Ser. 3, xcii: 392, figs. 193-195 (1932). G. Tayl. in New Fl. and Silva vi: 49 (1933).

Description. *Polycarpic. Plant* up to 3 ft. in height. *Basal leaves* in a dense rosette; lamina more or less oblong, up to 11 in. in length (including the petiole, which may attain 6·5 in. in length) and 1·75 in. in breadth, truncate or slightly cordate at the base, rounded to subacute at the apex, coarsely and broadly serrate at the margin, more or less densely covered with short bristles interspersed with long rufous bristles. *Upper cauline leaves* sessile, lanceolate-oblong to triangular-lanceolate, more or less stem-clasping and auriculate at the base, otherwise similar to the lower leaves. *Uppermost cauline leaves* similar to the lower leaves, arranged in a false whorl. *Flowers* arising in a 5–6 flowered terminal umbelliform inflorescence and also singly in the axils of the upper stem-leaves; pedicels up to 3 in. in length, densely covered with spreading bristles especially towards the apex. *Petals* 4, ovate to suborbicular, up to 2 in. in length and 1·5 in. in breadth, pale yellow. *Stamens* numerous; filaments filiform, whitish; anthers orange, ultimately brown. *Ovary* ovoid to oblong-ellipsoid, densely covered with more or less appressed rufous bristles; style distinct, up to 0·3 in. in length; stigma capitate, 4-lobed, green.

Geographical Range. Known only in cultivation; probably a garden hybrid.

* G. Tayl. in Gard. Chron., Ser. 3, lxxxv: 66 (1929).

M. auriculata is a problematical plant inasmuch as its origin is obscure and its claim to specific status is questionable. Only two plants were raised, and these appeared promiscuously in a batch of *M. aculeata* seedlings, the seed having been obtained from Kashmir. It was thought possible that the plants might have originated from Nepal seed which had been sown at the same time, but this is improbable as all the species in cultivation from that country can now be correlated with field specimens. This is not so with *M. auriculata*, and it is very questionable if Nepal is the true home of the plant. It flowered for the first time in 1930 and has continued to do so each year.

Several features prompt one to assume that *M. auriculata* is a hybrid. Support for such a supposition is derived in the first place from its spontaneous appearance. Then, no evidence of its occurrence in nature is known, and further the plant has so far failed to produce fertile seed. It is possible to suggest parents whose combined characters might give rise to such a plant as *M. auriculata*. There is a very strong habit resemblance between *M. auriculata* and *M. betonicifolia*, and indeed, there is no obvious structural difference between the two. It would appear that the latter species is the dominant parent in a possible combination. It should be noted that *M. betonicifolia* is generally perennial and *M. auriculata* differs only in retaining a dense basal rosette of leaves throughout the winter, in having yellow flowers, and to some extent in the character of the pubescence. These characters may have been derived from the yellow-flowered *M. paniculata*, in which the leaves persist during the winter and from which the pubescence character may have been acquired. Until attempts to secure a hybrid between these parents yield positive results this possible origin of *M. auriculata* must remain an open question.

19B. ×**MECONOPSIS COXIANA**

(*M. betonicifolia* Franch. ♂ × *M. violacea* Kingdon-Ward ♀)

×MECONOPSIS COXIANA G. Tayl. in New Fl. and Silva vi: 45, fig. 19 (1933).

DESCRIPTION. *Polycarpic. Plant* up to about 3 ft. in height. *Basal leaves* persisting in a dense rosette throughout the winter, the inner leaves being carried up by growth of the axis at time of flowering; lamina elongate-oblong to oblong-lanceolate, up to about 8 in. in length (including the petiole) and 1·5 in. in breadth, tapering at the base into a broad petiole which may attain 2 in. in length, obtuse at the apex, irregularly crenate or serrate at the margin or occasionally pinnatifidly lobed towards the base, more or less densely covered on both surfaces with spreading rufous bristles. *Cauline leaves* sessile, the upper stem-clasping and more or less auriculate, otherwise similar to the basal leaves. *Flowers* borne on simple pedicels from the axils of the uppermost leaves and in 1–3-flowered cymules from the axils of the lower leaves; uppermost pedicels ebracteate; pedicels up to 6 in. in length, densely covered with spreading bristles. *Petals* 4, more or less obovate, acute at the apex, up to 1·6 in. in length and 1·2 in. in breadth, light-blue. *Stamens* numerous; filaments white, filiform; anthers orange. *Ovary* oblong or ellipsoid-oblong, densely covered with obliquely spreading ultimately rufous hairs; style stout and distinct, twisted, up to 0·2 in. in length; stigma with 4–5 radiating green lobes.

GEOGRAPHICAL RANGE. A garden hybrid which appeared spontaneously.

This hybrid appeared spontaneously in a batch of *M. violacea* seedlings and flowered at Glendoick, Perthshire, in 1933. The influence of *M. betonicifolia* is reflected particularly in the polycarpic habit, while *M. violacea* is apparently responsible for the twisted style. In the display of the flowers there is a distinct break from either parent, as they are commonly sessile or borne on very short pedicels at the apex of the flowering branch.

19C. ×**MECONOPSIS MUSGRAVEI**

(*M. betonicifolia* Franch. ♂ × *M. superba* King ex Prain ♀)

×MECONOPSIS MUSGRAVEI G. Tayl. in New Fl. and Silva vi: 46, fig. 20 (1933).

DESCRIPTION. *Polycarpic. Plant* up to 24 in. in height, the stem more or less densely covered with spreading rufous hairs. *Basal leaves* petiolate; lamina oblong, up to 3 in. in length and 1·75 in. in breadth, cuneate to cordate at the base, obtuse to rounded at the apex, usually with broad obtuse serrations at the margin, more or less densely covered on both surfaces with soft hairs; petiole about 1 in. in length. *Cauline leaves* sessile; lamina oblong to triangular-lanceolate, auriculate and stem-clasping at the base, otherwise similar to the basal leaves. *Flowers* up to 8, arising singly in the axils of the upper cauline leaves; pedicels up to 3 in. in length, more or less densely covered with spreading rufous hairs. *Petals* 4, ovate to suborbicular, up to 2 in. in length and 2 in. in breadth, white. *Stamens* numerous; filaments filiform, whitish; anthers orange-yellow. *Ovary* ellipsoid, densely covered with obliquely spreading hairs; style distinct, up to 0·25 in. in length; stigma capitate, prominently 5–6-lobed, the lobes whitish or flushed with pale-purple.

GEOGRAPHICAL RANGE. A garden hybrid obtained by deliberate crossing.

The successful mating of the parents which produced this hybrid was accomplished by C. T. Musgrave, after whom the plant is named, at Godalming, Surrey, and the resulting hybrid is one of outstanding merit. At first sight *M. Musgravei* very closely resembles *M. superba*, but the polycarpic habit and auriculate stem-leaves show unmistakably the influence of *M. betonicifolia*. Owing to difficulty in obtaining seed from *M. superba*, the raiser was led to the possibility of crossing the species with *M. betonicifolia*, and this has proved a happy combination. The pure white of the flowers together with the polycarpic habit will be sufficient to commend it to horticulturists. Again in this hybrid, as elsewhere in the genus, there is demonstrated the recessive character of blue-coloured flowers. *M. Musgravei* produced fertile seed, and there appears to be no reason why it should not become established in gardens.

19D. ×MECONOPSIS SARSONSII

(*M. betonicifolia* Franch. ♀ × *M. integrifolia* (Maxim.) Franch. ♂)

Meconopsis Sarsonsii Sarsons ex Gard. Chron., Ser. 3, lxxxvii: 414 (err. "*Sarsonii*") (1930). Gard. Chron., Ser. 3, lxxxviii: 11, fig. 7 (1930). Journ. Roy. Hort. Soc. lvi: xxvii (1931). G. Tayl. in New Fl. and Silva vi: 50, fig. 21 (1933).*

Description. *Monocarpic or polycarpic. Plant* about 3 ft. in height. *Flowers* borne singly in the axils of the aggregated uppermost cauline leaves and also of the upper leaves; pedicels densely hairy. *Petals* 4, sulphur-yellow. *Stamens* numerous; filaments filiform; anthers golden-yellow. *Ovary* ellipsoid-oblong, densely hairy; style up to 0·2 in. in length; stigma with 4–6 radiating, more or less decurrent lobes.

Geographical Range. A garden hybrid raised by deliberate crossing, but which has also appeared spontaneously.

The plant on which the original description was based proved to be monocarpic, but the hybrid also appeared spontaneously in a batch of *M. betonicifolia* seedlings at the Royal Botanic Garden, Edinburgh, in 1930, and has flowered during the last three years. In habit *M. Sarsonsii* very closely resembles its seed parent, but the yellow flower-colour asserts the presence of *M. integrifolia*.

20. MECONOPSIS GRANDIS

Meconopsis grandis Prain in Journ. As. Soc. Bengal lxiv, 2: 320 (1895); in Ann. Roy. Bot. Gard. Calcutta ix, 1: 2, tab. 2 (1901); Novic. Ind.: 122 (1905); in Gard. Chron., Ser. 3, xxxvii: 369, fig. 157 (1905); in Ann. of Bot. xx: 352 (1906); in Bull. Misc. Inf. Kew 1915: 167 (1915); in Countr. Life liv: 111 (1923). Bulley in Gard. Chron., Ser. 3, xxvii: 352 (1900); *op. cit.* xxxvii: 397 (1905); in Fl. and Sylva iii: 82 (1905). Bull. Misc. Inf. Kew 1901, App.: 95 (1901). Gumbleton in Gard. Chron., Ser. 3, xxxvi: 305 (1904). Mottet in Jardin xx: 101 (1906); in Rev. Hort. xii: 265 (1912). Fedde in Engl., Pflanzenr. iv, 104: 263, fig. 35 D (1909). Jenkins in Garden lxxviii: 240 (1914). Farrer, Engl. Rock-Gard. i: 476, tab. 47 dextr. (1919). Irving in Garden lxxxvii: 170 (1923). Harley in Garden lxxxix: 70 (1925); in Journ. Roy. Hort. Soc. liii: 224, fig. 31 (1928). Kingdon-Ward in Gard. Chron., Ser. 3, lxxix: 439 (1926); in Ann. of Bot. xl: 544 (1926). L. H. Bailey, Stand. Cycloped. Hort., New Ed. ii: 2019 (1927). Harrow in Gard. Chron., Ser. 3, lxxxiv: 151, fig. 64 (1928); in New Fl. and Silva ii: 152, fig. 56 (1930). Journ. Roy. Hort. Soc. liii: liv (1928). L. H. and E. Z. Bailey, Hortus: 390 (1930). Wehrhahn, Gartenstaud. i: 470 (1930). Hay in Gard. Chron., Ser. 3, xcii: 409 (1932). Stapf in Curt. Bot. Mag. cxlvi: tab. 9304 (1933).

Description. *Polycarpic. Tap-root* narrowly dauciform or root-system fibrous. *Stem* rigidly erect, more or less densely bristly, the bristles spreading or slightly deflexed, at the base densely covered with persistent leaf-bases interspersed with rufous barbellate bristles, from about 15 in. to 48 in. in height.

* By error the name was here ascribed to Mulligan.

Basal and lower cauline leaves petiolate (petiole up to 7 in. in length, sheathing at the base); lamina narrowly oblanceolate to lanceolate- or elliptic-oblong, tapering into the petiole at the base, acute or subacute at the apex, distantly and irregularly serrate or with broad crenations at the margin, rufous bristles scattered on both surfaces. *Upper cauline leaves* sessile; lamina lanceolate or oblong-lanceolate, entire coarsely serrate or crenate at the margin. *Uppermost leaves* (commonly 3) aggregated in a false whorl at the level of which the pedicels arise. *Flowers* usually few (commonly not more than 3), produced in succession from the axils of the uppermost leaves or occasionally of the lower cauline leaves (commonly in cultivated specimens borne on basal scapes); pedicels (at least in fruiting specimens) attaining 18 in. in length. *Petals* commonly 4, but up to 9, suborbicular or broadly obovate, up to 2·75 in. in length and 2·5 in. in breadth, purple or rich blue. *Stamens* numerous; filaments filiform, whitish; anthers yellow. *Ovary* ovoid or oblong, glabrous to more or less densely hairy; style usually distinct, up to 0·5 in. in length; stigma clavate, 4–6-lobed (lobes often very strongly decurrent on the style), green. *Capsule* narrowly ellipsoid-oblong, splitting by 4–6 (most commonly 4) valves for a short distance from the apex. *Seeds* more or less reniform, testa with longitudinal rows of shallow pits. (Plate XVI.)

Geographical Range. Eastern Nepal, through south-central Tibet and Sikkim to Bhutan, at altitudes from 10,000–17,000 ft. Originally described from Sikkim.

The original description was based by Prain on specimens obtained by native collectors (1887) and also by Watt (1881) and Gammie (1892), all from the Jongri district of Sikkim where, apparently, the species occurs in some abundance between the altitudes of 10,000 and 12,000 ft. According to Gammie, *M. grandis* is found in this area only as a cultivated plant about the dwellings used in summer by shepherds. They are not primarily concerned with the aesthetic qualities of the plant, but grow it rather for the extraction of oil from the seeds, although the properties of this oil are not recorded. It has also been stated that the species is not truly native in Sikkim, but was originally introduced there from Nepal. Its occurrence in that kingdom has only recently been confirmed, and in Nepal the plant does not appear to be so robust as in Sikkim, and the colour of the flowers is given on the field tickets as purple in contrast to the blue colour usually attributed to the Sikkim specimens. It may also be observed that the ovary of the Nepal plants is much more elongated and less hairy, but these characters are hardly sufficient to merit taxonomic distinction. *M. grandis* was also collected in Tibet by the second Mount Everest Expedition of 1922 on stony soil at an altitude of 16,000 ft. By its discovery in 1933 by Ludlow and Sherriff the known geographical range has been extended eastwards into Bhutan. These collectors state that the species attains a height of 4 ft., and inhabits hillsides among small bushes.

It appears that Prain was responsible for the introduction of the species into this country and, to judge from a remark of his,* it flowered in the Royal Botanic

* Prain in Ann. of Bot. xx: 364 (1906).

Garden, Edinburgh, in 1895. When grown here it seems to lose the involucre-like whorl of leaves, at least to some extent, and the flowers tend to be produced on long basal scapes. The Nepal form flowered in cultivation for the first time in 1932, and from a horticultural point of view was regarded as distinctly disappointing, being of much smaller stature than is usually associated with *M. grandis* and with flowers of a very inferior wine-purple. There are indications that this form will improve in cultivation and opinions regarding its horticultural merit may require modification. It may be observed that in the natural state the occurrence of both colour forms is confirmed by the statements of native collectors.

Examination of the herbarium specimens emphasises the close affinity of this species with *M. simplicifolia*. *M. grandis* is distinguished by its much larger flowers with usually not more than four petals, although the terminal flower often has more, and its leafy stem. In cultivation the leafy character of the stem is not constant, and a more reliable distinction is to be found in the colour of the filaments, which are always white in *M. grandis* and coloured in *M. simplicifolia*. The two species may further be distinguished by their seeds, those of *M. grandis* having the seed-coat pitted in a longitudinal manner, whereas those of *M. simplicifolia* are very densely papillose.

Farrer has recorded* a hybrid between *M. grandis* and *M. latifolia* (*sinuata* "*latifolia*"), but he gave no precise data of its occurrence further than that it appeared in Ireland. The plant was stated to be polycarpic with blue flowers of a colour intermediate between that of the parents.

20A. ×MECONOPSIS BEAMISHII

(*M. grandis* Prain ♀ × *M. integrifolia* (Maxim.) Franch. ♂)

MECONOPSIS BEAMISHII Prain in Bull. Misc. Inf. Kew 1915: 166 in obs. (1915). G. Tayl. in New Fl. and Silva vi: 49 (1933).

[*Meconopsis integrifolia* × *M. grandis* Paine in Gard. Chron., Ser. 3, 1; 22, fig. 14 (1911).]

[*Meconopsis hybrid grandis* × *pseudointegrifolia* Harley in Quart. Bull. Alp. Gard. Soc. ii: 54, tab. opp. 55 infr. (1933).]

DESCRIPTION. *Polycarpic*. *Plant* up to about 4 ft. in height. *Basal leaves* up to 10 in. in length (including the petiole, which may attain about 3 in. in length) and 1·5 in. in breadth; lamina more or less oblanceolate, tapering at the base into the petiole, acute at the apex, entire at the margin. *Uppermost cauline leaves* aggregated in a false whorl. *Flowers* arising in an umbelliform inflorescence at the level of the uppermost leaves or accompanied by 1–2 basal scapes; pedicels up to 11 in. in length. *Petals* 6–8, obovate, up to about 3 in. in length and 2·5 in. in breadth, yellow throughout or with a purple blotch at the back of each petal towards the base. *Stamens* numerous; filaments yellowish and flushed with

* Farrer, Engl. Rock-Gard. i: 483 (1919).

purple; anthers bronze-yellow. *Ovary* ellipsoid, more or less densely bristly; style obsolete or up to 0·25 in. in length; stigma 4–6-lobed, the lobes decurrent. *Capsule* ellipsoid-oblong, more or less densely covered with the persistent hispid bases of bristles, splitting by 4–6 valves.

Geographical Range. Known only in cultivation, a garden hybrid raised originally by deliberate crossing.

The first successful mating of the species which produced this hybrid was accomplished by R. H. Beamish in his garden at Glounthaune, Co. Cork, the resulting plant flowering in 1906 and persisting until the winter of 1914–1915. *M. Beamishii* has since appeared spontaneously in the Royal Botanic Garden, Edinburgh, and has continued to flower there for several years.

In appearance the hybrid closely resembles *M. integrifolia*, but the influence of *M. grandis* has induced the perennial habit and more vigorous growth. The presence of *M. grandis* is further reflected in the purple marking at the base of each petal, though this feature is not constant. Of the hybrids known in the genus between blue-flowered and yellow-flowered species this is the only one which shows any indication of blue in the flower colour. Usually in such a combination the yellow-coloured parent is completely dominant and decides the flower-colour of the hybrid.

20B. ×**MECONOPSIS HYBRIDA**

(*M. grandis* Prain ♂ × *M. simplicifolia* (D. Don) Walp. ♀)

Meconopsis hybrida Puddle ex Gard. Chron., Ser. 3, lxxvii: 406 in obs. (1925).

It is impossible to give a detailed description of this hybrid as it has disappeared from cultivation and no specimens were preserved. From available accounts it appears that *M. hybrida* attained a height of over four feet and had brilliant blue flowers up to six inches in diameter. A proportion of the plants raised were polycarpic, but these gradually died out. The hybrid was raised by F. C. Puddle at Bodnant, Tal-y-Cafn, Wales.

Ser. iii. **PRIMULINAE**

Meconopsis ser. Primulinae Prain in Journ. As. Soc. Bengal lxiv, 2: 319 (1896) emend., quoad sp. 9.

Meconopsis sect. *Primulinae* (Prain) Fedde in Engl., Pflanzenr. iv, 104: 259 (1909) pro parte, quoad sp. 11.

Species 3, distributed from central Nepal to north-western Yunnan (see Fig. 8). Type-species: *Meconopsis primulina* Prain.

In this series the flowers are borne in the axils of the upper stem-leaves or, when the flowers are solitary, the peduncles are leafy, while the tap-root is short and usually napiform.

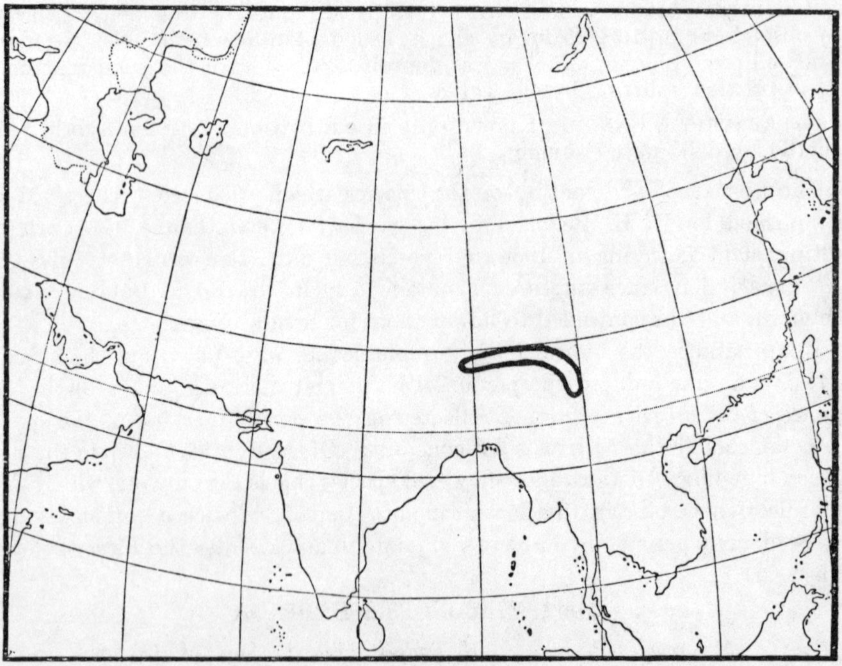

FIG. 8.—MAP SHOWING THE GEOGRAPHICAL RANGE OF THE SERIES *Primulinae*.

21. MECONOPSIS FLORINDAE

MECONOPSIS FLORINDAE Kingdon-Ward in Garden xc: 96 in obs. (Feb. 1926); in Gard. Chron., Ser. 3, lxxix: 307 in obs., fig. 232 dextr. (Apr. 1926); in Ann. of Bot. xl: 537 (July 1926); in Journ. Roy. Hort. Soc. lii: 23, 233 (1927).

DESCRIPTION. *Monocarpic. Tap-root* dauciform, up to 1·5 in. in length. *Stem* weak, usually glabrous but occasionally sparsely hairy, attaining 18 in. in height. *Basal leaves* few and soon withering; lamina more or less oblanceolate (and then entire or sinuate or broadly crenate at the margin) or bipinnatifid or bipinnatisect, gradually tapering at the base into the petiole (petiole attaining 1 in. in length and broadened at the base), subacute to rounded at the apex, up to about 1·5 in. in length and 0·5 in. in breadth, usually glabrous but rarely very sparsely hairy, glaucous on the under surface. *Lower cauline leaves* similar to the basal leaves. *Upper cauline leaves* serrate at the margin, more or less stem-clasping at the base, otherwise similar to the other leaves. *Flowers* numbering 2–6, semipendulous, arising in the axils of the upper cauline leaves (bracteal leaves often displaced so that the flowers appear to be ebracteate); pedicels attaining 6 in. in length (at least in fruiting specimens), slightly expanded and sparingly bristly immediately under the flowers. *Petals* usually 5–7 (rarely 4), ovate or obovate, acute to rounded at the apex, and usually slightly and irregularly denticulate, up to 0·6 in. in length and 0·4 in. in breadth, pale-yellow. *Stamens* numerous; filaments more or less filiform, "colourless"; anthers pale-orange. *Ovary* ovoid to ellipsoid-oblong, glabrous or sparsely bristly; style distinct, attaining almost 0·25 in. in length; stigma subclavate or with the lobes more or less free, yellow. *Capsule* ellipsoid-oblong, glabrous or sparsely bristly, splitting by 3–5 (according to Kingdon-Ward 4–6) valves to about one-third of its length.

Geographical Range. Confined to south-eastern Tibet, at altitudes from 11,000–13,000 ft. Originally described from Tra La, south-eastern Tibet.

This rare species, apparently restricted to a very limited area in south-eastern Tibet and at present known only from a single locality, was discovered by Kingdon-Ward in 1924. *M. Florindae* is closely related to *M. lyrata* and, as in that species, shows very considerable variation in the leaf-shape, even in the limited amount of material available. Kingdon-Ward's species is distinguished by having yellow flowers, more numerous stamens, and shorter and broader capsules. *M. Florindae* is a woodland plant, and although seeds were sent to this country there is no record of the successful flowering of the species.

22. MECONOPSIS LYRATA

Meconopsis lyrata (Cummins and Prain) Fedde [in Engl., Pflanzenr. iv, 104: 246 (1909), *nomen synonymum*] ex Prain in Bull. Misc. Inf. Kew 1915: 142 (1915). Kingdon-Ward in Gard. Chron., Ser. 3, lxxix: 306 (1926); *op. cit.* lxxxii: 506 (1927); in Ann. of Bot. xl: 539 (1926); *op. cit.* xlii: 855 (1928); Pl. Hunt. Edge World: 263 (1930).

Cathcartia lyrata Cummins and Prain ex Prain in Journ. As. Soc. Bengal lxiv, 2: 325 (1896). Prain in Ann. Roy. Bot. Gard. Calcutta ix, 1: 5, tab. 7 (1901); Novic. Ind.: 127 (1905); in Ann. of Bot. xx: 369 (1906). Fedde in Engl., Pflanzenr. iv, 104: 246, fig. 33 E (1909). Farrer, Engl. Rock-Gard. i: 210 (1919). Hand.—Mazz., Symb. Sin. vii: 335 (1931).

Cathcartia polygonoides Prain in Journ. As. Soc. Bengal lxiv, 2: 326 (1896); in Ann. Roy. Bot. Gard. Calcutta ix, 1: 6, tab. 8 (1901); Novic. Ind.: 128 (1905); in Ann. of Bot. xx: 369 (1906). Fedde in Engl., Pflanzenr. iv, 104: 246, fig. 33 L (1909). Farrer, Engl. Rock-Gard. i: 210 ("*polygonoeides*") (1919).

Meconopsis polygonoides (Prain) Prain in Bull. Misc. Inf. Kew 1915: 143 (1915).

Meconopsis compta Prain in Bull. Misc. Inf. Kew 1918: 212 (1918). Kingdon-Ward in Gard. Chron., Ser. 3, lxxix: 306 (1926); in Ann. of Bot. xl: 539 (1926). Forrest in Countr. Life liv: 653 (1923).

Description. *Monocarpic. Tap-root* usually napiform but sometimes narrowly elongated, up to 2·5 in. in length. *Stem* weak, glabrous or sparsely hairy (the hairs weak and more or less crisped), 2–20 in. in height. *Basal leaves* few and soon withering; lamina very various in shape, ovate, oblong-ovate, spathulate or oblanceolate, cordate obtuse or rounded at the base and decurrent into the petiole (petiole linear, attaining 3 in. in length, expanded into a sheathing base), acute to broadly rounded at the apex, entire or variously incised or lobed at the margin, sometimes pinnatifid or pinnatisect, up to 1·5 in. in length and about 0·75 in. in breadth, glabrous or sparsely hairy on both surfaces, usually somewhat glaucous beneath. *Cauline leaves* on the lower part of the stem with long petioles but becoming sessile and more or less stem-clasping on the upper part; lamina ranging from lanceolate elliptic or oblanceolate to ovate or oblong-ovate, up to 2·5 in. in length and about 1 in. in breadth, occasionally entire at the margin but usually more or less deeply lobed, otherwise similar to the basal leaves. *Flowers* 1–5, semipendulous, borne singly in the axils of the upper cauline leaves (rarely on a basal scape which is leafy at least towards the base); pedicels (at least in fruiting specimens) up to 8 in. in length, occasionally only 1 terminal flower produced and the lower flowers replaced by vegetative buds. *Petals* normally 4, but occasionally 5 or 6, ovate to obovate, up to 0·75 in. and almost 0·6 in. in breadth, rounded to acute at the apex and generally minutely notched, pale blue or rarely pink, pale-rose or white. *Stamens* about 12–36; filaments filiform or very narrowly linear, of the same colour as the petals; anthers golden-yellow. *Ovary* oblong or ellipsoid-oblong to narrowly oblong, glabrous; style varying from almost obsolete to 0·25 in. in length; stigma subclavate, green. *Capsule* narrowly oblong or subcylindric, splitting by 3–4 valves for about one-third of its length. *Seeds* falcate-ellipsoid, testa with shallow longitudinally arranged pits, but pitting sometimes obscure and then testa appears to be longitudinally wrinkled.

Geographical Range.—North-western Yunnan to central Nepal, at altitudes from 10,000–16,000 ft. Originally described from Sikkim.

The most striking feature of this species is the wide range of form assumed by the leaves. This is more marked in specimens from the eastern area of its distribution, where the leaf-shape is very diverse, the plants from the western regions being much more stable. The pale-blue colour and size of the flowers are more or less constant throughout.

M. lyrata was originally described under *Cathcartia* and based on several collections from Sikkim, while in the same publication *C. polygonoides* was founded on specimens from the Chumbi district of Tibet. The latter species, but poorly represented in herbaria and then only by the original collections, was stated to differ from *C. lyrata* in having ovate-lanceolate leaves and lanceolate petals which were acute and entire at the apex. A further species, *M. compta*, was described by Prain from material obtained by Forrest at Sarong in south-eastern Tibet. This species was recognised as intermediate between the Sikkim and Chumbi plants, although said to differ from both in having 24 stamens instead of 16. Much more material is now available and shows that the three forms described as species are so closely interrelated that they must be regarded as belonging to one species. The characters of leaf-shape, petal-shape, and number of stamens formerly depended upon for their separation are so unstable that they cannot be used for taxonomic differentiation.

M. lyrata, in some of its forms, closely resembles *M. lancifolia* var. *concinna*, but the latter is distinguished by its larger dark-purple flowers, which are usually borne on simple basal scapes.

Seeds of *M. lyrata* were obtained in Nepal in 1932 and sent to this country, but it is doubtful if the species would ever arouse much interest in horticultural circles because of its weak growth and small flowers. It is a plant of stony alpine meadows and scree slopes.

In several of the westerly representatives of this species the unusual occurrence of bulbils in the axils of the stem leaves may be observed. Such forms are usually more slender plants which probably become prostrate, so that the bulbils are enabled to take root and thus propagate the plant vegetatively. A similar phenomenon is found in *M. chelidonifolia*, but otherwise appears to be absent throughout the *Papaveraceae*.

23. MECONOPSIS PRIMULINA

MECONOPSIS PRIMULINA Prain in Journ. As. Soc. Bengal liv, 2: 319 (1896); in Ann. Roy. Bot. Gard. Calcutta ix, 1: 3, tab. 3 (1901); Novic. Ind.: 121 (1905); in Gard. Chron., Ser. 3, xxxvii: 369 (1905); in Ann. of Bot. xx: 350 (1906); in Bull. Misc. Inf. Kew 1915: 160 (1915); in Countr. Life liv: 111 (1923). Fedde in Engl., Pflanzenr. iv, 104: 260, fig. 35 C (1909). Farrer, Engl. Rock-Gard. i: 477 (sub *M. lancifolia*) (1919). L. H. Bailey, Stand. Cycloped. Hort., New Ed. ii: 2019 (1927). Wehrhahn, Gartenstaud. i: 469 (1930).

DESCRIPTION. *Monocarpic. Tap-root* dauciform, napiform, or narrowly elongated, up to about 3 in. in length and 0·3 in. in thickness. *Basal leaves* apparently soon withering and at time of flowering represented by a dense tuft of persistent membranous leaf bases. *Cauline leaves* all arising towards the base of the stem, the lower ones petiolate, the upper sessile; lamina more or less oblanceolate to elliptic, up to 3 in. in length (including the petiole, which may attain 1·5 in. in length) and 0·5 in. in breadth, glabrous or nearly so to more or less densely bristly on both surfaces. *Flowers* usually 3 (very rarely solitary), borne on axillary pedicels up to 10 in. in length; pedicels glabrous to sparsely covered with deflexed bristles. *Petals* 4–8, variable in shape but usually more or less obovate, up to 1 in. in length and 0·4 in. in breadth, blue. *Stamens* numerous; filaments filiform, of the same colour as the petals; anthers golden-yellow. *Ovary* more or less ellipsoid-oblong, glabrous or very sparsely covered with appressed bristles; style distinct, up to 0·2 in. in length; stigma subclavate, 4-lobed, lobes more or less decurrent. *Capsule* narrowly obovoid to narrowly oblong-ellipsoid, splitting by 4 valves.

GEOGRAPHICAL RANGE. Bhutan and neighbouring regions of Tibet, at altitudes from 13,000–15,000 ft. Originally described from Bhutan and the Chumbi district of Tibet.

This species was described by Prain from specimens gathered by native collectors, and it appears to be a rare plant, since no further record of its occurrence was known until Cooper obtained it in western Bhutan in 1914.

The closest affinity of *M. primulina* is with *M. lyrata*, of which, when more material becomes available for examination, it may prove to be a geographical form. At present it appears to differ from that species in having a dense tuft of persistent leaf bases, in the shape of the leaves, and in having the flowers borne on long, usually almost basal, pedicels.

There is a record* of the successful flowering of *M. primulina* in this country, but investigation has shown that the plant concerned was raised from seed obtained by Kingdon-Ward on the Litang River Divide in south-western Szechuan and was really *M. lancifolia* var. *concinna*.

Ser. iv. DELAVAYANAE

Meconopsis ser. Delavayanae G. Tayl., ser. nov.†

Meconopsis ser. *Primulinae* Prain in Journ. As. Soc. Bengal lxiv, 2: 319 (1896) pro parte, quoad sp. *M. Delavayi*.

Meconopsis sect. *Primulinae* (Prain) Fedde in Engl., Pflanzenr. iv, 104: 259 (1909) pro parte, quoad sp. 12.

Species 1, *Meconopsis Delavayi* (Franch.) Franch. ex Prain, confined to Yunnan (see Fig. 9).

The single species constituting this series was latterly included by Prain in his series *Bellae*, but it merits separate recognition as a series on account of its caespitose habit, due to branching of the rootstock, each branch bearing a single terminal flower.

24. MECONOPSIS DELAVAYI

Meconopsis Delavayi (Franch.) Franch. ex Prain in Journ. As. Soc. Bengal lxiv, 2: 311 in adnot. (1896); Novic. Ind.: 113 in adnot. (1905). Prain in Gard. Chron., Ser. 3, xxxvii: 369 (1905); in Ann. of Bot. xx: 350 (1906); in Bull. Misc. Inf. Kew 1915: 165 (1915). Fedde in Engl., Pflanzenr. iv, 104: 260 (1909). Forrest in Gard. Chron., Ser. 3, l: 51, fig. 24 (1911); in Countr. Life liv: 652, fig., 2 figs. on 653 (1923). Mottet in Rev. Hort. xii: 205 (1912). Gard. Chron., Ser. 3, liii: 357 (1913). Gard. Mag. lvi: 394 (1913). Garden lxxvii: 275, fig. on 274 (1913). Bull. Misc. Inf. Kew 1914, App.: 72 (1914). Journ. Roy. Hort. Soc. xxxix: cxxxii (1914). Farrer, Engl. Rock-Gard. i: 475, tab. 47 sinistr. (1919). Irving in Garden lxxxvii: 170 (1923). Kingdon-Ward, Myst. Riv. Tibet: 48 (1923); in Gard. Chron., Ser. 3, lxxix: 340 (1926); in Ann. of Bot. xl: 540 (1926). L. H. Bailey, Stand. Cycloped. Hort., New Ed. ii: 2018 (1927). Harrow in New Fl. and Silva ii: 152, fig. 55 (1930). Wehrhahn, Gartenstaud. i. 470 (1930). Hand.:—Mazz., Symb. Sin. vii: 336 (1931).

Cathcartia Delavayi Franch. in Bull. Soc. Bot. Fr. xxxiii: 390 (1886); Pl. Delav. i: 42 (1889). Bretschneider, Hist. Europ. Bot. Discov. China ii: 886 (1898).

* Gard. Chron., Ser. 3, lxxv: 322 (1924). Journ. Roy. Hort. Soc. l: li (1925).

† Herbae polycarpicae, radice ramosa ramis gracilibus caespitosis, foliis omnibus basalibus, scapis l-floris radicis ramos terminantibus.

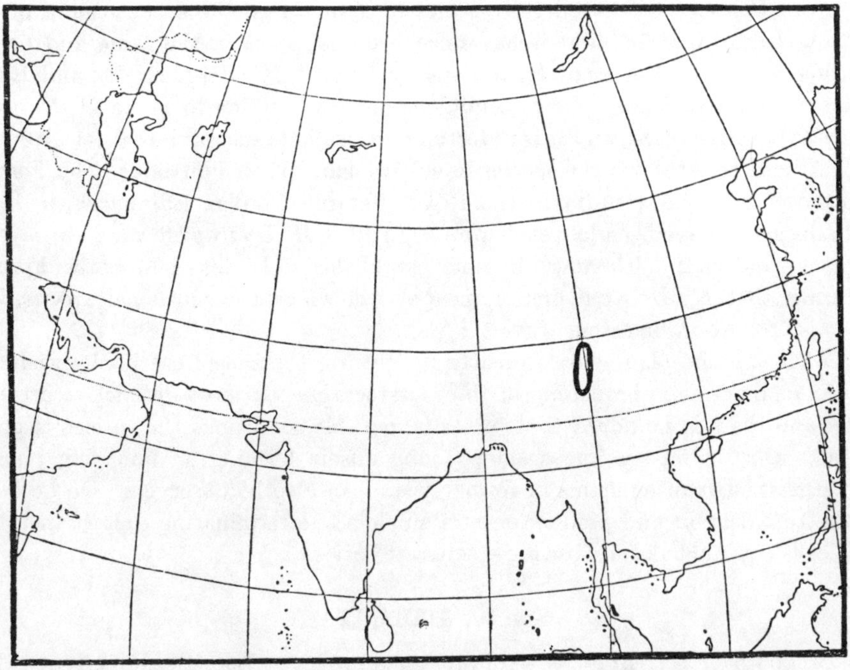

FIG. 9.—MAP SHOWING THE GEOGRAPHICAL RANGE OF THE SERIES *Delavayanae*.

DESCRIPTION. *Polycarpic*. *Tap-root* long and slender, up to 10 in. in length and passing upwards into a short stem which is usually branched and caespitose. *Leaves* all basal and aggregated at the apex of the tufted stems, attaining 6 in. in length (including the petiole) and 1·5 in. in breadth; lamina broadly ovate to narrowly oblanceolate, abruptly decurrent or gradually tapering at the base into a long linear petiole which may attain 5 in. in length, acute to rounded at the apex, entire at the margin, glabrous or very sparsely bristly on both surfaces, glaucous on the under surface. *Flowers* semipendulous, borne singly on slender terminal basal scapes; scapes up to 8 from a single plant, 1·25–11 in. in length (up to 24 in. in fruiting specimens), glabrous to sparsely bristly. *Petals* usually 4 but occasionally 6 or 8, ovate or obovate or suborbicular, acute to rounded at the apex, up to 1·25 in. in length and about 1 in. in breadth, deep-purple, rarely rose-coloured. *Stamens* numerous; filaments filiform, of the same colour as the petals; anthers orange. *Ovary* narrowly oblong-ellipsoid, glabrous; style up to 0·25 in. in length, occasionally almost obsolete; stigma capitate or subclavate. *Capsule* narrowly oblong or subcylindric, attaining 2·5 in. in length and 0·25 in. in breadth, splitting by 3 (occasionally up to 5) valves for a short distance from the apex. *Seeds* falcate-oblong, testa smooth or longitudinally striate. (Plate XVII.)

GEOGRAPHICAL RANGE. Confined to mid- and north-western Yunnan, at altitudes from 10,000–14,000 ft. Originally described from north-western Yunnan.

Père Delavay discovered this species in Yunnan on the eastern flank of the Likiang Range in 1884, and it has since been collected in the same and neighbouring regions on limestone formations by Forrest, Handel-Mazzetti, and Rock. The neat habit and deep-purple pendulous flowers combine to make *M. Delavayi* a most attractive plant, and it is unfortunate that little success has so far attended efforts made to establish the species in cultivation. It was introduced by Forrest and flowered in this country in the Royal Botanic Garden, Edinburgh, in 1913, but appears to have been lost soon after. In 1933 *M. Delavayi* flowered in several gardens, and may ultimately become established. In his field notes Forrest indicates that *M. Delavayi* prefers meadows in which the soil is calcareous, but it is also found on limestone screes.

Although the plant varies greatly in stature, the caespitose habit produced by the characteristic branching of the rootstock gives a most distinctive appearance, and there is no doubt that under favourable conditions the species is polycarpic. Herbarium specimens show young offsets forming on flowering plants, and persistent fruiting stems of former years can also be observed. On account of the tufted habit and production of a single scape terminating each branch the species is regarded as constituting a separate series.

Ser. v. **ACULEATAE**

Meconopsis ser. Aculeatae Prain in Journ. As. Soc. Bengal lxiv, 2: 313 (1896).

Meconopsis ser. *Primulinae* Prain in Journ. As. Soc. Bengal lxiv, 2: 319 (1896) pro parte, quoad spp. *M. Henrici* et *M. lancifolia.*

Meconopsis sect. *Aculeatae* (Prain) Fedde in Engl., Pflanzenr. iv, 104: 255 (1909).

Meconopsis sect. *Primulinae* (Prain) Fedde in Engl., Pflanzenr. iv, 104: 259 (1909) pro parte, quoad spp. 9–10.

Species 13, occurring from western Kansu to north-western Yunnan and northern Upper Burma and westwards along the Himalayas and through southern Tibet to Kashmir and Chitral (see Fig. 10). Type-species: *Meconopsis aculeata* Royle.

This series, the largest and most widespread in the genus, includes several species which are so closely related that their exact delimitation is a matter of great difficulty. All members of the *Aculeatae* are monocarpic with a succulent tap-root and the majority are furnished with stiff bristles or pungent spines. The flowers are borne on simple basal scapes or in bracteate or ebracteate simple inflorescences. Within the series considerable diversity is shown in the shape of the capsule, which varies from subglobose to narrowly subcylindric and then may be up to twelve times as long as broad.

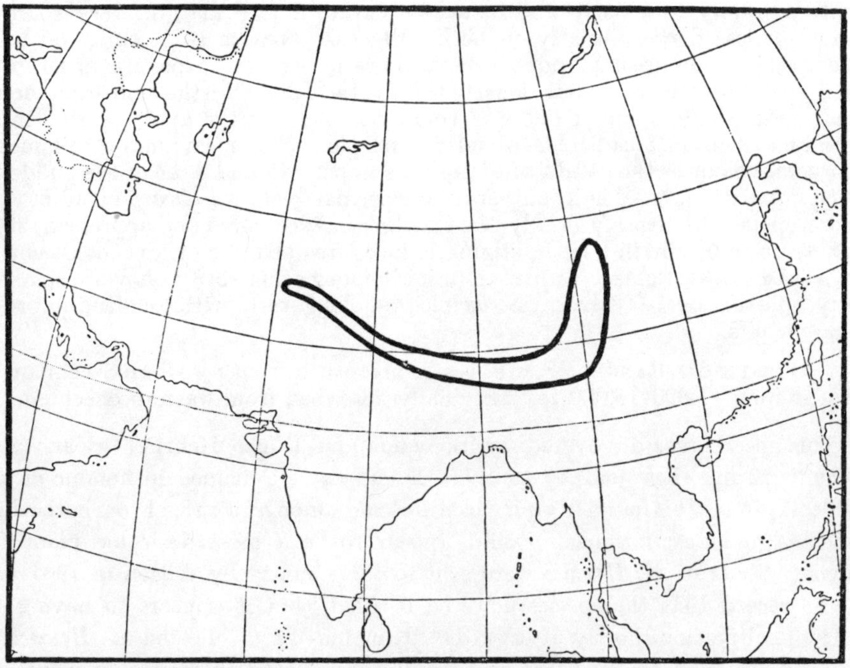

FIG. 10.—MAP SHOWING THE GEOGRAPHICAL RANGE OF THE SERIES *Aculeatae*.

25. MECONOPSIS HENRICI

MECONOPSIS HENRICI Bur. and Franch. in Journ. de Bot. v: 19 (1891); in Bonvalot, Tibet Inconnu: 467 (1892). Prain in Journ. As. Soc. Bengal lxiv, 2: 319 (1896); Novic. Ind.: 121 (1905); in Gard. Chron., Ser. 3, xxxvii: 369 (1905); in Ann. of Bot. xx: 350 (1906); in Bull. Misc. Inf. Kew 1915: 160 (1915); in Countr. Life liv: 110 (1923). Bretschneider, Hist. Eur. Discov. China ii: 913 (1898). E. H. Wilson in Journ. Roy. Hort. Soc. xxix: 660 (1905); West. China i: 138 (1913) Pl. Hunt. ii: 164 (1927). J. H. Veitch, Hort. Veitch.: 423 (1906). Bull. Misc. Inf. Kew 1907, App.: 72 (1907). Fedde in Engl., Pflanzenr. iv, 104: 259 (1909). Farrer, Engl. Rock-Gard. i: 477, tab. 48 sinistr. (1919) sub. *M. lancifolia*. Kingdon-Ward, Rom. Pl. Hunt.: 219 (1924): in Gard. Chron., Ser. 3, lxxix: 340 (1926). Limpr. f. in. Fedde, Repert. Sp. Nov., Beih. xii: 383 (1922). L. H. Bailey, Stand. Cycloped. Hort., New Ed. ii: 2019 (1927). Wehrhahn, Gartenstaud. i: 470 (1930).

DESCRIPTION. *Monocarpic*. *Tap-root* short and stout, napiform or narrowly dauciform, up to 3 in. in length. *Leaves* all basal, up to 6 in. in length (including the petiole, which may attain 2·5 in. in length) and about 0·5 in. in breadth; lamina more or less oblanceolate or oblong-oblanceolate, gradually tapering at the base into a linear petiole, acute or rounded at the apex, entire sinuate or rarely irregularly and distantly serrate at the margin, very sparsely to more or less densely bristly on both surfaces. *Flowers* 1–11, borne on basal scapes (very rarely arising from a central flowering-stem); scapes up to 20 in. in length, sparsely to more or less densely bristly, the rufous bristles spreading or reflexed. *Petals* 5–9, ovate or obovate, round to obtuse at the apex, up to 2 in. in length and 1·5 in. in breadth, deep-violet or purple. *Stamens* numerous; filaments of the same colour as the petals, filiform in the upper half and more or less suddenly dilated into a linear basal half; anthers orange or pale-yellow. *Ovary* ovoid or subglobose, sparsely to densely bristly, the bristles straw-coloured and appressed; style distinct, up to 0·4 in. in length; stigmatic lobes free or more or less coalescent to form a subclavate stigma. *Capsule* ellipsoid-oblong or narrowly obovoid, sparsely bristly, splitting by 4–6 valves. *Seeds* falcate-oblong, testa with longitudinal rows of shallow pits.

Geographical Range. South-western Kansu to south-western Szechuan, at altitudes from 11,000–15,000 ft. Originally described from western Szechuan.

This species was discovered by Bonvalot and Prince Henri d'Orléans near Tatsienlu during their journey through China, and it is named in honour of the latter collector. It is found in alpine pastures and amongst scrub. From herbarium specimens and descriptions it would appear to be a most desirable plant for gardens. Seeds of *M. Henrici* were sent to this country by Wilson in 1904 and it is on record that the species flowered in 1906,* but it appears to have been lost from cultivation shortly afterwards. Kingdon-Ward collected *M. Henrici* in 1921, and although his seed was successfully germinated the resulting plants do not seem to have reached maturity. Recently (1932) Rock has obtained the species in south-western Szechuan, but apparently no seeds were gathered.

In having the staminal filaments dilated in their lower half, *M. Henrici* can be at once distinguished from all other members of the series *Aculeatae*. It seems desirable to regard *M. psilonomma* as belonging to this species and to recognise two varieties within *M. Henrici*.

KEY TO THE VARIETIES

Flowers borne on basal scapes or rarely in an ebracteate inflorescence, numbering up to 11 . . . . var. α. *genuina*.
Flowers solitary . . . . var. β. *psilonomma*.

Var. α. **genuina** G. Tayl., var. nov.†

Meconopsis principis Bulley in Fl. and Sylva iii: 84 (1905).

Meconopsis Wardii Kingdon-Ward in Gard. Chron., Ser. 3, lxxii: 268 (1922), *nomen nudum et provisorium*.

Description. *Flowers* borne on basal scapes (or rarely on ebracteate inflorescence), numbering up to 11.

* Prain in Ann. of Bot. xx: 329 (1906).

† Based on *M. Henrici* Bur. and Franch., *sensu orig.*

Geographical Range. Western Szechuan at altitudes from 12,000–15,000 ft.

Var. β. **psilonomma** (Farrer) G. Tayl., var. nov.

Meconopsis psilonomma Farrer in Gard. Chron., Ser. 3, lvii: 110 in obs. (1915); in Journ. Roy. Hort. Soc. xlii: 84 (1916); Eav. World ii: 167, tab. opp. 168 (1917); Engl. Rock-Gard. ii: 479 (1919); apud Irving in Bull. Alp. Gard. Soc. i: 193 (1932). Prain in Bull. Misc. Inf. Kew 1915: 160 (1915). Rehder and Kobuski in Journ. Arn. Arboret. xiv: 14 (1933).

Description. *Flowers* borne singly on basal scapes.

Geographical Range. Confined to south-western Kansu, at altitudes from 11,000–13,000 ft.

M. psilonomma was described by Farrer from specimens which he had collected in the foothills of the Min S'an Mountains above Ardjeri in 1914 in western Kansu, where it is apparently confined to a limited area. Farrer's original set of specimens was stolen, but those available show such a close resemblance to *M. Henrici* that it is not considered desirable to treat *M. psilonomma* as a separate species. The collector observed that *M. psilonomma* invariably had single basal pedicels, and this character, in conjunction with the geographical segregation of the plant, appears sufficient to sustain varietal rank. It should be noted, however, that in weakly developed plants of *M. Henrici* the flowers may be solitary but this is a very rare occurrence. Seed of this variety was collected by Farrer's Chinese servants, but it was subsequently reported that it had "failed miserably in cultivation."

26. MECONOPSIS FORRESTII

Meconopsis Forrestii Prain in Bull. Misc. Inf. Kew 1907: 316 (1907); *op. cit.* 1915: 157 (1915); in Hook. Ic. Pl. xxxi: tab. 3034 (1915). Forrest in Gard. Chron., Ser. 3, l: 51 (1911); in Countr. Life liv: 615 (1923). Farrer, Engl. Rock-Gard. ii: 478 (1919). L. H. Bailey, Stand. Cycloped. Hort., New Ed. ii: 2019 (1927). Hand.—Mazz., Symb. Sin. vii: 336 (1931).

Description. *Monocarpic. Tap-root* dauciform, up to 4 in. in length and about 0·5 in. in thickness at the top. *Leaves* usually all basal; lamina oblanceolate or elliptic-oblong to almost linear, up to 8 in. in length (including the petiole, which may attain 1·5 in. in length) and 0·8 in. in breadth, gradually tapering at the base into the petiole, which is somewhat membranous and sheathing at the base, rounded to subacute at the apex, entire or slightly sinuate at the margin, sparsely covered on both surfaces with golden-brown bristles. *Flowering-stem* rigidly erect, sometimes very stout at the base and tapering towards the apex, more or less densely covered with stiff spreading or slightly deflexed golden-brown bristles, from 5 in. to 24 in. in height. *Flowers* 3–7, without subtending bracts; pedicels pendant or deflexed at first but spreading at the time of flowering, rarely exceeding 1 in. in length but becoming rigidly erect in fruit and lengthening up to 3 in. *Petals* 4 (rarely 5), ovate or obovate, up to 1 in. in length and 1 in. in breadth, pale-blue or pale-purplish-blue. *Stamens* numerous; filaments filiform, purplish; anthers orange or orange-yellow. *Ovary* narrowly ellipsoid-oblong, glabrous or sparsely bristly; style very short or obsolete; stigma 3–4-lobed. *Capsule* rigidly erect, narrowly subcylindric, glabrous or sparsely bristly, up to 2·5 in. in length, splitting by 2–4 valves for about a third of its length. *Seeds* more or less falcate-ellipsoid, testa obscurely pitted. (Plate XVIII.)

GEOGRAPHICAL RANGE. South-western Szechuan and north-western Yunnan, at altitudes from 10,000–14,500 ft. Originally described from north-western Yunnan.

It is unfortunate that this species, which commemorates one who has contributed so much to our knowledge of the genus, is not in cultivation. Seeds were obtained by Forrest in 1914, and although they were successfully germinated the plants failed to reach maturity. That *M. Forrestii* would be a desirable plant in cultivation is obvious from examination of the field specimens.

The species occurs only in a limited area, and was discovered by Forrest in 1906 on the eastern flank of the Likiang Range in sheltered positions on rich meadow land. It has subsequently been collected in neighbouring localities by the original collector and also by Schneider, Handel-Mazzetti, and Rock.

The long narrow fruiting capsules, which are borne stiffly erect, and the almost constant presence of four petals, form the most distinctive features of this species.

27. MECONOPSIS IMPEDITA

MECONOPSIS IMPEDITA Prain in Bull. Misc. Inf. Kew 1915: 162 (1915). Farrer, Engl. Rock-Gard. ii: 478 (1919). Forrest in Countr. Life liv: 653 (1923). Kingdon-Ward in Gard. Chron., Ser. 3, lxxix: 340 (1926); *op. cit.* xciii: 242 (1933); in Ann. of Bot. xlii: 855 (1928); Pl. Hunt. Edge World: 301 (1930). Harley in Journ. Roy. Hort. Soc. liii: 226 (1928). Hand.-Mazz., Symb. Sin. vii: 336 (1931).

Meconopsis impedita var. *Morsheadii* Prain in Bull. Misc. Inf. Kew 1915: 163 (1915). Kingdon-Ward in Gard. Chron., Ser. 3, lxxvii: 394 (1925); *op. cit.* lxxix: 340 (1926); *op. cit.* lxxxii: 506 (1927); in Garden xc: 115 (1926); in Ann. of Bot. xl: 536 (1926); *op. cit.* xlii: 859 (1928).

Meconopsis Morsheadii (Prain) [Farrer, Engl. Rock-Gard. ii: 478 in obs., 479 (1919), *nomen synonymum*] Kingdon-Ward in Ann. of Bot. xlii: 859 in obs. (1928); Pl. Hunt. Edge World: 301 (1930).

Meconopsis impedita var. *rubra* Kingdon-Ward in Gard. Chron., Ser. 3, lxxxii: 151 in obs. (1927).

Meconopsis rubra Kingdon-Ward in Gard. Chron., Ser. 3, lxxxii: 506 in obs. (1927); *op. cit.* xciii: 242 (1933); in Ann. of Bot. xlii: 857 (1928); Pl. Hunt. Edge World: 107 (1930).

DESCRIPTION. *Monocarpic. Tap-root* elongated and tapering, up to 12 in. in length and 0·5 in. in thickness. *Stem* short and stout, usually covered at the base with remnants of persistent leaf-bases. *Leaves* all basal, attaining 7 in. in length (including the petiole, which is long and linear) and 1 in. in breadth, sparsely to more or less densely prickly; lamina elliptic or more or less oblanceolate to linear or spathulate, entire sinuate or irregularly or pinnately more or less deeply lobed at the margin (lobes rounded to acute at the apex), glaucous on the under surface. *Flowers* pendulous, up to 21 on a single plant, produced singly on slender basal scapes up to 12 in. in length (lengthening up to 18 in. in fruit) and usually more or less densely covered with weak spreading prickles. *Petals* 4–10, but rarely less than 6, usually obovate or suborbicular, up to 1·25 in. in length and 0·7 in. in breadth, reddish-purple or dark-violet to almost black. *Stamens* numerous; filaments filiform, of the same shade or darker than the petals; anthers cream, orange, golden, or yellow. *Ovary* ellipsoid, ellipsoid-oblong, or narrowly obovoid, sparsely to densely prickly (very rarely glabrous), prickles at first appressed but ultimately spreading; style distinct and usually slender, up to 0·4 in. in length; stigma capitate, cream-coloured or green. *Capsule* narrowly obovoid to narrowly oblong-ellipsoid, up to 1·5 in. in length and 0·4 in. in breadth, usually more or less densely covered with spreading prickles, splitting most commonly by 3–4 (rarely by 5) valves for a short distance from the apex. *Seeds* falcate-ellipsoid, testa striate or obscurely longitudinally pitted. (Plate XIX.)

Geographical Range. North-western Yunnan, northern Upper Burma, and south-eastern Tibet, at altitudes from 10,000–15,000 ft. Originally described from north-western Yunnan.

M. impedita was described by Prain in 1915 from specimens collected by Monbeig, Forrest, Maire, and Kingdon-Ward in north-western Yunnan. In its natural state it occurs on screes, grassy slopes, moist alpine meadows, and in crevices on grassy ledges of granitic cliffs. The species has been in cultivation in this country but has never become thoroughly established. At present, however, attempts are being made to reintroduce it from seeds collected by Rock in 1932.

Around *M. impedita* are aggregated a group of extremely critical species whose separation from it and from each other is a matter of great difficulty. *M. pseudo-venusta* appears to be the most closely related, and in several respects it is intermediate between *M. impedita* and *M. venusta*, but it is distinguished from the former by having usually glabrous leaves, more rigid pedicels, and occasional agglutination of the scapes. The affinity of *M. impedita* with *M. venusta* is also very close, but the more deeply divided leaves, which are usually glabrous, and the 4-petalled flowers serve to distinguish the latter species. In the forms of *M. lancifolia* which have the flowers borne on basal scapes there is a close approach to *M. impedita*, but in mature specimens the scapes are rarely so numerous and the plants never so robust or so pubescent as in typical *M. impedita*. *M. horridula*, when found at higher altitudes, commonly produces basal scapes only and then presents a close resemblance to *M. impedita*. The latter species, however, is never so pungently prickly and further differs in the shape of the capsules and the number of their valves.

28. MECONOPSIS VENUSTA

Meconopsis venusta Prain in Bull. Misc. Inf. Kew 1915: 164 (1915) emend.: in Hook. Ic. Pl. xxxi: tab. 3036 (1915) pro parte. Farrer, Engl. Rock-Gard. ii: 480 (1919). Forrest in Countr. Life liv: 653 (1923). Kingdon-Ward in Gard. Chron., Ser. 3, lxxix: 340 (1926). Hand.-Mazz., Symb. Sin. vii: 336 (1931).

Meconopsis leonticifolia Hand.-Mazz. in Anz. Akad. Wiss. Wien. Math-Naturv. Kl. lvii: 340 (1926).

Description. *Monocarpic or polycarpic. Tap-root* stout, fusiform or gradually tapering, up to 9 in. in length and 0·75 in. in breadth. *Stem* stout and thick, up to 4 in. in length and 0·5 in. in thickness, covered (more obviously towards the apex) with remnants of persistent leaf-bases. *Leaves* all basal, up to 4·5 in. in length (including the petiole) and about 1 in. in breadth; lamina pinnatifid or pinnatisect (the lobes most commonly rounded at the apex), rarely spathulate or elliptic and then entire at the margin, glabrous on both surfaces or very rarely with a few spines on the under surface, usually conspicuously glaucous on the under surface. *Flowers* up to 15 produced on one plant, borne singly on basal pedicels; pedicels 2·5–7 in. in length, but elongating to 12 in. in fruit, glabrous or rarely very sparsely spiny. *Petals* 4, obovate to suborbicular, rounded to subacute at the apex, up to 1·6 in. in length and 1·1 in. in breadth, pale blue, deep purplish-wine or pale-lilac. *Stamens* numerous; filaments filiform, of the same colour as the petals; anthers orange-yellow. *Ovary* narrowly ellipsoid or ellipsoid-oblong, sparsely to more or less densely covered with usually spreading spines; style distinct, up to 0·25 in. in length; stigma capitate or subclavate or with the 3–4 lobes free. *Capsule* narrowly oblong or subcylindric, sparsely to more or less densely covered with spreading spines (spines ultimately deciduous), up to 3·75 in. in length and 0·25 in. in breadth, splitting by 3–4 (very rarely 2) valves to about a third of its length. *Seeds* narrowly oblong or ellipsoid-oblong, testa with fine longitudinal wrinkles. (Plate XX.)

Geographical Range. Confined to north-western Yunnan, at altitudes from 12,000–14,000 ft. Originally described from the Chung-hsien Plateau and mountains north-east of the Yangtze bend, north-western Yunnan.

This distinctive species was discovered by Forrest in 1913 on the mountains north-east of the Yang-tse bend, and although he subsequently collected fruiting material there appears to be no record of the successful cultivation of the plant in this country. That it is most desirable for introduction is obvious from herbarium specimens. The relatively large flowers are freely produced from an attractive rosette of deeply lobed glaucous leaves. To judge from the leaf-remnants present along the stem, the species appears either to be perennial or to require some years to come to maturity. The former alternative is probable, as in one of Forrest's specimens the stem is branched, and while one branch bears the fruits of the previous year the other branches are producing flowers of the current year.

M. venusta is very restricted in its distribution. It is found on stony alpine pastures in limestone country in north-western Yunnan, and appears to have been collected only by Forrest and Handel-Mazzetti.

In no specimen has more than four petals been observed and this character, together with the glaucous long-petiolate leaves and stout tap-root, forms the most characteristic feature of the species. The affinity of *M. venusta* is with *M. impedita*, from which it differs in having usually glabrous and very glaucous leaves, stouter pedicels, narrower and longer capsules and constantly four petals.

29. MECONOPSIS PSEUDOVENUSTA

MECONOPSIS PSEUDOVENUSTA G. Tayl., sp. nov.*

Meconopsis venusta Prain in Bull. Misc. Inf. Kew 1915: 164 (1915) pro parte.

DESCRIPTION. *Monocarpic. Tap-root* stout and elongated, rarely branched, up to at least 4 in. in length and 1 in. in thickness. *Rootstock* stout, up to 5·5 in. in length and 0·5 in. in thickness, covered with fibrous remains of persistent leaf-bases. *Leaves* all basal or carried up the flowering-stem for a short distance; lamina ovate or elliptic or more or less lanceolate to narrowly oblanceolate, cuneate at the base, acute to rounded at the apex, usually more or less deeply pinnatifid or bipinnatifid (lobes acute to rounded at the apex) rarely entire or sinuate at the margin, glabrous or very rarely with a few bristles on the upper surface or on the midrib on the lower surface; petiole linear, up to 4·5 in. in length. *Flowers* borne on basal pedicels, which are occasionally agglutinated at the base, or on ebracteate flowering-stems accompanied by basal pedicels; pedicels up to 8 in. in length (attaining 14 in. in fruiting specimens), glabrous to more or less densely covered with spreading bristles. *Petals* 4–10, elliptic to obovate or suborbicular, cuneate at the base, rounded to acute at the apex, purple. *Stamens* numerous; filaments filiform, of the same colour as the petals; anthers orange-yellow to dark-brown according to age. *Ovary* ellipsoid or ellipsoid-oblong, sparsely to more or less densely covered with appressed or spreading prickles, very rarely glabrous; style distinct, up to 0·25 in. in length; stigma capitate or subclavate. *Capsule* narrowly obovoid to narrowly ellipsoid, up to 1·2 in. in length and 0·3 in. in breadth, more or less densely covered with spreading prickles, splitting by 3–4 valves for a short distance from the apex. *Seeds* somewhat falcate-ellipsoid, testa obscurely longitudinally pitted. (Plate XXI.)

GEOGRAPHICAL RANGE. South-eastern Tibet to north-western Yunnan and south-western Szechuan, at altitudes from 12,000–14,000 ft. Described from the mountains north-east of Chung-hsien, north-western Yunnan.

The collections now referred to *M. pseudovenusta* were previously included in *M. venusta*, from which they differ most markedly in the character of the fruit, and as their removal from that species leaves it a remarkably homogeneous unit,

* *M. venustae* Prain proxima, sed ab ea discrepat petalis plerumque pluribus (usque ad 10), capsula anguste obovoidea ellipsoideave usque ad 3 cm. longa et c. 1 cm. diametro, floribus interdum caule florigero ebracteato suffultis. Typus in Herb. Hort. Bot. Reg. Edin., a G. Forrest (n. 16658) jn Yunnan boreali-occidentale anno 1918 lectus.

the course adopted appears to be desirable. While in *M. venusta* the petals are constantly four and the flowers are borne on basal scapes, in the new species the petals vary in number from four to ten and frequently the scapes are agglutinated or the flowers are borne in ebracteate inflorescences. The salient feature, however, which separates the two species is in the fruit, which is narrowly oblong or subcylindric and from four to five times as long as broad in *M. venusta*, whereas in *M. pseudovenusta* the length of the capsule never reaches four times the breadth and it is narrowly obovoid to narrowly ellipsoid. The species agree in having a well-developed rootstock covered with persistent fibrous leaf-bases, and it appears that some years elapse before flowers are produced.

M. pseudovenusta is also very closely related to *M. impedita*, from which it differs principally in having usually glabrous and more deeply lobed leaves.

M. pseudovenusta is found in open stony pastures, and has the appearance of a desirable garden plant.

30. MECONOPSIS GEORGEI

Meconopsis Georgei G. Tayl., sp. nov.*

Description. *Monocarpic. Tap-root* narrowly elongated, up to about 3 in. in length and 0·5 in. in thickness. *Leaves* aggregated near the base of the flowering-stem, a few carried up the stem for a short distance and subtending the lower flowers; lamina more or less oblanceolate, gradually tapering at the base into the linear petiole, acute to rounded at the apex, entire or slightly sinuate at the margin, up to 6 in. in length (including the petiole, which may attain 2 in. in length) and 0·75 in. in breadth, glabrous to sparsely covered on both surfaces with more or less pungent prickles, glaucous on under surface. *Flowering-stem* attaining 13 in. in height, almost glabrous to more or less densely prickly, the prickles spreading. *Flowers* up to 10, borne on long usually prickly pedicels which attain 8 in. in length, upper flowers ebracteate, lower flowers borne in the axils of the upper stem-leaves. *Petals* 5–8, obovate, obtuse to acute and usually minutely denticulate at the apex, up to 1·5 in. in length and 1·0 in. in breadth, yellow. *Stamens* numerous; filaments filiform; anthers orange-yellow to more or less black according to age. *Ovary* ellipsoid to ellipsoid-oblong, usually densely covered with straw-coloured ultimately spreading prickles; style distinct, up to 0·25 in. in length; stigma capitate or subclavate. *Capsule* ellipsoid-oblong, covered with spreading prickles, splitting by 3–5 valves for a short distance from the apex. *Seeds* more or less falcate-ellipsoid testa, irregularly wrinkled and obscurely pitted. (Plate XXII.)

Geographical Range. Confined to north-western Yunnan, at altitudes from 12,000–14,500 ft. Described from the Fu-chuan Shan, Mekong-Yantze divide, north-western Yunnan.

* Inter species ser. *Aculeatarum* petalis sulphureis valde distincta. *Herba* biennis altitudinis usque ad 32·5 cm. attingens. *Foliorum* lamina plus minusve oblanceolata, glabra vel sparse spinosa. *Petala* 5–8, sulphurea. *Capsula* ellipsoideo-oblonga, spinis patentibus munita, 3–5 valvis dehiscens. *Testa* rugosa vel obscure foveolata. Typus in Herb. Hort. Bot. Reg. Edin., a G. Forrest (n. 30100) in Yunnan boreali-occidentale anno 1931 lectus.

The specific epithet commemorates George Forrest, who discovered the species in the Fu-chuan mountains in 1931 during his last expedition. It was collected the following year by Rock in the same mountains, and specimens have also been sent to this country by Forrest's native collectors. As seed accompanied these collections it may be hoped that the species, which in nature grows on screes, will become established in gardens. It is quite unlike the other yellow-flowered members of the genus in having harsh prickles, while the flowers are borne on comparatively long pedicels arising near the base of the stem.

M. Georgei is closely related to *M. lancifolia* and *M. horridula*, but is at once distinguished from these species, and from the other members of the series *Aculeatae*, by having yellow flowers.

31. MECONOPSIS LANCIFOLIA

Meconopsis lancifolia (Franch.) Franch. ex Prain in Journ. As. Soc. Benga lxiv, 2: 311 in adnot (1896); Novic. Ind.: 113 in adnot (1905). Prain in Ann. of Bot. xx: 349 (1906); in Bull. Misc. Inf. Kew 1915: 157 (1915). Fedde in Engl., Pflanzenr. iv, 104: 259, fig. 35 P (1909). Farrer, Engl. Rock-Gard. i: 477 (1919). Forrest in Countr. Life liv: 652 (1923). Kingdon-Ward in Gard. Chron., Ser. 3, lxxiii: 107 (1923); *op. cit.* lxxix: 340 (1926). L. H. Bailey, Stand. Cycloped. Hort., New Ed. ii: 2019 (1927). Wehrhahn, Gartenstaud. i: 470 (1930).

Cathcartia lancifolia Franch. in Bull. Soc. Bot. Fr. xxxiii: 391 (1886); Pl. Delav. i: 43 (1889). Bretschneider, Hist. Eur. Bot. Discov. China ii: 886 (1898).

Description. *Monocarpic. Tap-root* short and stout to fusiform or narrowly elongated, up to 10 in. in length and 0·5 in. in thickness. *Leaves* most commonly all basal but occasionally a few are carried up the flowering-stem for a short distance, up to 9 in. in length (including the petiole, which may attain 3 in. in length) and 1 in. in breadth; lamina oblanceolate or narrowly oblanceolate to elliptic-lanceolate or narrowly linear, occasionally spathulate or obovate, tapering at the base into the petiole, which is often broad and linear, acute to rounded at the apex, entire or sinuate at the margin or pinnately or bipinnately lobed (lobes rounded to acute at the apex), glabrous to densely bristly or subspiny on both surfaces, glaucous on the lower surface. *Flowering-stem* (when present) up to 20 in. in height, often much swollen towards the base, glabrous to densely bristly or spiny (bristles or spines spreading or slightly reflexed). *Flowers* borne singly on basal scapes or arising on an ebracteate flowering-stem (often accompanied by basal pedicels) or the lower flowers borne in the axils of leafy bracts; pedicels up to 8 in. in length, glabrous to densely spiny. *Petals* 4–8 (up to 11, according to Farrer), obovate or suborbicular to ovate, rounded to acute and often minutely denticulate at the apex, up to 1·5 in. in length and 1·2 in. in breadth, deep-purple, or violet, or very rarely light-blue. *Stamens* numerous; filaments filiform, of the same colour as the petals; anthers orange or pale-yellow to grey or black according to their age. *Ovary* oblong or ellipsoid-oblong to ovoid or obovoid, glabrous to densely bristly or spiny; style distinct, up to 0·6 in. in length (at least in fruiting specimens); stigma capitate or subclavate. *Capsule* narrowly obovoid or oblong-ellipsoid to narrowly oblong or subcylindric, glabrous to densely bristly or spiny, splitting by 3–5 (rarely 2–6) valves for about a third of its length. *Seeds* more or less reniform or falcate-ellipsoid, testa longitudinally wrinkled or obscurely pitted. (Plate XXIII.)

GEOGRAPHICAL RANGE. South-western Kansu to south-eastern Tibet, northern Upper Burma and north-western Yunnan, at altitudes from 11,000–16,000 ft. Originally described from north-western Yunnan.

Considerable difficulty has been experienced in deciding the limits of this extremely polymorphic species, and as accepted here it embraces a wide range of forms. I have tried in vain to find satisfactory characters with which to separate these, but rather than recognise several critical and unsatisfactory subordinate units, a course which sometimes would entail splitting single collections, I have confined further segregation to the recognition of two varieties. At first sight several forms seemed to be separable on morphological as well as geographical grounds, but after critical study of the whole range of material it has been impossible to accord these any taxonomic status. It seems that continued interbreeding may have contributed to the existence of this plexus and obscured any obvious characters which might have been used for diagnostic purposes. A knowledge of the genetical constitution of the several forms would undoubtedly be of great service in their elucidation, but as yet, unfortunately, none is found in cultivation.

M. lancifolia shows an obvious affinity with *M. horridula*, but whereas in the latter species the leaves are carried up the flowering-stem and show a transition to scaly bracteate leaves on the upper part of the stem, in *M. lancifolia* the leaves are generally all basal and the flowers either entirely ebracteate or subtended on the lower part of the stem only in the axils of conspicuously leafy bracts. A further difference is to be found in the shape of the capsules which are generally broadest above the middle in *M. lancifolia* and always at least twice as long as broad.

In Yunnan there is a distinct tendency for the species to have lobed or divided leaves and flowers with four petals borne on basal scapes, and plants which show this combination of characters have been recognised as *M. concinna*. There are so many transitional specimens, however, in which the leaves are entire and in which the flowers are borne on ebracteate flowering-stems that the plants generally referred to *M. concinna* are scarcely worthy of separate specific rank, though the character of basal scapes with the tendency to produce lobed leaves appears sufficient to merit varietal status.

In one of the extreme forms, of which most of the specimens from Upper Burma are representative, there is a strong development of spreading spines on the leaves, stem, pedicels, and fruits, but this spiny character is so intimately intergraded through all degrees of spinosity that it is quite unreliable as a basis for any subdivision of the species. These spiny specimens also show a tendency to develop lobed leaves, but, again, all intermediate states are found and not necessarily with spines, so that no taxonomic significance can be attached to the character.

It was suggested by Prain in 1906 that it might prove advisable to merge *M. Henrici* with *M. lancifolia*, but, although they are certainly closely related, the expanded filaments characteristic of the former species are sufficient for it to merit separate recognition.

I have thought it desirable to reduce *M. eximia*. The plants referred to this species, on account of their more robust habit, larger flowers with six to eight petals, and densely hairy ovary, appeared to be distinct, but while these characters in association give a distinctive facies to the specimens, the whole series now available demonstrates a complete transition to typical *M. lancifolia*. The character of anther-colour has been used to separate them, but this varies so much with age that it is quite unsatisfactory for diagnostic purposes.

Examination of the type-collection of *M. lepida* and comparison with the range of forms found in *M. lancifolia* has shown that the two cannot be regarded as specifically distinct. Farrer's specimens from the mountain of Lei-Go-S'an (Thundercrown) in south-western Kansu, on which Prain based his original description of *M. lepida*, although they show constancy in having entire leaves and flowers with seven to eight petals borne on a definite inflorescence, are identical with several of the more southerly representatives, and indeed are very similar to Delavay's original plants of *M. lancifolia*.

So far as I am aware there is no authentic record of this species in cultivation, as the plant figured in 1923* as *M. lancifolia* does not appear to be accurately identified, and probably represents *M. Delavayi*. There is no doubt that the form which has been described as *M. eximia*, with large deep purple flowers, would be a very desirable addition to gardens, but no success attended Forrest's efforts to introduce it. In several gardens plants have been grown under the name *M. eximia*, but all that I have had the opportunity of examining proved to be forms of *M. horridula*. Field notes indicate that *M. lancifolia* prefers stony alpine meadows and screes on limestone formations on " the less sunny exposures." Herbarium specimens suggest that it is often a weakly plant, and the common presence of a bulbous root indicates difficulty in its cultivation.

KEY TO THE VARIETIES

Lamina undivided or very rarely lobed at the margin; flowers borne on an ebracteate flowering-stem . . . . var. α. *solitariiflora*.

Lamina deeply lobed but occasionally entire at the margin; flowers borne on basal scapes . . . . var. β. *concinna*.

* Garden lxxxvii: 293, fig. (1923).

Var. α. **solitariiflora** Fedde, Repert. Sp. Nov. xvii: 197 (1921).

[*Meconopsis Wardii* Kingdon-Ward, Land Blue Poppy: 138 in obs. (1913), *nomen nudum.*]

Meconopsis lepida Prain in Bull. Misc. Inf. Kew 1915: 158 (1915); in Countr. Life liv: 111 (1923). Farrer in Journ. Roy. Hort. Soc. xlii: 83 (1916); *tom. cit.*: 339 (1917); Eav. World ii: 16, tab. opp. 16 (1917); Engl. Rock-Gard. ii: 478, 506 (1919); apud Irving in Bull. Alp. Gard. Soc. i: 192, tab. 93 (1932).

Meconopsis eximia Prain in Bull. Misc. Inf. Kew 1915: 159 (1915); in Countr. Life liv: 111 (1923). Farrer, Engl. Rock-Gard. ii: 478 (1919). Forrest in Countr. Life liv: 653 (1923).

[*Meconopsis lancifolia* var. *Limprichtii* Fedde ex Limpr. f. in Fedde, Repert. Sp. Nov., Beih. xii: 383 (1922), *laps pro* var. *solitariiflora.*]

[*Meconopsis eucharis* Farrer ex Irving in Bull. Alp. Gard. Soc. i: 192 in obs. (1932), *nomen synonymum.*]

Description. *Tap-root* fusiform and elongated, up to 10 in. in length. *Leaves* all basal or carried up the flowering-stem for a short distance; lamina narrowly oblanceolate, elliptic-lanceolate or more or less obovate, entire sinuate or very rarely lobed at the margin. *Flowering-stem* up to 17 in. in height, commonly swollen towards the base, glabrous to densely bristly or spiny. *Flowers* up to 12, borne on an ebracteate flowering-stem (or the lower flowers occasionally borne in the axils of leafy bracts), often accompanied by basal pedicels. *Petals* 4–8.

Geographical Range. South-western Kansu to south-eastern Tibet, northern Upper Burma and north-western Yunnan, at altitudes from 11,000–16,000 ft.

Fedde based his description of *M. lancifolia* var. *solitariiflora* on specimens collected by Limpricht in eastern Tibet in 1914. Under the variety are included the forms which have hitherto been referred to typical *M. lancifolia*, together with the plants formerly regarded as *M. lepida* and *M. eximia*.

Seeds of this variety have recently been received from Rock, and attempts are at present being made to establish the plant in cultivation.

Var. β. **concinna** (Prain) G. Tayl., var. nov.

Meconopsis concinna Prain in Bull. Misc. Inf. Kew 1915: 163 (1915); in Hook. Ic. Pl.: tab. 3035 (1915); in Countr. Life liv: 111 (1913). Farrer, Engl. Rock-Gard. ii: 477 (1919). Forrest in Countr. Life liv: 653 (1923). Irving in Gard. Chron., Ser. 3, lxxviii: 425, fig. 174 (1925). Kingdon-Ward. in Gard. Chron., Ser. 3, lxxix: 340 (1926). Hand.-Mazz., Symb. Sin. vii: 336 (1931).

Description. *Tap-root* short, napiform or fusiform, about 1 in. in length, rarely elongated and then never exceeding 4 in. in length. *Leaves* all basal; lamina very variable in shape, oblanceolate, oblong-oblanceolate, elliptic-oblanceolate, spathulate or narrowly linear, entire or sinuate at the margin but (usually some at least) pinnately or bipinnately lobed. *Flowers* borne singly on basal scapes. *Petals* usually 4.

GEOGRAPHICAL RANGE. South-western Szechuan to north-western Yunnan, at altitudes from 11,000–15,000 ft.

Unfortunately this charming little plant, seldom above 6 in. in height and with relatively large flowers, is not at present in cultivation, but seeds have recently been received in this country from Rock. It is probable that the plant which received the Award of Merit of the Royal Horticultural Society in 1924 under the name *M. primulina** was really *M. lancifolia* var. *concinna*, as the herbarium specimens corresponding to Kingdon-Ward's seed number belong to this variety.

In its leaf-shape *M. lancifolia* var. *concinna* is one of the most variable members of the genus, and on one plant the leaves may range from entire at the margin to bipinnately lobed. The variety cannot be regarded as absolutely defined from *M. lancifolia* var. *solitariiflora*, and the two more or less merge, particularly through the forms described as *M. lepida*.

32. MECONOPSIS HORRIDULA

MECONOPSIS HORRIDULA Hook. f. and Thoms., Fl. Ind. i: 252 (1855); in Hook. f., Fl. Brit. Ind. i: 118 (1872). Walp., Ann. Bot. Syst. iv: 171 (1857). Prain in Journ. As. Soc. Bengal lxiv, 2: 313 (1896); Novic. Ind.: 115 (1905); in Ann. of Bot. xx: 348 (1906); in Bull. Misc. Inf. Kew 1915: 152 (1915); in Countr. Life liv: 110 (1923). Bulley in Fl. and Sylva iii: 83 (1905). Fedde in Engl., Pflanzenr. iv, 104: 257, fig. 35 K (1909). Farrer in Gard. Chron., Ser. 3, lix: 86 (1916); Engl. Rock-Gard. i: 476 (1919); *op. cit.* ii: 479 (1919); Rainbow Br.: 168, 232 (1921). Kingdon-Ward in Gard. Chron., Ser. 3, lxxix: 308 (1926); in Ann. of Bot. xl: 538 (1926). Wehrhahn, Gartenstaud. i: 469 (1930).

Meconopsis racemosa Maxim. in Bull. Acad. Imp. Sc. St.-Pétersb. xxiii: 310 (1877); Fl. Tangut. i: 36, tab. 9 figs 1–6, tab. 23 fig. 26 (1889). Franch. in Bull. Soc. Bot. Fr. xxxiii: 390 (1886). Bretschneider, Hist. Eur. Bot. Discov. China ii: 971 (1898). Besant in Garden lxviii: 384, fig. (1905). Bulley in Fl. and Sylva iii: 84 (1905). Prain in Gard. Chron., Ser. 3, xxxvii: 369 (1905); in Ann. of Bot. xx: 332 (1906); in Countr. Life liv: 111 (1923). Bull. Misc. Inf. Kew 1905, App: 82 (1905). Mottet in Rev. Hort. v: 205 (1905); *op. cit.* xii: 205 (1912); in Jardin xx: 101 (1906); Gard. Chron., Ser. 3, xlii: 30, fig. 12 (1907). Journ. Roy. Hort. Soc. xxxiii: lviii (1908). Fedde in Engl., Pflanzenr. iv, 104: 258, fig. 35 M (1909). T. Smith in Gard. Chron., Ser. 3, xlvi: 91, fig. 40 (1909). Irving in Garden lxxv: 510, fig. (1911); *op. cit.* lxxxvii: 170 (1923). Darlington in Journ. Roy. Hort. Soc. xxxvii: 635 (1912). E. H. Wilson, West. China i: 138 (1913); *op. cit.* ii: 9 (1913). Jenkins in Garden lxxviii: 240 (1914). Farrer in Gard. Chron., Ser. 3, lix: 86, fig. 33 (1916); Engl. Rock-Gard. i: 480 (1919); *op. cit.* ii: 479 (1919); Rainbow Br.: 168, 232 (1921); apud Irving in Bull. Alp. Gard. Soc. i: 195, tab. 95 (1932). Limpr. f. in Fedde, Repert. Sp. Nov., Beih. xii: 383 (1922).

* Gard. Chron., Ser. 3, lxxv: 322 (1924). Journ. Roy. Hort. Soc. l: li (1925).

Kingdon-Ward in Gard. Chron., Ser. 3, lxxix: 308 (1926). L. H. Bailey, Stand. Cycloped. Hort., New Ed. ii: 2018 (1927). Silva Tarouca and Schneider, Freiland-Staud.: 249 (1927). Harley in Journ. Roy. Hort. Soc. liii: 225 (1928). Wehrhahn, Gartenstaud. i: 469 (1930). Rehder and Kobuski in Journ. Arn. Arboret. xiv: 15 (1933).

Meconopsis horridula var. *typica* Prain in Journ. As. Soc. Bengal lxiv, 2: 313 (1896); Novic. Ind.: 115 (1905); in Bull. Misc. Inf. Kew 1915: 152 (1915). Kingdon-Ward in Gard. Chron., Ser. 3, lxxviii: 191 (1925).

Meconopsis horridula var. *racemosa* (Maxim.) Prain in Journ. As. Soc. Bengal lxiv, 2: 313 (1896); Novic. Ind.: 115 (1905); in Ann. of Bot. xx: 348 (1906); in Bull. Misc. Inf. Kew 1915: 152 (1915). Irving in Garden lxxv: 510, fig. (1911). Kingdon-Ward in Gard. Chron., Ser. 3, lxxviii: 191 (1925); in Ann. of Bot. xl: 538 (1926). Hand.-Mazz., Symb. Sin. vii: 336 (1931).

Meconopsis horridula var. *rudis* Prain in Journ. As. Soc. Bengal lxiv, 2: 314 (1896); Novic. Ind.: 116 (1905).

Meconopsis sinuata var. *Prattii* Prain in Journ. As. Soc. Bengal lxiv, 2: 314 (1896); Novic. Ind.: 116 (1905).

[*Meconopsis racemosa* var. *sinuata* E. H. Wilson in Journ. Roy. Hort. Soc. xxix: 660 in obs. (1905), *nomen nudum.*]

Meconopsis rudis (Prain) Prain in Ann. of Bot. xx: 347 (1906); in Curt. Bot. Mag. cxl: tab. 8568 (1914); in Bull. Misc. Inf. Kew 1915: 150 (1915); in Countr. Life liv: 111 (1923). Fedde in Engl., Pflanzenr. iv, 104: 256 (1909). Bull. Misc. Inf. Kew 1915, App.: 71 (1915). Forrest in Journ. Roy. Hort. Soc. xlii: 43, fig. 14 (1916); in Countr. Life liv: 614, fig. 3 (1923). Farrer, Engl. Rock-Gard. ii: 480 tab. 50 dextr. (1919); Rainbow Br.: 232 (1921). Harley in Garden lxxxix: 70, fig. (1925); in Journ. Roy. Hort. Soc. liii: 225 (1928). Kingdon-Ward in Gard. Chron., Ser. 3, lxxix: 308 (1926). L. H. Bailey, Stand. Cycloped. Hort., New Ed. ii: 2018 (1927). L. H. and E. Z. Bailey, Hortus: 390 (1930). Wehrhahn, Gartenstaud. i: 469 (1930). Hand.-Mazz., Symb. Sin. vii: 336 (1930).

Meconopsis horridula var. *abnormis* Fedde in Engl., Pflanzenr. iv, 104: 258 (1909).

Meconopsis Prattii (Prain) Prain in Curt. Bot. Mag. cxl: sub tab. 8568 in obs. (1914); *op. cit.* cxli: tab. 8619 (1915); in Bull. Misc. Inf. Kew 1915: 149 (1915); in Countr. Life liv: 111 (1923). Gard. Chron., Ser. 3, lviii: 329 (1915). Farrer in Gard. Chron., Ser. 3, lix: 86, fig. 34 (1916); in Journ. Roy. Hort. Soc. xlii: 85 (1916); *tom. cit.*: 338 (1917); Eav. World i: 301, tab. opp. 302 (1917); *op. cit.* ii: 185 (1917); Engl. Rock-Gard. i: 480, tab. 49 sinistr. (1919); *op. cit.* ii: 479, 507 (1919); Rainbow Br.: 168, 232 (1921). Bull. Misc. Inf. Kew 1916, App.: 63 (1916). E. T. Ellis in Journ. Roy. Hort. Soc. xliii: 563 (1919). Irving in Garden lxxxvii: 170 (1923). Forrest in Countr. Life liv: 653 (1923). Kingdon-Ward, Rom. Pl. Hunt.: 160 (1924); in Garden xci: 340, fig. (1927); in Gard. Chron., Ser. 3, lxxix: 308 (1928). Harley in Garden lxxxix: 72, fig. on 70 (1925); in Journ. Roy. Hort. Soc. liii: 225 (1928). Silva

Tarouca and Schneider, Freiland-Staud. 1927: 249 (1927); *op. cit.* 1933: 243, fig. 246 (1933). L. H. and E. Z. Bailey, Hortus: 390 (1930). Cox, Pl. Introd. Farrer: 41 (1930). Bull. Alp. Gard. Soc. i: 193 (1932).

Meconopsis rudis var. *intermedia* Prain in Bull. Misc. Inf. Kew 1915: 151 (1915). Farrer, Engl. Rock-Gard. ii: 480 (1919).

Meconopsis racemosa forma *horridula* Farrer, Engl. Rock-Gard. i: 480 in obs., tab. 50 sinistr. (1919).

[*Meconopsis duriuscula* Prain in Countr. Life liv: 111 in obs. (1923), *nomen nudum.*]

[*Meconopsis rigidus* Harley in Garden lxxxix: 70, fig. med. (1925), *nomen nudum.*]

Meconopsis Prattii alba Harley in Garden lxxxix: 70, fig. on 71 (1925).

[*Meconopsis rigidiuscula* Kingdon-Ward in Gard. Chron., Ser. 3, lxxix: 308 in obs. (1926), *nomen synonymum.*]

Meconopsis Prainiana Kingdon-Ward in Garden xc: 115, fig. (Feb. 1926); in Gard. Chron., Ser. 3, lxxix: 308, fig. 232 med. (Apr. 1926); in Ann. of Bot. xl: 540, tab. 16 fig. 1 (1926); in Journ. Roy. Hort. Soc. lii: 24 (1927).

Meconopsis calciphila Kingdon-Ward in Gard. Chron., Ser. 3, lxxxii: 506 in obs. (1927); in Ann. of Bot. xlii: 862 (1928); Pl. Hunt. Edge World: 302 (1930).

DESCRIPTION. *Monocarpic. Tap-root* dauciform, fusiform or narrowly elongated, up to 11 in. in length and 1 in. in thickness. *Base of stem* covered with persistent leaf-bases usually interspersed with prickles. *Basal and lower cauline leaves* up to 10 in. in length (including the petiole, which may attain about 5 in. in length) and 1·5 in. in breadth; lamina elliptic to oblanceolate or linear-oblong, rarely ovate or lanceolate, acute to rounded at the apex, gradually (or rarely abruptly) decurrent at the base into the broad linear petiole, entire sinuate or irregularly lobed at the margin, more or less densely covered on both surfaces with pungent spines which vary in colour from yellow to purple and commonly arise from a purple base, prickles more or less uniform or interspersed with smaller ones. *Upper cauline leaves* or bracts sessile, the uppermost becoming reduced to scales. *Flowers* numerous, borne singly in the axils of the leaves, which towards the apex of the stem are much reduced and the uppermost flowers are ebracteate, flowering stem attaining 3·5 ft. in height, usually accompanied by scapes arising from the axils of the basal leaves; occasionally central flowering-stem absent and flowers borne on basal scapes only; pedicels up to 9 in. in length, but usually when borne on a central stem never exceeding about 4 in., covered with spreading spines. *Petals* 4–8, obovate to suborbicular, usually at least minutely denticulate at the apex, up to 1·8 in. in length and 1·4 in. in breadth, light-blue to claret or rarely white. *Stamens* numerous; filaments filiform, of a somewhat darker colour than the petals; anthers buff to grey-black according to age. *Ovary* ellipsoid-oblong or narrowly ellipsoid-oblong to subglobose, densely covered with appressed or obliquely spreading spines, spines usually straw-coloured but commonly darker and purple at the base; style distinct, up to 0·5 in. in length, swollen towards the base, commonly longitudinally ridged; stigma capitate or subclavate, lobes more or less decurrent. *Capsule* ellipsoid or ellipsoid-oblong to subglobose, more or less densely covered with appressed, spreading or reflexed spines, splitting by 4–9 (though most commonly by 5–6) valves for a short distance from the apex. *Seeds* reniform, testa with longitudinal rows of shallow pits. (Plate XXIV.)

Geographical Range. From western Kansu to north-western Yunnan, through Upper Burma, south-eastern Tibet, Bhutan and Sikkim to central Nepal at altitudes from 10,000–19,000 ft. Originally described from Sikkim.

The polymorphic character of this species is reflected in the somewhat extensive synonymy, several of the forms having been given specific or varietal rank. It is in the disposition of the flowers that the most evident variation is displayed. These may be borne on simple basal scapes or on a central flowering axis which is bracteate towards the base and ebracteate towards the apex, but all transitions are found between these extremes. The western representatives are usually smaller in stature and show a higher proportion of forms in which only basal scapes are produced, but these also occur in the extreme north-eastern limit of the species (in Kansu), and, it may be observed, all forms may be found growing in association in the field. Marked variation is also shown in the number and colour of the petals, in the texture of the leaves and colour of their spines, and also in the shape, pubescence, and dehiscence of the capsule.

The species was described in 1855 from specimens collected in Sikkim, in which the flowers are borne on basal scapes or on scapes more or less agglutinated to form a central flowering stem, forms which do not represent the most familiar state of the plant. In the original diagnosis the authors stated that the petals were normally four, but were occasionally multiplied. In 1877 Maximowicz published a brief description of a new species, *M. racemosa*, based on specimens collected by Przewalski in Kansu, which he separated from *M. horridula*, as it had five to eight petals and the flowers arranged on a central flowering-stem. The extensive series of specimens now available shows that neither of these characters is sufficient to warrant specific separation, and indeed comparison of Przewalski's type-collection with the original specimens of *M. horridula* shows that the two are specifically indistinguishable. Unfortunately the name *M. racemosa* has been in common use among horticulturists, as it was based by Maximowicz on the form which happens to be most commonly cultivated, but the older name, *M. horridula*, must take precedence.

Prain in 1896 included *M. racemosa* under *M. horridula*, but recognised it as a variety on account of the presence of a central flowering-stem, although he expressly stated that a complete transition could be traced to the typical condition with basal scapes only. It is, however, impossible to regard Maximowicz's species even as a variety of *M. horridula*, as the forms are so intimately intergraded.

Two further species must be added to the synonymy. These are *M. rudis* and *M. Prattii*, whose separation from each other and from the form known as

M. racemosa has presented difficulties to horticulturists. The former was originally described by Prain as a variety (*rudis*) of *M. horridula* based on a plant collected by Delavay in the Likiang district of Yunnan. It was said to be characterised by having a tall thick stem, leaves very thick and subentire at the margins, and with small capsules arising on a much-expanded torus. Later, when further material became available, it was accorded specific rank (*M. rudis*). While it must be admitted that field specimens from the Likiang Range, the type-locality of *M. rudis*, have a distinctive facies due to the association of several characters, I have been unable to segregate the plant as a definable taxonomic unit. In these Likiang plants the leaves are usually conspicuously spotted with purple or bear purple spines, are often lobed at the margin and in addition have a glaucous appearance. It appears that they must be regarded as belonging to a localised strain whose separate recognition as a taxonomic entity is undesirable. They occur along with forms which grade completely into typical *M. horridula*, and it may be observed that the presence of purple spots at the base of the spines is not confined to these Likiang forms, as they are also to be found on specimens from central Nepal.

M. Prattii was originally described by Prain as a variety (*Prattii*) of *M. sinuata*, and was based on specimens collected by Pratt near Tatsienlu, Szechuan. In 1906 the same author placed *M. sinuata* var. *Prattii* under *M. rudis* in consequence of the receipt of fruiting material. Later, however, in deference to the opinion of Wilson, who had studied the species in the field, Prain again separated the plant, but as a species (*M. Prattii*), and published an amplified description. The leaf-texture, degree of pungency of the spines, colour of the anthers and stigma, were regarded as diagnostic characters sufficient to separate *M. Prattii* from its nearest relatives, but when these are tested by herbarium and cultivated specimens they are found to break down, so that the putative species can be considered only as a form of *M. horridula*.

A particularly robust form collected by Kingdon-Ward in 1924 at Temo La was described by him as *M. Prainiana*, but I have been unable to find any structural character of this plant to merit for it even varietal rank, and I believe that it is merely a luxuriant state of *M. horridula*. The same author has described one of his collections from Upper Burma as *M. calciphila*, but here again I have been unable to observe any satisfactory character sufficient to sustain separate taxonomic identity for this plant.

Although several previous attempts had been made to introduce *M. horridula* to cultivation, it appears that its definite establishment in this country dates from about 1904, and although it has been grown under different names the correct epithet has never been applied to it. The species, under cultivation, is subject to very considerable variation, particularly in the colour and disposition of the flowers. Indeed, even if seed is carefully saved from good forms, it is rarely possible to raise a uniform batch of plants, and for this reason *M. horridula* is apt to prove a disappointment. Occasionally most attractive plants are produced when the central flowering-stem is damaged, as this appears to stimulate the growth of the lower and basal pedicels, which lengthen and produce flowers more or less at the same level, thus avoiding the rather unattractive fruiting-stem of the more normal plant. This suggests that *M. horridula* might be a better garden plant if induced to assume this form by pinching out the central flowering-stem as it is about to elongate.

The species, in addition to being the most widely distributed member of the genus, occurs throughout the greatest altitudinal range and indeed reaches the upper limit of flowering-plant vegetation. It was collected by the Mount Everest Expedition in 1921 at an elevation of 19,000 feet, and under the severe conditions prevailing at that height is much reduced in stature, consisting of a small basal rosette and several basal scapes hardly an inch in height. When it is considered that, under favourable conditions, *M. horridula* may attain three and a half feet in height, its extreme variability is again exemplified.

33. MECONOPSIS LATIFOLIA

Meconopsis latifolia (Prain) Prain in Bull. Misc. Inf. Kew 1915: 146 (1915); in Countr. Life liv: 111, fig. (1923). E. A. Bowles in Garden lxxx: 332, fig. on 333 (1916). Bull. Misc. Inf. Kew 1916, App.: 63 (1916). Farrer, Engl. Rock-Gard. i: 482, tab. 46 infr. (1919); *op. cit.* ii: 478 (1919). Irving in Garden lxxxvii: 171, fig. (1923). Maxwell, Flowers: 186 (1923). Harley in Garden lxxxix: 72 (1925): in Journ. Roy. Hort. Soc. liii: 225 (1928). Kingdon-Ward in Gard. Chron., Ser. 3, lxxix: 308 (1926); in Garden xci: 340 (1927). Harrow in Garden lxxxviii: 360, fig. (1924); in New Fl. and Silva ii: 148 (1930).

Meconopsis sinuata var. *latifolia* Prain in Curt. Bot. Mag. cxxxiv: tab. 8223 (1908). Bull. Misc. Inf. Kew 1909, App.: 95 (1909). Irving in Garden lxxvi: 316, fig. (1912). Jenkins in Garden lxxviii: 240 (1914). L. H. Bailey, Stand. Cycloped. Hort., New Ed. ii: 2018 (1927). Wehrhahn, Gartenstaud. i: 469, fig. (1930).

[*Meconopsis sinuata* (non Prain) Irving in Gard. Chron., Ser. 3, xliv: 202, fig. 88 (1908).]

[*Meconopsis aculeata* (non Royle) T. Smith in Gard. Chron., Ser. 3, xlvi: 91, figs. 38–39 (1909): in Garden lxxv: 226, fig. (1911).]

Meconopsis psilonomma (non Farrer) Wehrhahn, Gartenstaud. i: 468, fig. (1930).]

Description. *Monocarpic. Tap-root* stout and elongated, more or less fusiform, attaining about 4 in. in length. *Basal and lower cauline leaves* up to 8 in. in length (including the petiole, which may attain 4 in. in length and is widened at the base) and about 2·5 in. in breadth: lamina more or less oblong to ovate or broadly lanceolate, usually cuneate but occasionally obtuse or rounded at the base, acute or obtuse at the apex, with broad, rounded, obtuse or subacute crenations at the margin or pinnately and coarsely serrate, sparsely covered on both surfaces with straw-coloured spines. *Upper cauline leaves* sessile, otherwise similar to the lower leaves. *Flowering-stem* attaining about 3·5 ft. in height, more or less densely covered with spreading spines. *Flowers* numerous, borne singly in the axils of the upper cauline leaves but sometimes throughout the length of the stem, bracteal leaves reduced towards the apex and several of the uppermost flowers ebracteate; pedicels slender, usually about 1 in. in length, densely covered with spreading spines. *Petals* 4, obovate or suborbicular, rounded and entire at the apex, up to 1·25 in. in length and 1 in. in breadth, pale-blue or rarely white. *Stamens* numerous; filaments filiform, deep-blue; anthers orange-yellow. *Ovary* ovoid, densely spiny, the spines straw-coloured and more or less appressed; style distinct, up to 0·25 in. in length; stigma oblong to globose. *Capsule* ellipsoid-oblong, more or less densely covered with spreading spines, splitting by 4–7 valves for a short distance from the apex. *Seeds* more or less reniform, testa with longitudinal rows of pits. (Plate XXV.)

Geographical Range. Confined to northern Kashmir, at altitudes from 10,000–13,000 ft. Originally described from a cultivated plant raised from seeds sent from northern Kashmir.

This very beautiful species flowered for the first time in this country in 1908, and its introduction was due to Appleton, who sent seeds to Kew in 1906. At first it was considered to be a variety of *M. sinuata* and was described and figured as such in "Curtis's Botanical Magazine." When ripe capsules of the plant were obtained, however, it became obvious that it differed from *M. sinuata* in having relatively short ellipsoid capsules and in the leaf shape. *M. latifolia* is also a much more floriferous species, for in *M. sinuata* not more than seven flowers are normally produced. The closest affinity of *M. latifolia* is with *M. aculeata*, from which it differs in having shorter pedicels and much less cut leaves.

Appleton observed that *M. latifolia* "is always found growing in the crevices of rocks or among loose piles of stone débris on stone slides and below cliffs. It likes the full sun, and springs to full growth after the snow melts off, while the ground is still damp." The plant is stated to attain a height of four feet under natural conditions.

By many horticulturists this is regarded as the finest species in cultivation, and it is certainly a plant of high merit which has not become as common in gardens as one would have expected.

M. LATIFOLIA × M. GRANDIS. See under *M. grandis* (p. 70).

33a. ×MECONOPSIS DECORA

(*M. latifolia* Prain ♀ × *M. napaulensis* DC. ♂).

Meconopsis decora Prain in Bull. Misc. Inf. Kew 1915: 143 (1915); in Countr. Life liv: 112 (1923). Gard. Chron., Ser. 3, lviii: 329 (1915). Bull. Misc. Inf. Kew 1916, App.: 62 (1916). Journ. Roy. Hort. Soc. xlii: xlv (1916); *tom. cit.*:

cxxviii (1916). Garden lxxx: 377 (1916). Hay in Garden lxxxii: 313 (1918). Farrer. Engl. Rock-Gard. ii: 477 (1919). Kingdon-Ward in Gard. Chron., Ser. 3, lxxix: 307 (1926).

DESCRIPTION. *Basal leaves* persisting in a dense basal rosette during the winter, up to 6·5 in. in length (including the petiole, which attains about 2 in. in length) and 1·5 in. in breadth; lamina oblong or elliptic-oblong, cuneate at the base, obtuse at the apex, irregularly serrate at the margin (the serrations acute to rounded at the apex), densely bristly on both surfaces. *Cauline leaves* sessile, auriculate and stem-clasping at the base, subacute to rounded at the apex, broadly and obtusely serrate at the margin, otherwise similar to the basal leaves. *Flowering-stem* up to 2 ft. in height, sparingly bristly. *Flowers* borne singly in the axils of the uppermost leaves and in 2–3-flowered cymes in the axils of the lower leaves; pedicels slender, up to 3·75 in. in length, bristly. *Petals* 4–6, obovate, about 1 in. in length and 0·7 in. in breadth, white or blue. *Stamens* numerous; filaments filiform, white; anthers golden-yellow. *Ovary* obovoid or ellipsoid, densely covered with whitish bristles; style distinct and slender, up to 0·2 in. in length; stigma capitate or subclavate, purplish.

GEOGRAPHICAL RANGE. Not known to occur under natural conditions.

*M. decora** was described from a cultivated specimen raised at Greenwich Park from seed said to have been collected by Bailey in the mountains between the Dibang and Dihang rivers, south-eastern Tibet. It was subsequently stated, however, that the precise source of the seed was unknown. Several plants were raised and flowered for a number of years, but never set seed; some had blue flowers, others white.

Shortly after the species was described, the opinion was expressed that the plant was a hybrid, and with this view Prain† concurred, the parents suggested being *M. latifolia* and *M. Wallichii.* These species are widely separated taxonomically, and until positive results are obtained by crossing them the exact identity of the hybrid must remain doubtful. It is a strange coincidence that the plant should arise independently in several gardens, but its whole history suggests hybridity.

34. MECONOPSIS SPECIOSA

MECONOPSIS SPECIOSA Prain in Trans. and Proc. Bot. Soc. Edin. xxiii: 257, tab. 2 (1907); in Bull. Misc. Inf. Kew 1915: 148 (1915); in Countr. Life liv: 111 (1923). Kingdon-Ward, Land Blue Poppy: 109 (1913); in Gard. Chron., Ser. 3, lxix: 79, fig. 35 (1921); *op. cit.* lxxix: 308 (1926); Myst. Riv. Tibet: 91, tab. opp. 88 (1923). Farrer, Engl. Rock-Gard. ii: 480 (1919). Forrest in Countr. Life liv: 652 (1923). Hand.-Mazz., Symb. Sin. vii: 335 (1931).

* I am indebted to Mr. T. Hay, who raised the type-plant, for several descriptive particulars which cannot be observed in the dried specimens.

† Prain in Countr. Life liv: 112 (1923).

Meconopsis Ouvrardiana Hand.-Mazz. in Anz. Akad. Wiss. Wien, Math.-naturv. Kl. lix: 247 (1922).

Meconopsis Cawdoriana Kingdon-Ward in Gard. Chron., Ser. 3, lxxix: 308, fig. 232 sinistr. (1926); in Ann. of Bot. xl: 536 (1926); in Journ. Roy. Hort. Soc. lii: 24 (1927).

Description. *Monocarpic. Tap-root* stout and elongated, more or less fusiform, attaining 1 ft. in length and about 1 in. in thickness. *Leaf-lamina* pinnatifid, usually with rounded sinuses between the lobes (lobes more or less oblong and usually rounded or occasionally subacute at the apex), reddish-brown spines scattered on both surfaces, glaucous on the under surface; lamina of the basal and lower cauline leaves tapering at the base into a broad petiole; lamina of the upper cauline leaves sessile. *Flowers* numerous, strongly fragrant, borne singly in the axils of the lower leaves, bracts towards the apex of the stem greatly reduced and several of the uppermost flowers are ebracteate; pedicels occasionally almost basal and agglutinated into a short stem, stout and covered with spreading reddish-brown spines, expanded under the flowers, in fruit prominently decurrent down the stem. *Petals* 4–8, obovate to suborbicular, rounded and entire at the apex, up to 1·7 in. in length and 1·5 in. in breadth, azure-blue to ruddy-purple. *Stamens* numerous: filaments filiform, of a darker shade of blue than the petals; anthers orange-yellow to yellowish-grey according to age. *Ovary* globose to ellipsoid, densely covered with dark reddish-brown spines; style distinct, stout, up to 0·4 in. in length, occasionally spiny towards the base; stigma capitate or subclavate, stigmatic lobes free or coalescing to form an oblong stigma. *Capsule* ellipsoid, covered with persistent often purple spines, splitting by 4–8 valves for a short distance from the apex. *Seeds* more or less reniform, testa with longitudinal rows of shallow pits. (Plate XXVI.)

Geographical Range. South-eastern Tibet and north-western Yunnan, at altitudes from 12,000–17,000 ft. Originally described from north-western Yunnan.

Unfortunately this very handsome species has failed to respond to cultural methods in this country adequately enough to show its real merit. *M. speciosa* was discovered by Forrest in north-western Yunnan in 1905 and it was raised from seed sent home by him, but I have been unable to ascertain whether the resulting plants were ever brought to maturity. All plants which I have seen growing under the name *M. speciosa* have been either *M. aculeata* or *M. latifolia*. Kingdon-Ward, Handel-Mazzetti, and Rock have subsequently collected the species, and their specimens confirm the favourable accounts given of the plant. Rock obtained seeds in 1932 and at present attempts are being made to reintroduce the species. The potentialities of *M. speciosa* can be judged from Kingdon-Ward's description of a field specimen; it " was 20 inches in height, crowned with twenty-nine flowers and fourteen ripening capsules, with five buds visible below—forty-eight flowers in all." Then, " each flower is between 3 and 4 inches in diameter, coloured brilliant azure blue, with the texture of Japanese silk, massed with old gold in the centre." Finally it should be observed that the flowers are fragrant, according to Forrest with a scent resembling that of hyacinths. The accompanying plate is of an average field specimen and gives an idea of the habit of the species.

M. speciosa has a limited geographical range and inhabits rocky alpine meadows and granitic and limestone screes. In certain localities it reaches the altitudinal limit of flowering plants and often shows the condition commonly associated with *M. horridula,* in which the pedicels are almost basal and agglutinated into a short stem.

The plant described as *M. Cawdoriana* differs in no respects from typical *M. speciosa.*

35. MECONOPSIS ACULEATA

MECONOPSIS ACULEATA Royle, Illustr. Bot. Himal.: 67, tab. 15 (Mar. 1834). Rennie, Mag. Bot. and Gard. ii: 64, tab. 28 n. 7 (May 1834). Walp., Repert. Bot. Syst. i: 110 (1842): Ann. Bot. Syst. iv: 171 (1857). Hook. f. and Thoms., Fl. Ind. i: 253 (1855); in Hook. f., Fl. Brit. Ind. i: 118 (1872). Hook. in Curt. Bot. Mag. xc: tab. 5456 (1864). Stewart, Punjab Pl.: 9 (1869). W. in Garden xiv: 280 (1878). Robinson, Engl. Fl. Gard.: 183 (1883), Nicholson, Illustr. Dict. Gard. ii: 341 (1886). D. in Garden xliii: 81 (1893). Bois, Dist. Hort. ii: 821 (1893–99). Prain in Journ. As. Soc. Bengal lxiv, 2: 314 (1896); Novic. Ind.: 116 (1905); in Ann. of Bot. xx: 347 (1906); in Bull. Misc. Inf. Kew 1915: 144 (1915); in Countr. Life liv: 111 (1923). Collett, Fl. Simla: 23 (1902). Bulley in Fl. and Sylva iii: 82 (1905). Mottet in Jardin xx: 100 (1906); in Rev. Hort. xii: 203 (1912). Strachey, Cat. Pl. Kumaon: 8 (1906). Fedde in Engl., Pflanzenr. iv, 104: 255, fig. 35 N (1909). Jenkins in Garden lxxviii: 240 (1914). Kirtikar and Basu, Ind. Med. Pl. i: 83, tab. 55 (1918). Farrer, Engl. Rock-Gard. i: 474 (1919). Canning-Wright in Garden lxxxvi: 177, fig. (1922). Irving in Garden lxxxvii: 170 (1923). Coventry, Wild Fl. Kashmir i: 25, tab. 13 (1923). Kingdon-Ward in Gard. Chron., Ser. 3, lxxix: 308 (1926). Harley in Garden xc: 250, fig. (1926); in Journ. Roy. Hort. Soc. liii: 226 (1928). L. H. Bailey, Stand. Cycloped. Hort., New Ed. ii: 2018 (1927). Wehrhahn, Gartenstaud. i: 469 (1930).

[*Meconopsis napaulensis* (non DC.) Honigberg., Thirty-five Years East ii: tab. 15 ("*Nepalensis*") (1852).]

Meconopsis Gulielmi-Waldemarii Klotzsch and Garcke, Bot. Ergebn. Reise. Prinz Waldem.: 129, tab. 36 (1862).

[*Meconopsis racemosa* (non Maxim.) Silva Tarouca, Freiland-Staud.: 150, fig. 201 (1910).]

Meconopsis aculeata var. *typica* Prain in Bull. Misc. Inf. Kew 1915: 144 (1915).

Meconopsis aculeata var. *nana* Prain *loc. cit.* (1915). Bull. Misc. Inf. Kew 1916, App.: 63 (1916). Farrer, Engl. Rock-Gard. ii: 477 (1919).

Meconopsis aculeata forma *normalis* Prain *tom. cit.*: 145 (1915). Farrer, *loc. cit.* (1919).

Meconopsis aculeata forma *acutiloba* Prain *loc. cit.* (1915). Farrer, *loc. cit.* (1919).

[*Meconopsis latifolia* (non Prain) Silva Tarouca and Schneider, Freiland-Staud. 1927: 249, fig. 272 (1927); *op. cit.* 1933: 243, fig. 248 (1933).]

Description. *Monocarpic*. *Tap-root* narrowly elongated or fusiform, up to about 5 in. in length. *Basal and lower cauline leaves* up to 11 in. in length (including the petiole, which may attain 6 in. in length and is expanded at the base) and about 2 in. in breadth; lamina irregularly pinnatifid (occasionally bipinnatifid) or pinnatisect, often with broad sinuses particularly between the lower lobes, sparsely covered on both surfaces with straw-coloured spines, lobes very variable in shape (more or less oblong and then obtuse or rounded at the apex to triangular and then acute at the apex). *Upper cauline leaves* sessile. *Flowering-stem* up to 2 ft. in height, more or less densely covered with spreading spines. *Flowers* borne singly on long, slender, spiny axillary pedicels (from 1–9 in. in length), bracteal leaves reduced towards the apex of the stem and several of the uppermost flowers ebracteate. *Petals* usually 4 (rarely up to 6), obovate or suborbicular, up to 1·5 in. in length and 1·5 in. in breadth, sky-blue or rarely varying to purplish-blue or red. *Stamens* numerous; filaments filiform, of a darker shade than the petals; anthers golden-yellow. *Ovary* subglobose or ellipsoid, more or less densely spiny, the spines straw-coloured and at first appressed but ultimately spreading; style distinct, up to 0·5 in. in length, in fruit swollen at the base; stigmatic lobes free or coalescent to form an oblong or globose stigma. *Capsule* subglobose to ellipsoid-oblong, more or less densely spiny, splitting usually by 4–6 (rarely 3–8) valves for a short distance from the apex. *Seeds* more or less reniform, testa with longitudinal rows of pits.

Geographical Range. From Hazara District, North-West Frontier Province, to Kumaun, at altitudes from 8,000–14,000 ft. Originally described from the western Himalayas from Kashmir to Garhwal.

This species has been in cultivation since 1864 when it flowered at Kew. The seed from which the original plants were raised was sent by Cleghorn from north-western India. According to the field notes available *M. aculeata* grows amongst damp rocks and screes and along stream sides. The plant is not often seen in gardens, and indeed its cultivation has not been attended with much success. Usually it is very variable and frequently quite unattractive.

Two varieties, one with two forms, have been recognised, but they are subject to so much intergrading that it is advisable to reduce them. The variety *nana* was described from cultivated specimens in which the usual tap-root was replaced by a fibrous root-system. It is not unusual, however, for species which normally have a tap-root to produce a fibrous root-system in cultivation. The two forms of the variety *typica* recognised by Prain were based on the shape of the leaf-segments and relative lengths of the pedicels, but these characters cannot be used satisfactorily for taxonomic differentiation.

36. MECONOPSIS NEGLECTA

Meconopsis neglecta G. Tayl., sp. nov.*

Description. *Monocarpic. Tap-root* dauciform, up to 5·5 in. in length and 0·5 in. in thickness at the top, passing upwards into a short stem which is invested below with persistent leaf-bases. *Leaves* all basal, up to about 4 in. in length (including the petiole, which may attain 2 in. in length) and 0·6 in. in breadth; lamina deeply pinnatifid (lobes oblong, rounded at the apex), sparsely covered on both surfaces and on the margin with more or less pungent spines. *Flowers* up to 12, borne on slender basal scapes; scapes up to 6 in. in length, sparsely spiny. *Petals* 4, broadly obovate or suborbicular, up to 0·8 in. in length and about 0·8 in. in breadth. *Stamens* numerous; filaments filiform; anthers yellow. *Ovary* ellipsoid, more or less densely covered with pungent spines; style distinct but very short, up to 0·05 in. in length; stigma capitate.

Geographical Range. Known only from Chitral State. Described from the Kafiristan border in the State of Chitral.

With the discovery of this species in Chitral the geographical limit of the genus is extended westwards, and it is probable that, as a result of future botanical exploration in this area, the western boundary of *Meconopsis* in Asia will be carried beyond India. Previous to this record of *M. neglecta* no species (apart from *M. cambrica*) had been found west of the River Indus.

The new species is based on a single flowering-specimen collected by Toppin, but no particulars of the date of collection, altitude, or flower-colour are given and only immature capsules are present. It may possibly represent a depauperate state of *M. aculeata*, but in the large series of specimens of that species which I have examined none can be seen in which the flowers are borne solely on basal scapes. The character of the inflorescence as a taxonomic character has been found to be quite untrustworthy in other members of the series *Aculeatae*, but the very much shorter style present in *M. neglecta* and its geographical isolation are additional characters which, though slight, help to separate the new species from *M. aculeata*. It may be shown that the plant here described is only a form of *M. aculeata*, when further material from the type-locality and from intervening areas is obtained, but at present it appears worthy of separate specific rank. *M. neglecta* also resembles *M. horridula*, especially in habit, but is readily distinguished from that species in having pinnatifid leaves.

* Inter ser. *Aculeatarum* species *M. aculeatae* proxima, sed ab ea floribus omnibus a scapis basalibus suffultis et stylo breviore distinguitur; *M. horridulae* etiam similis sed foliorum lamina pinnatifida differt. Typus in Herb. Kew., a S. M. Toppin (n. 761) in Chitral fine Kafiristan ad occidentem lectus.

37. MECONOPSIS SINUATA

MECONOPSIS SINUATA Prain in Journ. As. Soc. Bengal lxiv, 2: 314 (1896) excl. var. *Prattii*; in Ann. Roy. Bot. Gard. Calcutta ix, 1: 5, tab. 6 (1901); Novic. Ind.: 116 (1905) excl. var. *Prattii*; in Ann. of Bot. xx: 347 (1906); in Bull. Misc. Inf. Kew 1915: 148 (1915); Fedde in Engl., Pflanzenr. iv, 104: 256, fig. 35 O (1909). Farrer, Engl. Rock-Gard. i: 481 (1919). L. H. Bailey, Stand. Cycloped. Hort., New Ed. ii: 2018 (1927). L. H. and E. Z. Bailey, Hortus: 390 (1930). Wehrhahn, Gartenstaud. i: 469 (1930).

Meconopsis sinuata var. *typica* Prain in Journ. As. Soc. Bengal lxiv, 2: 314 (1896); Novic. Ind.: 116 (1905).

DESCRIPTION. *Monocarpic. Tap-root* dauciform, narrow and elongated, sometimes over 1 ft. in length. *Stem* more or less densely covered with spreading or slightly deflexed spines, 9–30 in. in height. *Basal leaves* few and often withered at time of flowering, up to about 7 in. in length (including the petiole) and 1·25 in. in breadth; lamina more or less obovate to oblanceolate, tapering at the base into a long flattened petiole (up to 2·5 in. in length), rounded at the apex, more or less deeply and irregularly lobed at the margin, sparsely covered on both surfaces with spinous bristles. *Lower cauline leaves* petiolate, narrowly oblanceolate or oblong-oblanceolate, otherwise like the basal leaves. *Upper cauline leaves* sessile, more or less auricled at the base and stem-clasping, otherwise similar to the basal leaves. *Flowers* from 4–8, borne singly in the axils of the upper stem leaves (bracteal leaves often displaced so that the upper flowers appear to be ebracteate); pedicels accrescent in fruit, attaining almost 9 in. in length, rigidly erect. *Petals* 4, obovate, subacute to rounded at the apex and slightly irregularly notched, up to 1·25 in. in length and 0·8 in. in breadth, blue, purple, or violet. *Stamens* numerous; filaments filiform; anthers orange-yellow. *Ovary* ellipsoid, more or less densely spinous, the bristles appressed; style distinct, slender, about 0·25 in. in length; stigma capitate. *Capsule* narrowly obovoid to oblong-ellipsoid, attaining 2 in. in length and 0·3 in. in breadth, prominently 3–4-ribbed, usually with persistent spreading spines, splitting by 3–4 valves sometimes to one-third of its length. *Seeds* more or less falcate-oblong, testa with longitudinal rows of shallow pits.

GEOGRAPHICAL RANGE. Central Nepal to Bhutan, at altitudes from 12,000–14,000 ft. Originally described from Sikkim and Bhutan.

On account of its poor flowering capacity (only one flower being expanded at a time) this species is hardly worthy of much horticultural consideration, and compares most unfavourably with the plant described originally as *M. sinuata* var. *latifolia* and now well known as *M. latifolia*.

In describing *M. sinuata* Prain recognised two varieties, var. *typica* and var. *Prattii*. The latter, originally from Szechuan, was subsequently accorded specific rank as *M. Prattii* Prain and is often grown in gardens under that name, although correctly it should be known as *M. horridula*. *M. sinuata* var. *typica*, which has never been in cultivation in this country, is confined to the area between central Nepal and Bhutan. It is closely related to *M. aculeata* and *M. latifolia*, but differs from both in leaf-shape and in having narrowly elongated capsules.

INSUFFICIENTLY KNOWN SPECIES OF SER. *PRIMULINAE* OR *ACULEATAE*

38. **MECONOPSIS ARGEMONANTHA**

MECONOPSIS ARGEMONANTHA Prain in Bull. Misc. Inf. Kew 1915: 161 (1915), Farrer, Engl. Rock-Gard. ii: 477 (1919). Kingdon-Ward in Gard. Chron., Ser. 3. lxxix: 340 (1926).

DESCRIPTION. *Leaves* up to 3·5 in. in length (including the petiole, which may attain 1 in. in length) and 0·5 in. in breadth; lamina narrowly oblong to narrowly elliptic-oblong, pinnately lobed towards the base (lobes subacute to rounded), sinuate towards the apex, very sparsely bristly on both surfaces, glaucous on the under surface. *Pedicels* attaining at least 3·5 in. in length, very sparsely bristly. *Petals* 6–8, obovate, rounded at the apex, about 1 in. in length and 0·6 in. in breadth, white. *Stamens* numerous; filaments filiform; anthers yellow. *Ovary* ellipsoid, more or less densely covered with appressed prickles. *Style* distinct, up to 0·4 in. in length. *Stigma* capitate.

GEOGRAPHICAL RANGE. Known only from south-eastern Tibet, at an altitude of 13,800 ft. Originally described from Mipak in the Tawang district of south-eastern Tibet.

It is impossible to decide the affinity of this plant with any degree of certainty, and it must remain a problematical species until more adequate material is accessible. Only fragments, comprising two flowers and two leaves, were collected by Bailey, and from these a proper conception of the plant cannot be obtained. All that it is possible to say is that it belongs either to the ser. *Primulinae* (to which Prain referred it) or to the ser. *Aculeatae*. The plant is notable for its white petals.

SER. vi. **BELLAE**

MECONOPSIS ser. BELLAE Prain in Journ. As. Soc. Bengal lxiv, 2: 321 (1896).

Meconopsis sect. *Bellae* (Prain) Fedde in Engl., Pflanzenr. iv, 104: 261 (1909).

Species 1, *Meconopsis bella* Prain, occurring from eastern Nepal to Bhutan (see Fig. 11).

In *M. bella*, the sole member of this series, the stigma is expanded at the base to form a conical structure over the apex of the obovoid or pear-shaped capsule. The basal scapes, in the fruiting stage, are generally prominently recurved. In its dwarf habit, dense covering of persistent leaf-bases investing the base of the stem, and finely-cut leaves, *M. bella* is quite a distinctive species.

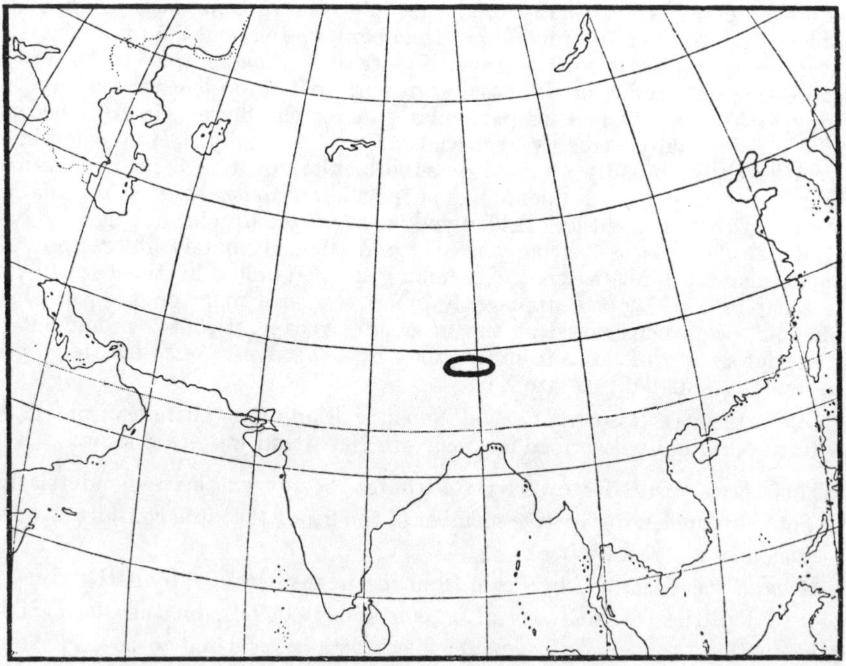

FIG. 11.—MAP SHOWING THE GEOGRAPHICAL RANGE OF THE SERIES *Bellae*.

39. MECONOPSIS BELLA

MECONOPSIS BELLA Prain in Journ. As. Soc. Bengal lxiii, 2: 82 (1894); *op. cit.* lxiv, 2: 321 (1896); in Ann. Roy. Bot. Gard. Calcutta ix, 1: 3, tab. 4 (1901); Novic. Ind.: 71, 123 (1905); in Gard. Chron., Ser. 3, xxxvii: 370 (1905); in Ann. of Bot. xx: 351 (1906); in Curt. Bot. Mag. cxxxiii: tab. 8130 (1907); in Bull. Misc. Inf. Kew 1915: 163 (1915); in Countr. Life liv: 110, 111 (1923). Bull. Misc. Inf. Kew 1905, App.: 82 (1905). Bulley in Fl. and Sylva iii: 82 (1905). Harrow in Gard. Chron., Ser. 3, xl: 198, fig. 81 (1906); in New Fl. and Silva ii: 152 (1930). Fedde in Engl., Pflanzenr. iv, 104: 261, fig. 35 J (1909). Mottet in Rev. Hort. xii: 205 (1912). Farrer, Engl. Rock-Gard. i: 474 (1919). Kingdon-Ward in Gard. Chron., Ser. 3, lxxix: 340 (1926). L. H. Bailey, Stand. Cycloped. Hort., New Ed. ii: 2018 (1927). Silva Tarouca and Schneider, Freiland-Staud.: 249 (1927). L. H. and E. Z. Bailey, Hortus: 390 (1930). Wehrhahn, Gartenstaud. i: 468 (1930).

DESCRIPTION. *Polycarpic*. *Tap-root* dauciform or narrowly and much elongated, up to about 9 in. in length and passing upwards into a short stout stem up to 2 in. in length and very densely covered with the fibrous remains of persistent petioles. *Leaves* numerous, all basal and crowded; petioles slender, up to 4 in. in length, expanded at the base, glabrous or provided with a few scattered bristles; lamina more or less irregularly pinnately or bipinnately lobed (the ultimate segments usually 3-fid, the lobes varying in shape from obovate to oblong and more or less rounded at the apex), up to about 2·5 in. in length and 1 in. in breadth, glabrous or very sparsely bristly. *Flowers* up to 18, borne singly in succession on slender simple basal scapes up to 4 in. in length; scapes usually bearing at least a few bristles particularly under the flowers, in fruit becoming lignified and usually strongly recurved. *Petals* normally 4, but sometimes 5 or very rarely 6, broadly obovate or suborbicular, up to 1·3 in. in length and 1·25 in. in breadth, pink, pale-blue or purple. *Stamens* numerous; filaments filiform, dark-purple; anthers golden-yellow. *Ovary* ellipsoid, oblong-ellipsoid or subglobose, glabrous or sparingly bristly and then ultimately glabrescent; style distinct, about 0·1 in. in length, becoming much swollen at the base in fruit; stigma capitate, 4–7-lobed, apparently green. *Capsule* more or less pear-shaped or obovoid, often constricted at the base into a stipe, with 4–7 prominent ribs, splitting for a short distance from the apex by 4–7 valves. *Seeds* falcate-ellipsoid, testa finely reticulated. (Plate XI.)

Geographical Range. Central Nepal to Bhutan, at altitudes from 12,000–16,500 ft. Originally described from eastern Nepal and western Sikkim.

This species with its dwarf tufted habit, deeply cut leaves, and relatively large flowers is such a distinctive member of the genus that it is considered worthy of inclusion in a series by itself.

M. bella was described by Prain from specimens obtained by native collectors from two localities at altitudes of 12,000 and 14,000 ft. on the Nepal-Sikkim frontier in 1888. For many years the species was considered to be very circumscribed in its distribution, but it is now known to occur along the Himalaya from central Nepal to Bhutan. The species was collected by Cooper in Bhutan in 1914, and the known range westwards was extended by the recent receipt of specimens from Nepal.

The history of the species in cultivation is rather a melancholy one. Seeds were sent to this country and other parts of Europe by King as long ago as 1888, but, although several attempts were subsequently made to introduce the plant, its horticultural merit remained unknown until 1906, when seed received early in 1904 from the Calcutta Botanic Garden produced flowering plants at the Royal Botanic Garden, Edinburgh. The species has since disappeared from gardens, but it is hoped that the recent acquisition of seeds from Nepal may be the means of reintroducing this charming garden plant.

From the field notes available it appears that *M. bella* prefers a northern exposure on moist, sheltered, mossy rock ledges or crevices and it is never found in any abundance in its native state. The rosette of leaves is closely applied to the surface of the rock, while the long tap-root penetrates into the crevices.

As figured in "Curtis's Botanical Magazine" the species appears to have more robust leaves, which are more regularly divided and devoid of the long slender petioles usually associated with field specimens.

Subgen. B. **DISCOGYNE**

Meconopsis subgen. Discogyne G. Tayl., subgen. nov.*

Meconopsis sect. *Polychaetia* Prain in Ann. of Bot. xx: 352 (1906) pro parte, quoad ser. 7.

Meconopsis ser. *Torquatae* Prain *tom. cit.*: 355 (1906).

Meconopsis subgen. *Polychaetia* (Prain) Fedde in Engl., Pflanzenr. iv, 104: 262 (1909) pro parte, quoad sect. 7.

Meconopsis sect. *Torquatae* (Prain) Fedde *tom. cit.*: 265 (1909).

Species 2, confined to south-central Tibet and the Indo-Himalaya from central Nepal to Bhutan (see Fig. 12). Type-species: *Meconopsis torquata* Prain.

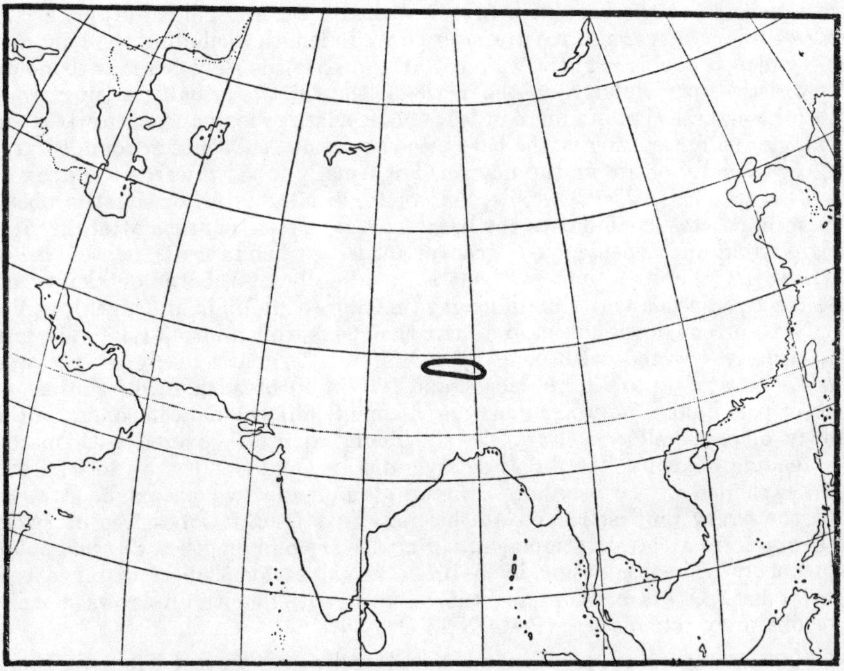

Fig. 12.—Map showing the Geographical Range of the Subgenus *Discogyne*.

The members of this subgenus are at once distinguished from all the other species by the presence of a flat disc surmounting the ovary. This disc gives to the fruit much the appearance of a *Papaver* capsule, but, in place of the radiating stigmatic rays associated with that genus, the stigma of the subgenus *Discogyne* is clavate or the lobes are more or less free and borne on at least a short style.

* A subgenere *Eumeconopsidi* stylo basi in discum glabrum lobatum explanato facile distinguitur.

40. MECONOPSIS DISCIGERA

Meconopsis discigera Prain in Ann. of Bot. xx: 356, tab. 24 fig. 12 (1906); in Bull. Misc. Inf. Kew 1915: 170 (1915); in Countr. Life liv: 110 (1923). Bull. Misc. Inf. Kew 1907, App.: 72 (1907). Fedde in Engl., Pflanzenr. iv, 104: 266 (1909). Farrer, Engl. Rock-Gard. i: 476 (1919). Kingdon-Ward in Gard. Chron., Ser. 3, lxxix: 459 (1926). L. H. Bailey, Stand. Cycloped. Hort., New Ed. ii: 2019 (1927). Cooper in New Fl. and Silva i: 240, fig. 72 (1929). G. Tayl. in Journ. of Bot. lxviii: fig. 4 (1930). Harrow in New Fl. and Silva ii: 151 (1930). Wehrhahn, Gartenstaud. i: 470 (1930).

Description. Apparently *monocarpic*. *Tap-root* dauciform and usually branched below, up to about 4 in. in length, passing upwards into a stout stem which is covered at the base with persistent leaf-bases and golden-brown bristles. *Basal leaves* in a very dense rosette, up to 7 in. in length (including the long linear petiole which becomes slightly widened at the base) densely beset with golden-brown bristles (particularly on the petiole), the bristles usually arising from a purplish-black base; lamina more or less oblanceolate or long and narrowly wedge-shaped, gradually tapering at the base into the petiole, subacute or rounded at the apex, occasionally entire at the margin, but usually lobed towards the apex and most often trilobed. *Bracts* sessile, lanceolate, usually entire or slightly lobed at the margin, otherwise similar to the basal leaves. *Flowering-stem* attaining 16 in. in height, stout and conspicuously grooved (at least when in fruit), densely bristly. *Flowers* 13–20 (the upper ones without subtending bracts), borne on simple more or less erect pedicels about 1 in. in length (in fruit about 1·5 in. in length); pedicels strongly decurrent down the stem and at the apex swollen into a relatively broad torus, densely covered with long spreading bristles particularly at the apex. *Petals* 4, obovate, up to 2 in. in length and 1·75 in. in breadth, dark-crimson, red, purple, or pale-blue. *Stamens* numerous; filaments filiform, dark in colour; anthers narrowly oblong, yellow. *Ovary* shortly oblong, densely covered with more or less spreading golden-yellow bristles; style distinct and slender, up to 0·25 in. in length, expanded at the base into a broad glabrous disc which extends over the top of the ovary and is fringed at the margin; stigmatic lobes free or twisted together to form a clavate stigma, equalling the style in length. *Capsule* oblong, conspicuously ribbed, splitting by 6–10 small valves for a short distance below the stylar disc. *Seeds* more or less reniform, testa with longitudinal rows of shallow pits or obscurely reticulate. (Plate XXVIII.)

Geographical Range. Central Nepal and south-central Tibet to Bhutan at altitudes from 11,000–16,000 ft. Originally described from Sikkim.

Prain based his description of this species on fruiting specimens collected by Cave at an altitude between 11,000 and 12,000 ft. on the mountain of Gucha La in western Sikkim in 1905. Some years later a native collector returned to the type-locality, and the flowering specimens which he obtained enabled Prain to amend his original description. He then stated that the flowers were yellow, although in a subsequent publication* he observed that this was incorrect. Recent collections

* Countr. Life liv: 111 (1923).

from Nepal and by the Mount Everest Expedition of 1922 have shown that the flower-colour is dark crimson, red, purple, or, as Cooper has recorded from Bhutan, blue. The species has been described as polycarpic, but the evidence for this statement is unsatisfactory. From herbarium specimens it appears that the plant may require some years to reach maturity, as below the dense basal tuft, which is so conspicuous a feature of the species, there are copious remains of leaves presumably produced in former years. Experience of members of the series *Robustae* in cultivation has shown that many persist for several years before producing flowers.

In the structure of the ovary and capsule *M. discigera* is exceedingly interesting. Along with *M. torquata* it has been referred to the subgenus *Discogyne*, the two species being characterised by the presence of a disc surmounting the ovary. Apart from the conspicuous style and more or less free stigmatic lobes the structure is remarkably like the typical condition of *Papaver*, where the ovary is also provided with a disc at the apex. The resemblance can be regarded only as superficial, as the very definite differences in the stylar characters preclude the assumption of any close relationship.

Seedlings of *M. discigera* were raised in this country in 1906, and in 1915 Prain observed that the species had become introduced to cultivation, and, although no details regarding the first date of flowering are given by him, there is a specimen in Kew Herbarium of a cultivated plant in flower which had been sent from the Royal Botanic Garden, Edinburgh, in 1917. A plant stated to be *M. discigera* and which proved to be monocarpic flowered at Edinburgh in 1930, but as the flowers were yellow its true identity is uncertain. Seeds of the species have recently been received from Nepal, and plants have been successfully raised from them. The herbarium specimens which accompanied them show that *M. discigera* is an extremely desirable garden plant, the flowers being freely produced along the length of the stem and completely concealing the apex. Field notes indicate that the species prefers gravelly situations where the drainage is rapid.

41. MECONOPSIS TORQUATA

Meconopsis torquata Prain in Ann. of Bot. xx: 355, tab. 24 fig. 11 (1906); in Bull. Misc. Inf. Kew 1915: 170 (1915). Fedde in Engl., Pflanzenr. iv, 104: 265 (1909). Farrer, Engl. Rock-Gard. i: 482 (1919). Wehrhahn, Gartenstaud. i: 470 (1930).

Description. *Monocarpic. Stem* covered at the base with the remnants of persistent leaf-bases. *Basal and lower cauline leaves* up to 5 in. in length (including the petiole), densely bristly especially on the lower part of the petiole (the bristles arising from a dark-coloured base); lamina oblanceolate, gradually tapering at the base into a linear petiole which is sheathing at the base, obtuse or subacute at the apex, entire or distantly and irregularly sinuate at the margin. *Bracts* sessile, irregularly lobed at the margin, otherwise similar to the basal leaves. *Flowering-stem* attaining 16 in. in height, stout, densely covered with spreading or slightly reflexed conspicuously barbellate bristles. *Flowers* about 25, densely aggregated towards the apex of the stem (the upper ones devoid of bracts), borne on simple densely bristly pedicels; pedicels up to about 0·25 in. in length, expanded at the apex into a broad torus. *Petals* 4, or perhaps more, more or less obovate, up to 1·5 in. in length and 0·75 in. in breadth, pale red, sparsely bristly on the outside. *Stamens* numerous; filaments filiform; anthers yellow. *Ovary* obovoid or ellipsoid-oblong, densely bristly (the bristles obliquely spreading); style very short or almost obsolete, expanded at the base into a glabrous reddish-purple disc which is sinuate and 8-angled at the margin; stigma clavate. *Capsule* obovoid or ellipsoid-oblong, more or less prominently ribbed, splitting for a short distance under the disc by 8 valves. *Seeds* ovoid, testa reticulated. (Plate XXVII.)

GEOGRAPHICAL RANGE. Known only from south-central Tibet at an altitude of 11,500 ft. Originally described from the valley of the river Kyi-chu, near Lhasa, south-central Tibet.

M. torquata was discovered by Walton in Tibet in 1904, and apparently this is the only known record of its occurrence. The species is obviously very closely related to *M. discigera*, the two being very similar in habit and characterised by the presence of a well-defined disc surmounting the ovary. *M. torquata* is, however, distinguished by its narrower oblanceolate leaves, the close aggregation of the flowers, almost sessile stigma, and presence of bristles at the back of the petals. This latter character is found in no other species of *Meconopsis*.

The remarks under *M. discigera* regarding its horticultural merit apply with equal force to *M. torquata* which has never been in cultivation.

SPECIES EXCLUDED FROM MECONOPSIS

MECONOPSIS CRASSIFOLIA Benth. in Trans. Hort. Soc., Ser. 2, i: 408 (1835)= **Stylomecon heterophylla** (Benth.) G. Tayl. See *M. heterophylla* (below).

MECONOPSIS DIPHYLLA DC., Reg. Veg. Syst. Nat. ii: 88 (1821)= **Stylophorum diphyllum** (Michx.) Nutt.

MECONOPSIS GLABRA Hook., Ic. Pl. viii: sub tab. 732, in syn. (1848) (laps. *pro M. heterophylla*)= **Stylomecon heterophylla** (Benth.) G. Tayl. See *M. heterophylla* (below).

MECONOPSIS HETEROPHYLLA Benth. in Trans. Hort. Soc., Ser. 2, i: 408 (1835)= **Stylomecon heterophylla** (Benth.) G. Tayl.*

* The full synonymy of *Stylomecon* and its only species is as follows:

STYLOMECON G. Tayl. in Journ. of Bot. lxviii: 140 (1930).

Meconopsis ser. *Anomalae* Prain in [Journ. As. Soc. Bengal lxiv. 2; 311 et 313 in ob (1896), *nomen nudum*] Ann. of Bot. xx: 344 (1906).

Meconopsis sect. *Anomalae* (Prain) Fedde in Engl., Pflanzenr. iv, 104: 253 (1909).

Stylomecon heterophylla (Benth.) G. Tayl. in Journ. of Bot. lxviii: 140, fig. 3 (1930).

MECONOPSIS PETIOLATA DC., Reg. Veg. Syst. Nat. ii: 87 (1821)= **Stylophorum diphyllum** (Michx.) Nutt.

Meconopsis heterophylla Benth. in Trans. Hort. Soc., Ser. 2, i: 408 (1835).
Meconopsis crassifolia Benth. *loc. cit.* (1835).
Stylophorum heterophyllum (Benth.) Steud., Nomencl. Bot., Ed. 2, ii: 650 (1841).
Stylophorum crassifolium (Benth.) Steud. *loc. cit.* (1841).
[*Meconopsis glabra* Hook., Ic. Pl. viii: sub tab. 732, in syn. (1848), *laps. pro M. crassifolia.*]
Papaver heterophyllum (Benth.) Greene, Pittonia i: 168 (1888).
Papaver crassifolium (Benth.) Greene, Man. Bot. San Francis. Bay: 9 (1894).
Papaver heterophyllum var. *crassifolium* (Benth.) Jepson, Fl. West. Mid. Calif. 209 (1901).

NOTES ON THE CULTIVATION OF THE INTRODUCED SPECIES

Meconopsis is a genus that is not so popular in gardens as it should be. It has long had the reputation of being difficult, a subject for a small number of gardens that possess exceptional soil and climatic conditions. Only lately has it come to be realised that many species are not so exacting as their reputation had led us to suppose.

In general the genus must stand high in the ranks of ornamental garden plants. Many of the species—and among them are included some of those that are quite easily grown—are of unsurpassed beauty with their lovely colouring and graceful habit, ideal plants for the woodland garden or more shady corners of the rock garden.

One of the main reasons for lack of success in the past is a belief, which has been fairly prevalent, that they are saxatile plants. They have been given positions in the ordinary rockery, often with full exposure to the sun. In such situations many have died a natural, or unnatural, death, to the disappointment of the gardeners, who have at once classed them among difficult plants.

In reality *Meconopsis*, in their likes and dislikes, are very similar to the Asiatic species of *Primula*. In *Meconopsis* as in *Primula* there are several species which have readily become established in gardens; of the former genus *P. Florindae*, *P. japonica*, *P. Bulleyana*, and *P. denticulata* may be mentioned as presenting no difficulties in cultivation, while in *Meconopsis* the same remark may be applied to *M. betonicifolia*, *M. napaulensis*, and *M. horridula*. *Primula Littoniana*, *P. Winteri*, and *P. nutans* ask for a little more consideration; so do *Meconopsis simplicifolia*, *M. latifolia*, and *M. quintuplinervia*. The comparison might be carried further, but it is sufficient to state that success in the cultivation of *Primulas* should ensure similar results with some of the species of *Meconopsis*.

Possibly the limits of conditions under which they can be successfully grown must be a little more closely defined than in the case of *Primulas*, but the limits of those in regular cultivation are by no means impossible to find in many gardens.

Before the garden behaviour of individual species is described I must mention some of the main conditions necessary for their successful cultivation.

Moisture and Soil

Of these conditions moisture and soil are important. It must be remembered that only a few species are perennial. Out of the same batch of seedlings a few may flower in the second year, a large proportion in the third, while some will wait until the fourth or even the fifth year before reaching maturity. Thus, these monocarpic species should not be treated as ordinary garden biennials in the belief that any position will suit so short-lived a plant. Positions should be found that conform as much as possible to their known requirements. As they have thick fleshy roots, they should not be moved once they are planted in their flowering positions. If they must be moved, this should be done while they are young and a big ball of soil lifted with the plants.

Meconopsis, like so many *Primulas*, are plants that like a dry bed in winter and moisture during the growing season; the former is even more important than the latter, as few will survive a wet sticky soil through several winters, while the dry summer of 1933 proved, rather surprisingly, to what an extent they will exist under exceedingly dry conditions. It is true that their stature and the size of the flowers suffered, but few perished unless the heat had been excessive.

It makes little difference whether the species belong to those sections where the foliage dies down completely in winter or to the series *Robustae* and *Superbae*, with their splendid flat winter-rosettes of leaves: in both cases the collar between the crown and the root system is particularly susceptible to winter rot, or rather spring rot, as a mild wet autumn seems to affect them less than similar conditions during February or March.

This at once brings us to the vital question of drainage, although I believe that in the case of *Meconopsis* the drainage of the top 2 inches of soil is just as important as conditions below that level. They are plants usually occurring in thin woodland or in alpine pastures, and it is only natural that stagnation in any form is fatal, but there is no necessity to make special preparation of the lower soil where good drainage already exists. Ordinary open loam is satisfactory so long as it is not of too poor a quality.

It is, however, just this point, that good loam suits them so well, which is sometimes so fatal in early spring. Occasionally there are certain climatic conditions under which ordinary loam as a surface soil is most unsuitable. It is not uncommon after a few nights of moderate frost to have heavy rain that beats down the surface opened by the frost to a hard impermeable skin. Possibly it is only an inch thick, but it is wet and sticky at exactly the point where the collar of the plant, its most vulnerable part, is in contact with the soil. These conditions, then, make the plant liable to that incurable disease, winter crown-rot. Prevention lies in making the top inch or so of the soil as porous as possible, so that no matter how heavy the rain may be it will not be beaten into a solid cake.

Sand is usually mentioned as a certain specific, but unless the sand is extremely sharp it will help to cake the soil. Powdered leaf-mould mixed with granulated peat is much better.

This stressing of the importance of the surface may sound unnecessary to those whose soil is naturally full of humus and so open that it does not cake, but I have seen many gardens with good ordinary loam that undoubtedly suffer severely from surface caking of the soil.

It is difficult to lay down hard-and-fast rules about moisture. A few, like *M. latifolia*, prefer drier conditions than others, whereas *M. violacea* seems to prefer, and *M. betonicifolia* will not object to, a moister climate. As a general rule many will grow and thrive under the same conditions as really flourishing *Primula Littoniana*, *P. pulverulenta*, *P. secundiflora*, or *Gentiana sino-ornata*. Many of them are perfectly ordinary herbs, liking ordinary soil and ordinary thin woodland.

As the genus prefers moderately dry winter conditions and a certain amount of moisture during the growing season, it might appear that the usual open scree would be a suitable home for them; but, with the exception of the series *Aculeatae* (comprising among others *M. horridula* in its many forms, *M. latifolia*, and *M. aculeata*), they are not plants adapted to scree-planting. They are inclined to be rich feeders and to resent the meagre nourishment of the scree by making ridiculously small growth.

Certainly many *Meconopsis* species seen in gardens are starved. Sometimes this is due to lack of moisture in the growing season, but often it is from lack of feeding. If it is remembered that the majority of them live in thin woodland or damp alpine meadows, rich in humus, it is obviously unfair to expect them to grow in ground that is never fed, a fault of many woodland gardens. Well-rotted cow dung suits the coarser species, such as *M. regia*, *M. paniculata*, *M. betonicifolia* and *M. napaulensis*, but an ample supply of leaf-mould will suit them equally well, or, to be generous, two large handfuls of dry guano may be added to every barrowful of leaf-mould. If this mixture is forked into the soil before each batch is planted, there will be sufficient nourishment to see them through their short life. They are deep-rooting plants, and surface mulching adds little to their food supply, although any of the good compound artificial manures forked in just before they begin their growth will improve them in a poor soil.

It is often said that *Meconopsis* will not grow in lime soils, but as far as I know this has never been proved conclusively with any particular species. Many species appear to resent chalk, but this is possibly due to insufficient drainage and climatic conditions. On the other hand, some occasionally grow in their wild state on limestone: examples are *M. quintuplinervia*, *M. horridula*, and *M. punicea*; while others, such as *M. latifolia* and *M. betonicifolia*, are known to be tolerant of lime. *M. Delavayi*, at present in cultivation, is found exclusively on limestone. *M. speciosa*, of which Rock has sent seed, is also occasionally found growing on limestone.

Lime is blamed for wastage and death, and many of us are only too much inclined to state that lime is the cause of failure. It is much more satisfying to blame the chemical composition of the soil, something over which we have no control, than to look for other causes, such as lack of drainage, too dry an atmosphere, or too much sun exposure.

Unfortunately lime poisoning is not always easy to distinguish with any certainty in the case of *Meconopsis*. The yellowing of the foliage, which is so often quoted as a certain sign that a calcifuge plant is being given an excess of lime, may also be caused by lack of moisture during the growing season, or may even show the effects of lack of drainage. A great deal of experiment on the subject of *Meconopsis* and lime still requires to be carried out.

Exposure

Exposure is also of the greatest importance with *Meconopsis*. Like any other plant, they may be severely damaged or even killed by severe late spring frosts, but many species are known to have stood almost zero conditions during winter without flinching. Indeed, I have never heard of a *Meconopsis* being killed by winter cold. It is rather the other way about; deaths in a hard winter of frost and snow are almost reduced to a minimum, a fact which may reassure those who live in cold districts.

What the species object to most is summer heat, and particularly heat without moisture in the atmosphere. This point of moisture in the atmosphere is stressed, as this is certainly the main reason for their usual failure in the south of England and in eastern and central Canada and the United States. It is possible to conserve or add moisture to the soil by growing them in a more spongy medium aided by copious watering, but an intensely dry atmosphere during May and June and July is much more difficult to counteract. Where heat and dry air are a regular combination during the growing season the only solution is to give the plants the coolest position possible, a north border or very nearly full shade in woodland. As one goes north and conditions become cooler, considerably more sun exposure can be given, certainly as much as half-shade. In cool climates it is inadvisable to grow them in a north border. Ripening of the plants in a wet autumn is then impossible, and the crowns will be much more likely to be attacked by winter crown-rot.

Where late spring frosts are common an easterly exposure should be avoided. If possible, they should be sheltered from wind, not only because many of them are tall-growing, but also because the substance of the petals is fragile and the flowers are easily tattered and torn by wind. In moderately sheltered situations staking is entirely unnecessary and should be avoided.

Meconopsis should be grown in groups whenever possible. Apart from the fact that many of the species are difficult to place as single plants, it must be remembered that the majority are monocarpic and that in order to ensure a regular succession seed must be collected and sown every year. It will be more likely that fertile seed will be set in a group of plants than in a solitary specimen. In addition, a few self-made hybrids have already turned up in gardens. As the species become more commonly grown it seems likely that more and more rogues will appear. It is much easier to keep a strain true by growing plants of one species in groups than if mixed planting is practised.

Raising from Seed

The raising of *Meconopsis* from seed is not difficult in the commoner species. The amount of seed borne is in most cases enormous, even in such a prolific family as the *Papaveraceae*. If the seed is fresh, the percentage of fertility is large and it germinates rapidly and freely.

Opinions differ about the relative advantages of autumn and spring sowing. If it is sown in autumn as soon as gathered, the percentage of seed germinating is certainly larger than in spring sowing. Some seedlings may be lost during winter, and sometimes autumn-sown plants are rather slow to start away again in the spring. Seed sown in the spring may not germinate so freely, but the seedlings will grow quicker as they have had no winter check as seedlings.

As a general rule it is a good plan to divide the seed and make a sowing in autumn and another in February. Thus you have two chances of success.

Seed should be sown thinly in an open and well-drained mixture of a third fibrous loam, a third sharp sand, and a third granulated peat moss or powdered leaf-mould. It is as well to cover the surface of the pan with a powdering of sharp sand. If the pan is placed in moderate heat and kept fairly moist, germination should take place in from three to six weeks.

Seedlings should be pricked off as soon as they have passed the cotyledon stage and are easily handled. The seedling boxes should contain the same mixture with, perhaps, a little less sand and a little more peat or leaf-mould. They should be planted at least 2 inches apart to allow for expansion, as they will have to remain in the boxes for several months at least, and possibly a year, depending on the time of sowing. As soon as they have settled down in the boxes, these should be removed to a cool house, and if autumn-sown left there until spring, when they should be placed in a cold frame with a north exposure. If sown in February, the seedling boxes should be removed by degrees to the cold frame as soon as fear of check is past.

It is better to grow them on in boxes than to plant the seedlings out direct into a cold frame, for the root disturbance is less when planted into their final positions from a box than from the soil in a frame, and the less the roots are disturbed the better.

The best time for final planting really rests on the size of the young plants and on local conditions. No rules can be laid down. The best months are April and August, but unless the young plants are really strong and fill their allotted space in the seedling box, it is better to wait until April and miss a possible flowering the following year than to plant them out in late summer or early autumn with the chance of loosing the entire batch during the winter. Never plant when the weather is too dry or too wet, as the first few weeks after the final planting are the most important.

Vegetative reproduction is possible in a few perennial species. This is mentioned under the several species concerned.

Blue is the colour of some of the most popular species, *M. napaulensis*, *M. simplicifolia*, *M. grandis*, *M. betonicifolia*, *M. latifolia*, and *M. horridula*, but it is an unstable colour in the genus. The intensity of the tone sometimes varies according to the temperature at the time when the buds are colouring; more often the chemical constitution of the soil has a direct bearing on the purity of the blue tones. Some gardens are lucky, others unlucky. Therefore there is no guarantee that seed of a particularly fine shade of blue in one garden will produce plants of an equally fine colour in another. As shades vary so much, consistent pulling up of all colours that do not reach a certain standard is the only method of perpetuating a good strain.

Individual Species

In dealing with individual species it would be waste of time even to suggest possible treatment for those which have barely arrived in cultivation, such as *M. impedita*, or those whose life in our gardens so far has been fleeting, such as *M. bella*. I have seen three-year-old plants of *M. bella*, wizened and unhappy, grown in pots for the sole reason that the owner had no idea of the proper conditions under which to grow them. This is through no fault of his. Here is a Himalayan *Meconopsis* of which the seed has been sent home at fairly frequent intervals. It has been tried by a number of gardeners and they have usually failed. The condition necessary for these species may yet be fulfilled. On the other hand, they may never be properly reproduced. It is no easy problem, when probably only a pinch of seed is received and half a dozen seedlings raised, to know what to do with them.

I have only one tentative suggestion to make; the possibility of a scree with a good deal of leaf-mould added in a position in half-shade. For some reason or another it has been the fashion to make screes in full sun. This certainly suits many European and American alpines, but scree-makers forget that conditions in many of the high hills of Asia are entirely different from those in the Rocky Mountains or the European Alps. In the latter the growing seasons are more or less sunny and often dry. In the monsoon areas of Asia, from which so many species of *Meconopsis*, *Primula*, and *Gentiana* come, the growing season is often completely sunless. Such plants will resent strong sunshine and a dry atmosphere. The value of a garden scree for such plants is limited to a controlled water supply and adequate drainage. It is the only possible means of imitating the climatic conditions to which they are accustomed; ample moisture during the growing season and a dry bed in winter, the closest imitation of a snow blanket that we can give them.

Of the 41 species of *Meconopsis* so far described, the following 15 may be said to be in general cultivation (by " general " is meant that they are in a sufficient number of gardens to guarantee with some certainty that the species will survive in cultivation): *M. cambrica*, *M. chelidonifolia*, *M. villosa*, *M. regia*, *M. Dhwojii*, *M. paniculata*, *M. napaulensis*, *M. violacea*, *M. simplicifolia*, *M. quintuplinervia*, *M. integrifolia*, *M. betonicifolia*, *M. grandis*, *M. horridula*, and *M. latifolia*.

Of the remaining 26 the following 4 species are not quite so certain, although there seems a probability that they will survive: *M. superba*, *M. longipetiolata*, *M. punicea*, and *M. aculeata*.

Of the remaining 22 species the following 7 are in doubtful cultivation or are either definitely difficult plants or are so newly introduced as to be untested: *M. primulina*, *M. Delavayi*, *M. Henrici*, *M. impedita*, *M. Georgei*, *M. bella*, and *M. discigera*.

This leaves 15 species which have never been in cultivation or have died out completely. To have 26 out of 41 known species in cultivation is a large proportion when compared to Asiatic *Primula* or *Gentiana*, and should help to prove that the cultivation of the genus is not beset with such very great difficulties as many gardeners imagine.

In the following paragraphs on individual species I have treated them according to their affinities, as many of the factors that apply to one plant in a section apply equally to others in the same section. Detailed descriptions would be redundant when each species is fully described elsewhere in this volume.

SECTION CAMBRICAE

M. cambrica : The native Welsh Poppy is so well known in gardens that it is unnecessary to give detailed particulars of its behaviour in cultivation. The species can be readily propagated by division of the dense tufts which it forms.

SERIES CHELIDONIFOLIAE

M. chelidonifolia : Although this has been in cultivation for a number of years it is still a rare plant in gardens. Perhaps more than any other species it must have a position in cool, moist woodland if it is going to be other than a poor straggling thing. When a group is growing well under these conditions and the soft yellow flowers can be clearly seen against a dark background it is an attractive and unusual plant. It is certainly more for the cool north than the warmer and drier south.

Seed is not set freely. Reproduction is most readily carried out by means of small vegetative buds that appear in the axils of the stem leaves below the flowers. As the flowers develop the stem bends over and becomes more or less prostrate, and if it is pegged down the bulbils root easily; or they may be treated as cuttings.

SERIES VILLOSAE

M. villosa : This has been grown for many years under its more common name of *Cathcartia villosa*. While it likes cool and fairly moist situations it will grow in the south, as is proved by the excellent plants at Wisley in a shady corner near the top of the rock garden. It is evergreen and the winter foliage is hairy. This means that it is susceptible to winter wet, and should really be protected by glass unless snow lies for long. Seed sets freely and germinates well.

M. villosa is an elegant plant with its deeply lobed leaves. The rich yellow of the flowers suits the pale green of the foliage. It is one of the few species of *Meconopsis* whose proportions make it almost as good as a specimen plant as when seen in the mass. Thus it has its value in the rock garden in positions too small for a group of larger species, while it is also a desirable woodland plant.

SERIES SUPERBAE

M. regia : As this new species from Nepal is extremely strong-growing, with mature leaves sometimes up to 30 inches in length, ample room should be allowed for expansion. Where they grow well, 2 feet should be given between each plant. The winter-rosettes are magnificent. The individual flowers are good in size and colour, but unfortunately too few open at a time to make *M. regia* one of the finest when in flower. Possibly this may be improved in time by selection. It is excellent for massed planting in thin woodland, but care should be taken that it is always in a position where its winter-rosettes can be clearly seen.

So far it appears to be absolutely hardy, as frost of just above zero has left it unscathed. Sun and drought after its full growth is completed do not seem to harm it, but it should have ample moisture and cool weather during the growing season.

During the dry summer of 1933 very few plants flowered. Even the remaining portions of batches planted out in 1931, of which about half flowered in 1932, did not show a flower spike. The reason for this lack of flower is unknown; it might be due to intensely dry conditions at the time when the flower buds should normally have developed.

M. superba: The required conditions for this fine white-flowered species are closely akin to those for *M. regia.* It is, however, not quite so amenable. It is inclined to be more susceptible to winter crown-rot. Also it is more irregular in flowering. Nevertheless it is a lovely thing, well worth growing.

Seed must be very fresh or it will not germinate at all freely.

Possibly in time its place may be taken by the hybrid ×*M. Musgravei*, of which it is the male parent. In addition to having the same white flowers ×*M. Musgravei* is perennial and appears to be good-tempered even in the south.

SERIES ROBUSTAE

M. paniculata: This tall yellow-flowered species bears rather a mediocre reputation owing to the fact that in some forms the flowers are so ridiculously small as to be worthless. There are, however, others with flowers over 2 inches in diameter and of good colour. These are well worth growing and make excellent plants in the woodland garden. Care should be taken to save seed only from the best forms. The winter-rosettes with their more or less finely cut foliage covered with silvery hairs are very handsome. As they are not so large as those of *M. regia*, young plants should be set about 1½ feet apart.

It stands drier conditions than others of the section, but there are differences of opinion about its survival during winter. In some gardens not a single plant has been lost even when planted in a fairly sticky soil; in others, where apparently conditions are the same, it is much addicted to winter crown-rot. On the whole, it is a plant of easy cultivation, and is not at all difficult to bring to flower. It is more regular in flowering during its third year than most of the other species, and it is only rarely that a plant or two out of a batch will wait until the fourth year before sending up its flower spike.

M. Dhwojii is still uncommon in cultivation, but seed sets so freely that in time it should be a common woodland plant. It seems to be easily grown, requiring very much the same conditions as *M. paniculata.* It is not a tall grower, and 14–16 inches is all that need be allowed between plants. Winter-rot is its greatest enemy, and the drainage must be perfect. It is a plant better suited to the woodland than the rock garden.

M. longipetiolata, another new species from Nepal, is better regarded as a woodland species than a rock garden plant. At least 2 feet should be allowed between each plant to show off its particularly graceful habit. In other respects its cultivation is exactly like that of *M. Dhwojii*.

M. violacea: This species definitely likes moister conditions and more shade and as definitely dislikes a dry and hot atmosphere. Of the series *Robustae* it is the least likely to grow well in the south, but in a soil rich in humus in a fairly moist and shaded woodland it will grow as vigorously as *M. napaulensis*. It is not so tall growing as either *M. napaulensis* or *M. paniculata*, and if planted together *M. violacea* should be in the foreground.

Seed is set fairly freely. Seedlings are not difficult to raise, but watering should be done with care. During winter the seed boxes should be kept as dry as those containing *M. napaulensis*, but as soon as growth commences the boxes should be kept shaded and well watered. The compost should contain a good proportion of granulated peat.

M. napaulensis: This has been consistently grown in gardens as *M. Wallichii*. In its best forms it is certainly a magnificent plant. Colour varieties may be divided into three groups, blue (the oldest in cultivation), a kind of dull port colour, and white tinged with blue. The first, blue, at its very best—and this is unfortunately rare—almost rivals a good blue *M. betonicifolia*. Opinions differ about colour selection of blue *Meconopsis*, as soil undoubtedly has, as in *Hydrangea*, a great deal of influence on the quality of the blue. I know of one garden where the addition of red in the blue is almost unknown, and yet seed produced from the best blue form in that garden may bring forth ugly magentas elsewhere. Possibly constant selection on scientific lines may in time produce a race of a real clear blue, but at the moment no such strain exists.

The red colour variety has been in cultivation for too short a time to judge whether it will produce a pure strain. Almost all the flowering plants that I have seen keep to the peculiar but attractive shade and there appears to be every chance of this colour remaining. Of the so-called white, also newly introduced from Nepal, there is more doubt. A bluish tinge is undoubtedly present, although it is sufficiently faint in many cases to be called white.

This has probably been the most popular of all *Meconopsis* until the arrival of *M. betonicifolia* and it is still the most stately. For woodland planting it is ideal. It likes a soil rich in humus and on the damp side in at least half shade in the south, but it is more susceptible than *M. paniculata* to winter-rot, particularly if planted too close. Where it grows strongly 1½–2 feet should be allowed between each plant. Seed is set very freely.

SERIES SIMPLICIFOLIAE

M. punicea : In colour this is one of the most striking of all *Meconopsis*. In general habit it is like *M. quintuplinervia* with wider open flowers, but it has not the vigour of the latter species. It is most certainly a plant for the north or west, and its position should be in more than half shade where it can have a cool root-run. One of the difficulties is to keep it from sending up a premature flower spike from a single crown. If this is allowed to mature, the plant usually dies. Every effort must be made to grow it on slowly so as to form multiple crowns before it attempts to flower. In order to conserve its strength early flower buds should be removed as soon as they appear. Unfortunately it appears to be a shy seeder.

M. quintuplinervia : The Harebell Poppy of Farrer is, perhaps, the most unassuming member of the genus, but owing to the freedom with which it flowers when happily situated and the delicate poise of its flowers it certainly has a place in the rock garden. The dull lavender-blue is only dull when compared with the brilliant shades of *M. betonicifolia* and *M. simplicifolia*. This *Meconopsis* should be grown on a cool ledge of the rock garden where its roots are either shaded by low shrubs or can creep under stones for coolness. In other respects it is an easily satisfied plant, growing equally well on limestone or granite soils. It does not damp off easily so long as the soil is gritty and the drainage good. It is not a plant for the woodland garden.

It is only seldom, in a hot summer like 1933, that seed is set in quantity, but the plants spread rapidly and increase is easy by division.

M. simplicifolia : Two strains are in cultivation, one sky blue, which is usually monocarpic, the other a deeper blue or blue-purple, which is usually perennial. Although quite hardy it suffers from winter crown-rot. More than any other species it requires a surface soil that does not cake, and, in addition, the main drainage must be perfect. It also dislikes a hot and dry atmosphere.

The best situations are on the north slope of a rock garden or in woodland bays among *Rhododendrons* where it can be sheltered from the sun for most of the day. It should always be planted in groups, 8 inches between each plant.

Seed is set very freely and seedlings are not difficult to raise so long as they are not coddled and spend most of their young life in the cold frame.

SERIES GRANDES

M. grandis : This splendid plant is always admired in the rock garden of the Royal Botanic Garden, Edinburgh, where it has now been growing for many years. The satiny and iridescent sheen of its large blue flowers is extremely uncommon in the hardy plant world. It is odd that with its fragile appearance flowers have been known to last for three weeks in water when cut just as the bud is opening. Although *M. grandis* is a very shy seeder, it is a true perennial, and vegetative reproduction is comparatively simple through separation of the side shoots from the parent plant.

Another colour form has lately been introduced from Nepal, equally perennial but not so large in stature and of rather a washy purple in colour. It is not nearly so fine as the original plants from Sikkim, but shows signs of improving.

M. grandis is quite hardy and should be grown in half shade where the lower stem and roots can be sheltered from the sun by nearby dwarf shrubs. It dislikes a hot and dry atmosphere; thus it is more a plant for the north than the south.

M. integrifolia : With its big yellow flowers this is one of the best species for the rock garden. In some gardens it is found to be particularly susceptible to winter crown-rot and it should always be planted with a surface soil that is not liable to cake. It is certainly influenced by the presence or absence of moisture. Drainage must be excellent, while drought during the growing season will cause it to wilt and die. In the south it should always be grown on the north side of the rock garden, if possible among, but not underneath, low-growing shrubs. These will help to keep the soil cool.

Plenty of seed is produced which germinates freely. Seedlings should be removed to a cold frame as early as possible.

M. betonicifolia : The most universally grown of all *Meconopsis*, and certainly the best for the ordinary garden. It will grow in almost any soil and in almost full sun or shade. Moist winter conditions do not seem to harm more than a small proportion of the plants, nor does it object strongly to the hot dry air of the south; but the drier the conditions the more shade should be given to it. It is really too tall and lush growing for the rock garden unless this is designed on a large scale where a big group can be planted in a bay towards the back. Almost anywhere in the woodland garden it seems at home and I would lay stress on its value as a plant for the ordinary herbaceous border so long as this is not too scorched by the sun.

The tones of its brilliant blue flowers only vary in the intensity of the colour: it is very rare that muddy or magenta shades are seen, and these may be caused by a touch of some other species in the strain. A proportion of every batch is usually perennial: some plants are known to have flowered for at least seven years and now form multiple crowns. The proportion of perennial plants seems to vary according to the speed with which the young plants are grown. Its behaviour in the seed pan and seedling box is admirable, so much so that one is inclined to force on its growth in the greenhouse in order to get bigger plants that flower earlier. The quicker they are grown the more monocarpic plants will be found in the batch.

A young plant that throws up a flowering-stem when it has only one crown will always die after flowering. If no effort is made to flower them the second year, a large percentage of a batch may send out side shoots. When this occurs the plant may live for years.

SERIES DELAVAYANAE

M. Delavayi : This, again, would seem to be a plant for the shaded scree. Having flowered in 1913 and then died, plants are again growing from a fresh importation of seed. They have survived in an open granite scree in a garden in the north, but are not vigorous, and do better in a shaded and cool sandy bed in the alpine house, where they have flowered for two years in succession. This, of course, is not a question of hardiness but of controlled light and moisture. In the wilds it is known to grow exclusively on limestone, so possibly a mixture of limestone and granite in a scree might be beneficial. As it is still in the experimental stage, little is known about its ultimate possibilities as a garden plant, but it is sufficiently charming to make it valuable if only we can learn its likes and dislikes.

SERIES ACULEATAE

M. horridula : Under this name is now collected the aggregate of such old specific names as *M. rudis*, *M. racemosa*, and *M. Prattii.* This group is often considered to have the poorest flowers of the genus, chiefly owing to the numerous forms in cultivation, many of which are extremely mediocre both in colour and size of flower. Nevertheless there are some good strains ranging from a pale blue through a clear blue to one of the best of all, a rather dull steely blue set off by a large white eye and black stamens. In the last the flowers are sometimes 4 inches across.

Up to the present no strain in cultivation is pure, and a varying proportion of rogues will appear in each batch of seedlings; but doubtless when more care is taken in selection this species will be much improved in the garden.

Occasionally most attractive plants are produced when the central flowering-stem is damaged. This appears to stimulate the growth of the lower and basal pedicels which lengthen and produce flowers more or less at the same level, thus avoiding the rather unattractive fruiting-stem produced by the more normal plant. This suggests that *M. horridula* might be a better garden subject if induced to assume this form by pinching out the central flowering-stem as it is about to elongate.

It is the quickest to flower of all *Meconopsis*; under favourable conditions a large proportion of any one batch will flower the second year from seed.

M. horridula is the most spiny of the genus, and this rightly implies that it does not object to more xerophytic conditions than other species. Indeed, once the strains have been improved it will doubtless become much more popular in southern gardens. In its best forms it certainly is worth growing, both in groups in the rock garden or in the foreground of the shrub border. In all cases plants should be spaced fairly close together, about 8 or 10 inches apart at the most.

Its cultivation presents no difficulty so long as the drainage is perfect. It does not object to sun, but it must be remembered that the more sun it is given the smaller will be the plant and the flowers.

M. aculeata : This is a rare species in cultivation, many of the plants grown as *M. aculeata* being *M. latifolia*. Although at its best *M. aculeata* is a fine plant, it is much more variable than *M. latifolia*, and usually is inferior to the best forms of *M. horridula*.

In cultivation it requires more moisture and is best grown at the base of a cleft in the rocks in rather more than half shade.

M. latifolia : This is the best species of all for dry situations. When it is thoroughly at home it seeds itself freely round the parent plants. In many gardens this self-seeding is so regular that there is no need to raise further supplies in pans and boxes. In fact, it is easier to raise plants by scattering a few seeds among rocks where they are going to flower than to raise them in pans and boxes. Although I have seen only a few plants in southern gardens, I see no reason why it should not be successful and take the place of others which prefer cooler and moister conditions.

The only point about its cultivation is drainage. This must be particularly good, especially in the top surface, as it has a strong objection to a hard, sticky skin on the surface of the soil. The medium should be gritty, with a proportion of leaf soil added to give nourishment.

It is a most beautiful plant when grouped towards the back of the rock garden, and is valuable as the shade of blue is less variable than in many other species. Plants will be larger and more flowers will be carried if it is grown in half-shade.

M. impedita : Seedlings of this extremely dark-coloured species are growing, but again nothing is known about its cultivation. It would seem that the shady scree with ample moisture during the spring might suit it. Although the colour is very dark, it seems probable from the herbarium specimens that it would make a desirable garden plant if it could be grown as it occurs in nature.

SERIES BELLAE

M. bella : Seedlings of this charming species are again in cultivation; whether they will come to maturity and survive is another matter. There is no suggestion to make other than the possibility of the shady scree (see p. 118).

If we could only learn how to treat it, this would certainly be a plant of great garden value. Its delicate foliage, low stature, and pink or light blue flowers, large for the size of the plant, give it a charm sometimes lacking in the larger species.

SUBGENUS DISCOGYNE

M. discigera : Seedlings are now in cultivation, and it is to be hoped that this fine plant, obviously very free-flowering from the herbarium material, will prove easy to establish, but this is very doubtful, as it certainly will take several years, possibly as many as six or seven, to flower from seed.

Nothing is known about its cultivation, although it is stated to have flowered once in this country. From its habitat it would appear to like conditions similar to *M. violacea*, cool woodland with perfect drainage and ample moisture during the growing season.

INDEX TO BOTANICAL NAMES

Names accepted in *Meconopsis* are in clarendon; synonyms of these are in italics. Other names mentioned are in roman.